In Defense of Globalism

In Defense of Globalism

Dalibor Rohac

ROWMAN & LITTLEFIELD
Lanham • Boulder • New York • London

Published by Rowman & Littlefield
An imprint of The Rowman & Littlefield Publishing Group, Inc.
4501 Forbes Boulevard, Suite 200, Lanham, Maryland 20706
https://rowman.com

6 Tinworth Street, London SE11 5AL, United Kingdom

British Library Cataloguing in Publication Information Available

Library of Congress Cataloging-in-Publication Data

Names: Rohac, Dalibor, 1983- author.
Title: In defense of globalism / Dalibor Rohac.
Description: Lanham : Rowman & Littlefield, [2019] | Includes
    bibliographical references and index. | Summary: "Countering our
    divisive times, this invaluable book makes the conservative case in
    favor of international organizations and cooperation. Moving beyond
    empty political rhetoric, Dalibor Rohac's meticulous research and clear
    analysis assess and explain the strengths, flaws, and relevant
    trade-offs of different forms of global governance"-- Provided by
    publisher.
Identifiers: LCCN 2019016800 (print) | ISBN 9781538120798 (cloth : alk.
    paper) | ISBN 9781538120804 (pbk. : alk. paper)
Subjects: LCSH: Globalization. | International organization. |
    International cooperation.
Classification: LCC JZ1318 .R635 2019 (print) | LCC JZ1318 (ebook) | DDC
    303.48/2--dc23
LC record available at https://lccn.loc.gov/2019016800
LC ebook record available at https://lccn.loc.gov/2019981210

Contents

Preface

I looked with great admiration upon the Ukrainian protesters who gathered on Kyiv's Maidan in the final weeks of 2013. Having seen my home country, Slovakia, shed an aspiring autocrat in 1998 and then quickly catch up with other countries of the region, both in domestic reforms and accession to the European Union and the North Atlantic Treaty Organization (NATO), I was hoping that Ukrainians would pull off the same feat. Although Ukraine has made significant strides since Maidan in emulating the example of other, more successful postcommunist countries, its progress has been uneven. The most important among the factors holding it back has been the aggression of its neighbor to the east: In February 2014, Vladimir Putin annexed Crimea and invaded eastern Ukraine, starting a protracted conflict that has cast a shadow on Ukrainian politics.

At that time, I was working as a researcher at the Cato Institute, Washington's premier libertarian think tank. My colleagues were by no means oblivious to the historic nature of the events taking place in Ukraine. In fact, in as early as March 2014, Cato cohosted the Emergence Economic Summit for Ukraine, a high-profile conference in Kyiv that made the case for bold economic reforms in the country. Some of the leading Eastern European reformers attended and have since played important roles in Ukraine's policy world.

Yet, although my Cato colleagues almost universally condemned Putin's actions, I was disappointed to see only muted suggestions as to what the West should do in response to Russian aggression, other than to provide moral support and organize conferences. "Ukraine is in a bad neighborhood," shrugged Cato's foreign policy scholar Doug Bandow, "and, like Finland during the Cold War, suffers from constraints not faced by other nations. The situation isn't fair, but Congress can't change geopolitical reality."[1] Not only were Russia's brazen actions supposedly triggered by previous provocations by the West—the suggestion that successive NATO enlargements encircled Russia and more recently the prospect of an association agreement with the European Union—there was no real reason for Western democracies to intervene in a conflict in a country that mattered much more to Russia than to the United States or the European Union. "Escalating a potentially endless conflict serves no one's interest," wrote Bandow.[2]

I did not find this perspective compelling. Yet I understood that it was coming from a deep-seated skepticism of an activist foreign policy and "entangling alliances," which has defined this segment of the political right for decades, long predating the quagmires in Iraq and Afghanistan. Libertarians and foreign policy realists have long seen America's role in the world as destabilizing and a source of unintended consequences. Instead of acting as a guarantor of international order, the United States should simply follow its narrow national security interests. While this parochial outlook has been prominent in the United States, it was not exclusive to America. Rather, it reflected a more general temptation of pro-market intellectuals and activists to shy away from questions of the international order. As Razeen Sally, a prominent British–Sri Lankan free-market economist, puts it in his 1998 book on classical liberal approaches to international political economy, classical liberalism "directs the observer's gaze to the national or domestic preconditions of international order, and conceives (national) policy action to a large degree in unilateral terms, that is, not predicated on the reciprocity of intergovernmental bargains."[3]

While the focus on domestic conditions for a liberal (in the classical sense) global order is warranted in many situations, in the beginning of 2014 it appeared as a massive blind spot. If anything, the experience of not only Ukraine but also postcommunist Eastern Europe as a whole illustrates just how important the international environment was to the success of pro-market reform efforts. Ukraine and Poland, for example, started from almost identical levels of economic development in the early 1990s. Depending on the metric one uses, Poland is now three to five times wealthier than Ukraine in per capita terms. That is primarily because successive Polish governments leveraged the prospect of their country joining the community of Western liberal democracies to implement economic and legal reforms that would be otherwise unpalatable due to the short-term social costs or the resistance of influential interest groups. In Ukraine, similar policy and institutional choices were simply not on the menu.

The brave men and women who gathered on the Maidan in those winter months of 2013 and 2014 understood this well. And so had, I later learned, earlier generations of free-market thinkers including Friedrich von Hayek. An Austrian economist who received the Nobel Prize in economics in 1974, Hayek made substantial contributions to legal theory and political philosophy and became the central figure of the free-market movement. But in addition to being an icon for me and my colleagues at the Cato Institute, Hayek also recognized "that it was one of the main deficiencies of nineteenth-century liberalism that its advocates did not sufficiently realize that the achievement of the recognized harmony of interests between the inhabitants of the different states was only possible within the framework of international security."[4]

It was the same lack of interest in the international preconditions needed for the realization of the free-market program on the part of many classical liberals and libertarians that ultimately drove me away from the "liberty movement," although most of my substantive views on domestic policies changed only marginally over that same period. Later in 2014, I penned a "libertarian"[5] (and in 2016 a "conservative"[6]) defense of the European project, arguing a Europe of sovereign nation-states without a common governance structure would not be a boon to free markets and individual autonomy. Without being a scholar of international relations, I have also questioned the embrace of the so-called foreign policy realism by most of my free-market colleagues and friends.[7]

When the late James Denton, editor of *World Affairs*, published my essay on such topics in April 2015,[8] he confessed to me that he had not paid much attention to libertarian foreign policy views, finding them "a bit wacky and ultimately irrelevant." Yet it was at that precise moment that those views started gaining traction far beyond the corridors of libertarian think tanks, isolationist publications, and fringe political figures such as Senator Rand Paul. What is Donald Trump's "America First" mentality if not a cruder version of the "realist" outlook that sees states as engaged in a zero-sum competition driven by the pursuit of power? There has always been a large contingent of conservatives skeptical of multilateralism and pooling of sovereignty, potentially attuned to such a message. Yet with the exception of a small number of divisive and contested issues, such as the role of the United States in the International Criminal Court, no US administration, Democratic or Republican, seriously questioned the value implicit in the architecture of the world's postwar institutions and America's role in them. Today is different. President Trump does not hide his contempt for the European Union,[9] which he sees as an organization "set up to take advantage of the United States."[10] He praises dictators and appears eager to scale back the US military presence overseas—by withdrawing troops from Syria and Afghanistan,[11] scrapping joint military exercises with key US allies,[12] or closing down military bases.[13] If any of those ideas in isolation would provoke a strong pushback just a few years ago, today's right has mostly made peace with the crude "realism" of the current Republican administration, if not with the president's mercurial style. Conservative pundits are questioning the value of NATO[14] and back the administration's economic protectionism, notwithstanding the GOP's age-old commitment to free trade.[15]

It has become somewhat of a cliché for authors to claim that their work is "personal." But that does not make it any less true in this case. And it has also become a bit cliché to claim that the world has become more dangerous in the current populist era in which the long-accepted tenets of international order and America's role in the world are called into question. But then again, overused stereotypes become overused for a reason, and there *is* something dangerous about the degree to which most have been desensitized to rhetoric and policy decisions that would have provoked major outcries only a few years ago. Because the questions that the critics of international cooperation raise are not inherently illegitimate, my goal in this book is not only, or primarily, to sound the alarm bell. Rather, it is to invite my friends on the political right—conservatives, classical liberals, and libertarians—to rethink their views on the international order, sovereignty, and international cooperation. The reason for such a rethink is simple. The single biggest risk of the present era lies not so much in the short-term damage that President Trump and others do to America's standing in the world and the Western-led international order, but rather the possibility that his zero-sum, protectionist outlook that ignores the role of international norms becomes the new normal for years to come.

To counter that risk, this book offers a new perspective on international cooperation, congruent with ideas of self-governance and individual autonomy that have long defined the political right. It argues that the existing institutions have been extraordinarily successful at making the world free, peaceful, and economically dynamic. Furthermore, unlike the common caricatures of international institutions as ossified, top-down impositions, this book sees them as constantly evolving and diverse orders featuring many different nodes of decision-making. Efforts to reform, strengthen, and adapt those institutions to the reality of today's world need to leverage precisely their self-governing, polycentric features.

In the current political environment in the United States and many other parts of the Western world, the direction of travel is exactly the opposite, particularly on the political right. To be sure, Trump's presidency has given rise to a small cottage industry of studies and intellectual and political initiatives focused on combating populism and authoritarianism. Such studies and initiatives focus both on questions of domestic policy, as well as on questions of international order. However, particularly in the latter case, those efforts only rarely question the shortcomings of existing institutions, much less deploy common analytical tools to understand them. It is precisely that gap that this book seeks to fill by revisiting questions of international cooperation using a toolbox of ideas that were once central to the classical liberal tradition.

Although I am sure that my colleagues at the American Enterprise Institute (AEI) will find a lot to disagree with on the following pages, this book could not have been written without the supportive, intellectually stimulating, and diverse environment that AEI provides. As a testimony to the organization's openness and intellectual freedom, I should note that large portions of the manuscript were written at the desk that I inherited from John Bolton after he had been appointed national security advisor to President Trump in March 2018. I am particularly grateful to my boss, Danielle Pletka, the head of AEI foreign policy and defense studies, for giving me ample space to explore ideas, regardless of the conclusions to which they will lead me, as well as to Gary Schmitt for numerous enlightening conversations about self-governance and national sovereignty.

Feedback from many individuals helped me improve the manuscript. I am particularly grateful for their comments to Irena Schneider, Fredrik Erixon, Vlad Tarko, Stefan Kolev, Inu Manak, and Jessica Wright. I initially explored some of the ideas presented in this book in my monthly column in *The American Interest*, skillfully edited by Damir Marusic, particularly in my 2018 essay on polycentrism and international institutions.[16] I also received helpful comments from Aurelian Craiutu, Michael McGinnis, Zhou Lu, Mostafa Beshkar, and other participants of my Tocqueville lecture at the birthplace of research into polycentric governance, the Ostrom Workshop at Indiana University Bloomington. My thinking has also been shaped by readings and conversations with participants at the Self-Governance and Civil Society conference, hosted by the Centre for the Study of Governance and Society at King's College London. Wesley Fox, Jon Rodeback, Lindsey Weiss, Lance Kokonos, Evan Abramsky, and David Pasmanik provided research and editorial assistance, and Olivier Ballou kindly designed the book's cover.

Chapter One

Every Country for Itself?

As the clouds over Europe were darkening, twenty-six high-profile intellectuals gathered in Paris in August 1938 to discuss the book published recently by American journalist Walter Lippmann, *The Good Society*. The attendees included the polymath Michael Polanyi; Austrian economists Ludwig von Mises and Friedrich von Hayek (who became the 1974 Nobel laureate); Jacques Rueff, the future advisor to President de Gaulle; as well as Wilhelm Röpke—one of the economists who would be credited with Germany's postwar growth miracle. The meeting, now known as the Walter Lippmann Colloquium, was a precursor of the postwar Mont Pelerin Society, convened by Hayek for the first time in 1947. In the popular imagination, both the Lippmann Colloquium and Mont Pelerin Society became associated with the term "neoliberalism," which was in fact coined at the Colloquium by German economist Alexander Rüstow.

Today, neoliberalism evokes policies of the Thatcher and Reagan years: cuts to government spending and top tax rates, privatization of state-owned enterprises and market liberalization, and the opening of economies to trade and capital flows. Yet Rüstow's idea of neoliberalism was somewhat different: a political program that would complement the traditional laissez-faire liberalism with a robust social safety net.[1] Needless to say, that vision—of mixed economies, combining markets, and sizable welfare states—has characterized advanced Western democracies of the postwar era, most notably of Germany.

Rüstow's neoliberal program, which assigned a substantial role to government, encountered a mixed reception among an explicitly free-market–minded group. But such minutiae of domestic economic policy were not the main driver of conversations at the 1938 meeting in Paris. Instead, the participants were concerned about how the excesses of nationalism, militar-

1

ism, and the rise of totalitarian ideologies could be countered. The agenda of the meeting thus included the question of "co-existence of liberal and totalitarian economies," "economic and psychologic policy of liberal states toward totalitarian ones," "economics of war," "economic policy of liberal states between themselves," and other pressing questions of international political economy.[2]

Although the Colloquium, which met again in January 1939, did not seek unanimity, most participants shared a basic perspective about how international affairs ought to be organized among free societies. That perspective revolved around the idea of international federalism: a rules-based system transcending national boundaries and curbing the destructive and protectionist capabilities of nation-states. One influential attendee of the Colloquium, the Austrian economist Ludwig von Mises—an iconic figure of the postwar libertarian movement in the United States—already had a history working for the leading voice of the Paneuropean Movement, the Count of Coudenhove-Kalergi. Later, after fleeing Nazi-occupied Europe, he lent support to the idea of an overarching federal structure binding free societies of the world in the first book he published after arriving in the United States. In 1944, Mises wrote that "[i]f the Western democracies do not succeed in establishing a permanent union, the fruits of victory will be lost again."[3] For small nations of Europe in particular, "[t]he alternative to incorporation into a new democratic supernational system is not unrestricted sovereignty but ultimate subjugation by the totalitarian powers."[4]

Another participant, Friedrich August von Hayek, argued that European nations needed to form an interstate federation. "The abrogation of national sovereignties and the creation of an effective international order of law is a necessary complement and the logical consummation of the liberal program," he wrote in 1939.[5]

Wilhelm Röpke, a German attendee, fled the Nazis to Istanbul and Geneva, before becoming the intellectual father of Germany's post–World War II economic reforms. Röpke saw Swiss-style federalism as a blueprint for the governance of Europe after the war. "[T]he political structure of Switzerland in its democratic, multi-national and federal character has attracted the attention of those who are looking for a model to be used in the political reconstruction of Europe after this war," he wrote. "Why should we not similarly regard the economic and social constitution of this country as a model at least as useful for the economic and social reconstruction of the West?"[6]

The ambition of this book is to revitalize this view of international affairs, long dormant on the center-right. It seeks to marry the federalist ideas that animated the Lippmann Colloquium with analytical tools developed by Elinor Ostrom, a Nobel laureate in economics who pioneered the study of polycentric orders, as well as her husband, Vincent—a prominent scholar of American federalism. As the latter noted in his 1991 book, *The Meaning of*

Democracy and the Vulnerabilities of Democracies, the semantic root of federalism is in the Latin word for a covenant or a treaty (*foedus*). "A covenantal theology was also referred to as a 'federal theology.' A federal system of governance is, then, a covenantal system of governance."[7] In contrast to those who see the nation-state as the natural and complete endpoint of history, international federalism extends covenantal relations to the international realm to create rules structuring interactions between states and other actors and to solve a variety of problems of collective action.

BACK TO THE 1930s?

This is not just an intellectual or academic exercise. The divide between those who see nation-states as somehow natural forms of governance and those who see value in international pooling of decision-making is among the most pressing dividing lines in politics today. Without overplaying parallels with the present, the world finds itself today in a situation that dangerously resembles the 1930s. Across Western democracies, populist leaders claiming to speak on behalf of *the people* and denouncing the supposedly self-serving and out-of-touch *elites* seek to upend the existing international order by scaling back international commitments. The repatriation of political control away from complex international organizations back to national capitals will have unintended consequences, not least the re-emergence of economic and political conflicts between governments.

The drivers of the current populist upsurge are not exactly a mystery. Just as in the aftermath of the Great Depression when economic hardship drove the rise of support for extremist politics, the West is experiencing a disappointingly sluggish recovery from a financial shock that has been blamed by many voters on political elites. The notion that the system is "rigged" and that economic power has become unduly concentrated is not without merit. Structural changes in Western economies have also created a gulf between the economically successful cosmopolitan elites living in urban capitals and the large swathes of the population who see themselves as being left behind by globalization and automation. In the United States, furthermore, trust in key political and nonpolitical institutions—including Congress, public schools, the media, and others—has been eroding for decades.[8]

There are good reasons not to overplay the similarities between today and the 1930s. But there are also bad reasons for doing so—especially complacency. In one sense, the current predicament is even more dangerous than the dynamics of the interwar period. Today, the collective memory of nationalism, protectionism, and war has faded away across the Western world. It is thus natural, especially for younger generations, to see the world's prosperity, openness, and relative peace as primitive, invariable facts of life. In the

United States, moreover, such complacency has been amplified by the perception that the country has been bearing the burden of maintaining the
world's peace and stability alone, without much help from its allies. The
costly wars in Iraq and Afghanistan showed the limits of America's ability to
foster political stability in distant parts of the world, leading many, including
some on the traditionally hawkish political right, to draw the lesson that
international entanglements should best be avoided.

Migration, driven both by rising incomes across the developing world and
by conflicts—most notably by the horrific civil war in Syria—has added fuel
to the fire of populism. Migration is a challenge both to poorer countries
experiencing brain drain and to host societies in the West, which are not
always in a position to integrate and assimilate large immigrant populations
and where political elites have long been in denial about the true views of
their electorates concerning the subject. Adding to the conflagration, the
2015 refugee crisis in the European Union created a sense of alarm that
democratically elected governments were not in control of events. That has
damaged trust in political institutions and in the European Union. It was also
exploited by demagogues and aspiring authoritarians such as Prime Minister
Viktor Orbán, who used the threat of (mostly nonexistent) immigration to
Hungary as a pretext for a dramatic consolidation of his power.[9]

For the emerging cohort of populist candidates and political leaders, globalism and international cooperation are useful scapegoats. Seen through the
prism of the populist dichotomy between the blameless "ordinary people"
and the corrupt "elites," any form of complicated international arrangements
is suspect, if not responsible for failures of domestic policy—particularly if
the said populists see the world in zero-sum terms. Unsurprisingly, the notion
that the United States is "being taken advantage of"—not only by its adversaries but, more significantly, by its allies—has been a persistent theme in
Donald Trump's rhetoric.[10] In his 2007 volume, *Think Big and Kick Ass*,
Trump claimed that the idea of win-win "is a bunch of crap. In a great deal,
you win—not the other side. You crush the opponent and come away with
something better for yourself."[11]

As president, Trump also stated that "NATO [was] as bad as NAFTA,"
referring to the North American Free Trade Agreement, which he blamed for
a number of economic problems in the United States, contending that the
European Union was established to "take advantage" of the United States and
was "worse than China" on trade.[12] Similarly, Marine Le Pen, the former
candidate for president of France called the European Union "deeply harmful" and "an anti-democratic monster," vowing "to prevent it from becoming
fatter, from continuing to breathe, from grabbing everything with its paws
and from extending its tentacles into all areas of our legislation."[13]

In more intellectual terms, Orbán explains his own opposition to "globalism":

National and globalist forces have never squared up to each other so openly. We, the millions with national feelings, are on one side; the elite "citizens of the world" are on the other side. We who believe in nation-states, the defense of borders, the family and the value of work are on one side. And opposing us are those who want open society, a world without borders or nations, new forms of family, devalued work and cheap workers—all ruled over by an army of shadowy and unaccountable bureaucrats. On one side, national and democratic forces; and on the other side, supranational and anti-democratic forces.[14]

This backlash against international cooperation on the political right has long been in the making. In France, for example, Le Pen's right-wing populist Front National (today's Rassemblement National) has been in existence since 1972, and parties rallying against "globalism" in some other European countries are even older. In 1992, Pat Buchanan sought the Republican nomination in the United States by running on an isolationist and protectionist platform that articulated many of the ideas recycled later by Trump and his supporters. Unsurprisingly, Buchanan himself welcomes the current nationalist revolt in Europe and predicts that "[i]f these trends continue . . . the idea of a United States of Europe dies, and with it the EU."[15]

ROOTS OF THE RIGHT'S PROBLEM

In 1992 the GOP was able to repudiate such ideas; its intellectual safeguards were much weaker in 2016. One reason is that the internationalist tradition on America's right atrophied over time, in part as a reaction to the lackluster results of wars in Iraq and Afghanistan. In libertarian circles, furthermore, foreign policy thinking had been long reduced to an uncritical embrace of crude realism. As a rough first approximation, realism posits the existence of self-interested sovereign nation-states as the basic units of analysis, disregarding both the rules that might constrain their behavior as well as the various governance structures that facilitate their cooperation—providing a perfect starting point for a Trump-like doctrine of unfettered national egoism.

Even across the more influential segments of America's conservative right, a knee-jerk distrust of international cooperation has long been a dominant operating principle. It reflects both the commitment of many conservative thinkers to the idea of national sovereignty and American exceptionalism and the fact that in many contexts international organizations and treaties have been seen as vehicles for progressive causes. Conservative thinkers critical of "global governance" include British philosopher Roger Scruton,[16] editor at *National Review* and former advisor to Margaret Thatcher and John O'Sullivan,[17] Israeli writer Yoram Hazony,[18] American legal scholars Jeremy Rabkin[19] and John Yoo,[20] and President Trump's national security advisor John Bolton.[21] For all their differences, these authors tend to see self-governing nation-states, unhindered by forms of governance transcending national borders, as the natural and indispensable building blocks of international order. Like Orbán and authoritarian populists, they see attempts to bind countries by treaty obligations, to pool decision-making authority, or to subject states to any kind of international supervision as inherently subversive of democracy.

In a 2000 article, for instance, Bolton warned against a "worldwide cartelization of governments and interest groups"[22] that results from attempts at pooling national sovereignty. The British conservative intellectual John O'Sullivan claimed that "global governance" "seeks to take ultimate political power (sovereignty) from democratic parliaments and congresses accountable to national electorates in sovereign states and vest it in courts, bureaucratic agencies, NGOs and transnational bodies that are accountable only to themselves or to other transnational bodies."[23] And at the time of NAFTA's ratification, the Republican Senator Jesse Helms warned that the agreement would give rise to "an international, environmental gestapo."[24]

To be fair, conservatives do not *always* reject international cooperation. Many of the figures cited are vocal supporters of NATO. They would also see unfettered national sovereignty as providing ample leeway for effective cooperation. As Rabkin writes,

> [N]ineteenth century diplomacy was remarkably effective in what it set out to do. Goods could be shipped almost anywhere. Letters could be delivered with stamps paid at the point of origin, telegrams sent in the same way. Merchants, scholars, even tourists could travel freely and with considerable security throughout Europe and through much of the rest of the world. This network of open trade and communication rested to a large extent on the treaties, built on the system of mutual concessions and equality of states and on the underlying premise that conflicts among states need not hinder communication among private citizens.[25]

Yet reducing international cooperation back to nineteenth-century–style diplomacy between sovereign states yields an antiquated and skewed perspective on international affairs. For one, the arrangements described were fragile and short-lived, precisely because they were not embedded in a system of binding rules of the game. As a result, they did not stop the creeping rise of protectionism, well underway by the end of the nineteenth century. Nor did they prevent the Great Depression, the rise of totalitarianism in the 1930s, or the two worst killing sprees in human history. It is, therefore, odd to single them out as models to emulate in the twenty-first century.

There is also a double standard in conservative thinking about international commitments. Most of the time (though no longer always) NATO gets a pass on the conservative right because it is seen as an alliance of sovereign nation-states. However, the effectiveness of its security guarantees is predicated on the willingness of governments to send their troops to fight and die in defense of other countries: a sacrifice far greater than the pooling of sovereignty needed to sustain, say, the European Union's common market.

Moreover, the efforts to disentangle the various, oftentimes overlapping, platforms for cooperation in the hope of returning to an era of untarnished national sovereignty are rarely compelling. It is naive, for instance, to believe that the United Kingdom's departure from the European Union has no bearing on the United Kingdom's commitments to NATO or to European security, notwithstanding British rhetoric to the contrary. Since the 2016 referendum, Brexit has crowded out all other subjects of public policy in the United Kingdom, including strategic thinking about threats from, say, the Middle East and North Africa. More significantly, if the United Kingdom ends up leaving the European Union in a disruptive way—which cannot be ruled out at the time of writing—it is obvious that the British willingness to defend its European allies would take a hit, and vice versa. It is mostly the same leaders and the same governments who are meeting at the European Council and at NATO summits. The notion that a loss of trust and acrimony experienced at one of those venues would be immaterial to decisions taken at the other is fanciful.

In the same vein, defenders of President Trump's harsh rhetoric about NATO have argued that his aim is not to damage the alliance but to strengthen it by making sure that European allies step up and start making meaningful investments into their security capabilities. They also point to the fact that America's military presence on NATO's Eastern flank has been boosted under the current administration in order to deter Russia's potential aggression. But Trump's style and rhetoric matter too, as does the erratic nature of the current White House, which has oftentimes sent out signals at odds with those coming from the State Department and the Pentagon. Healthy, viable alliances require trust and a sense of mutual understanding and respect, which are nowhere to be found in Trump's treatment of European allies.

NO ORDER WITHOUT LEADERSHIP

These disparate developments are illustrative of the fact that leading Western nations, particularly the United States, are less keen today to play their traditional roles as guarantors of the international order. On both sides of the Atlantic, there is less willingness to entertain new international commitments—and in fact, an active reconsideration of some of the existing ones, as we have seen with Brexit and with Trump's NAFTA and the Paris Agreement. In Europe in particular, the willingness to shape the continent's neighborhood—the post-Soviet space, the Balkans, or the Middle East and North

Africa region—is limited to the stalled enlargement agenda and to ad hoc arrangements, such as the 2016 EU agreement with Erdoğan's Turkey. While the United States has not adopted a completely passive posture on the world stage—it has, most prominently, started to confront China in ways not seen under previous administrations—both outsiders and insiders find Washington's foreign policy priorities confusing and erratic.

As a result, the world finds itself in a dangerous place. In the interwar period a preeminent global power, the United Kingdom, was not able to shoulder the burden of its global responsibilities. That enabled revisionist powers—Germany and Italy—to fill the void. Today, as the West is scaling back on its international commitments, its adversaries are busily expanding their influence. Given the many fora and dimensions within which international affairs can be shaped, efforts to return to the imagined cocoons provided by national sovereignty are bound to encourage the West's adversaries to further expand their influence and usher in a world order in which democratic capitalism, rule of law, and economic openness will be the exceptions, rather than the basic operating principles of civilized societies.

It is not enough for the West to respond with military might, sanctions, or other displays of hard power if revisionists are spreading their influence through means of economic integration and forms of international governance that emulate those developed earlier by Western democracies. Take China's Belt and Road Initiative. The investment projects conducted under its auspices are not just driven by economic considerations—after all, overland transport of goods makes no more sense today than it did at the time of the original Silk Road. Instead, its driving motor is the ambition of the Chinese regime to lock smaller countries into a position of economic dependence through irreversible decisions about transport and energy infrastructure. Likewise, Russia is using its natural gas exports as a tool of political leverage, alongside nuclear power projects—such as Rosatom's expansion of the Paks power plant in Hungary, financed through a loan from a Russian-led multilateral lending organization, the International Investment Bank.

Both China and Russia have built international organizations that resemble those created by Western powers after the Second World War. Most prominent among them is the Asian Infrastructure Investment Bank, which a number of Western nations joined as founding members. The bank provides financing and other forms of assistance to Chinese-led projects under the auspices of the Belt and Road Initiative. The Kremlin, in turn, has founded the Eurasian Economic Union as a response to the European project—except, of course, that it is a project of Russia's political domination over the lesser autocracies in the post-Soviet space.

This book's aim is to make an intellectual case for robust and deep forms of international cooperation between and within free societies of the world. One can call such cooperation, for the lack of a better term, *globalism*. To be sure, globalism is a term coined initially by critics of globalization and deep international cooperation. As a result, its use is often imprecise and loaded with emotions. Much of this book focuses on globalism defined primarily by institutions, organizations, norms, and other governance structures spanning across national borders—rather than free global flows of goods, services, capital, and people. That is not because that latter set of ideas is not worth defending, nor because the two sets of ideas would be unconnected, but because making the case for globalization involves engaging in a different intellectual exercise. In chapter 5, therefore, we take the argument in favor of free trade as a given, relying on the overwhelming consensus existing among academic economists. To be sure, reasonable people might disagree about the appropriate degree of openness of societies to, say, capital flows or immigration. But even in the latter case, the controversy revolves not so much around the economic benefits of free flows of labor, which are substantial,[26] but rather around the political dynamic that seemingly uncontrolled migration might set in motion.[27] As a result, the term globalism, as employed throughout this book, is compatible with a wide array of policies, instead of being a shorthand for an uncompromising embrace of openness. This book's contribution lies in making the case for the necessity of covenantal arrangements, between countries and other actors, for addressing various cross-border policy challenges.

At the same time, this book is not agnostic about the feasibility or costs of policies that would seek to undo the existing degree of economic interconnectedness. A return to tariffs and discriminatory regulatory practices that were widespread before the postwar efforts at trade liberalization would reduce global trade flows and standards of living in both advanced and developing economies. Contrary to President Trump's claim that "trade wars are good, and easy to win,"[28] a recent study of tariffs, covering 151 countries between 1963 and 2014, concludes that "tariff increases also result in more unemployment, higher inequality, and real exchange rate appreciation, but only small effects on the trade balance."[29] Another study by the Peterson Institute estimated that the 2009 tariffs imposed by the Obama administration on Chinese tire imports into the United States saved a maximum of 1,200 jobs in US manufacturing, but at a whopping price tag of at least $900,000 per job in direct economic costs.[30] Considering President Trump's penchant for tariffs, the lesson does not seem to have been learned. His own steel tariffs, designed to respond to the perceived problem of Chinese overcapacity, have disproportionately affected small and poor steel-producing countries, rather the ones that the administration sees as true culprits.[31]

Although there are reasons to treat the movement of people differently from the movement of goods or services, restrictive immigration policies have economic costs too—particularly in societies coping with unfavorable demographic changes. In other cases, such as that of capital mobility, effective restrictions are often not even practical. Today, financial capital can move between countries via a number of different channels ranging from banking systems to encrypted and decentralized online platforms. The world has already learned the hard way over the course of the past decade that regulatory and fiscal decisions taken in, say, Iceland and Greece can produce dramatic financial consequences elsewhere.

More important, capital can be understood in expansive terms to include a variety of factors of production including human skills, or human capital. Thanks to new information and communication technologies, it is now possible to rely much more on distant human labor than ever before. Technological substitutes for face-to-face communication are abundant and essentially free, and international travel has also become cheaper and more convenient.[32] There is, furthermore, a rising degree of substitutability between different types of mobility. A company might decide to hire cheap immigrant labor at home, or it might decide to move some of its manufacturing to a developing country—in that case, mobility of final goods and mobility of labor act as substitutes.

WELCOME TO THE FLAT WORLD

Unsurprisingly, due to such changes and the increased openness of the global economy, the outsourcing of both manufacturing and certain types of services has proceeded rapidly. To be sure, the bold predictions about the end of conventional workplaces and the rise of telework have not fully materialized. Location still matters, as illustrated by the skyrocketing property prices in prosperous urban areas in advanced economies around the world. Yet the rising mobility facilitated by falling costs of transport and communication has led to a significant "flattening" of economic activity, to use a term associated with Thomas Friedman's best-selling (and oft-derided) book.[33] In the past, as legal scholar Gillian Hadfield argues, most corporations acted as self-contained "boxes"[34] in which decisions were taken by fiat and whose operations were mostly confined to individual countries. Today, companies span vast distances and numerous jurisdictions to the extent that it is sometimes impossible to identify them as "American" or "German." General Electric operates in 170 countries, IKEA has stores in thirty-seven countries, and the supply and assembly of Apple products occurs in thirty countries.[35]

Toyota pioneered the new approach to managing supply chains: instead of micromanaging every step of the production process, as was necessary in the old corporate "boxes," it simply defined the essential characteristics of components it was buying and allowed its suppliers to make autonomous production decisions. Today, production of Boeing's Dreamliner relies on a network of some one thousand suppliers, organized through intricate contract relationships.[36] The emerging economic relationships in the "flat" global economy are "as difficult to nail down as jelly,"[37] Hadfield argues. Their complexity, fluidity, and disregard for national borders puts a strain on national legal systems, which were designed to govern much simpler business models and contractual relationships, typically taking place within the territory of one country.

Furthermore, more and more economic activity takes place online, outside of effective national control. Cross-border data bandwidth, for instance, grew 148 times between 2005 and 2017.[38] National governments can respond by seeking to assert control over it. However, doing so would result in a balkanization of the internet and would, in turn, require governments to engage in an unpopular and costly race against new technologies, platforms, and evolving methods of encryption. To some extent, that is the race that the Chinese government has engaged in by constructing its Great Firewall, insulating Chinese nationals from subversive content and cracking down on internet privacy. Likewise, the EU standards on data protection have forced some international sites to hide their content from European users. However, considering the enormous benefits of an integrated internet and the costs of erecting effective barriers, it is implausible that the world would end up with myriad perfectly insulated internet spaces. But whatever the final outcome, the transnational character of the internet needs adequate tools of governance to deal with questions of cybersecurity, privacy, protection of intellectual rights, and so forth.

Besides creating new forms of economic interaction beyond the control of national governments, technological progress can be a source of new dangers for humankind. In a recent paper, philosopher Nick Bostrom conceptualizes innovation as a lottery involving balls of different colors. "Over the course of history, we have extracted a great many balls—mostly white (beneficial) but also various shades of gray (moderately harmful ones and mixed blessings). The cumulative effect on the human condition has so far been overwhelmingly positive and may be much better still in the future."[39] However, it is possible that a technology will be invented that will pose a grave danger to the civilization that invents it—a black ball. Under different laws of physics, it is imaginable that nuclear weapons could have played that role.

One concern of scientists involved in the Manhattan Project during the Second World War, for example, was that their models could not rule out the possibility that a man-made nuclear explosion would trigger a self-sustaining thermonuclear reaction in the surrounding air or water, effectively igniting the atmosphere.[40] Even though that outcome did not happen, it is possible to imagine many different destabilizing scenarios, such as the emergence of technologies that would make nuclear weapons or other weapons of mass destruction cheap and easy to produce. That way, not only could a wider array of governments acquire and use them, but criminal and terrorist organizations would be in a position to do so as well.

Whatever the odds of such technologies emerging in the near future, proliferation is already a serious problem even if weapons of mass destruction are generally difficult to produce and hide. Proliferation is, furthermore, only one item on a long list of challenges that cross national borders and will continue to do so in the future. International terrorism, including jihadist networks in Europe, pay little attention to national borders. Their communication networks and ability to orchestrate low-intensity yet deeply destabilizing attacks would not cease even if European countries ended the free movement of people within the European Union or passportless travel within the Schengen Area. Similarly, cybersecurity is an area in which thinking purely in terms of territorial nation-states makes little sense. Vulnerable computer systems can be attacked from anywhere, with little cost, by unfriendly governments or nonstate actors.

The same reasoning can be applied to threats posed by pandemics, climate change, ocean pollution, disappearing biodiversity, or the management of the seabed, Antarctica, and outer space. Defenders of the nation-state are either silent or revert to magical thinking about how such "global commons" could be governed by individual governments acting in isolation. And at their worst—typically on the subject of climate change—some proponents of national sovereignty are inclined to argue that the challenges in question are either nonexistent or vastly exaggerated, notwithstanding an overwhelming scholarly consensus.

This book's defense of globalism rejects the central tenet of nationalism: namely, that political and cultural, or ethnic, boundaries always have to coincide. In fact, the relationship between the two has always been a complex and indirect one. Moreover, the following chapters also provide a rebuttal to a crude version of foreign policy realism that has grown in influence in recent years, along with the rise of nationalism in Western democracies. Associated with names such as Hans Morgenthau[41] and Kenneth Waltz,[42] realism presents a bleak vision of an anarchic international system in which states emerge as the only relevant actors. Its logic forces states to pursue their national interest understood best as power. No international organizations, treaties, or shared values or morality can pierce through this harsh, zero-sum reality. Realism has a descriptive and analytical dimension to it, seeking to depict the world through the state-centric prism of countervailing threats, domination, and spheres of influence. More important, it also carries a normative component, teaching its followers that any deviations from the self-interested behavior of states are futile and potentially counterproductive.

One way in which realism goes wrong is in ignoring the "flat," transnational nature of today's world. There is a much greater diversity of actors in the international arena than just governments. The character of most of the challenges that such actors face extends far beyond simple interstate interactions. More fundamentally, realism fails on empirical grounds by being unable to account for effective cooperation between states, which has deepened dramatically over the past decades. It cannot explain why states adhere to international norms, especially in situations where such behavior is not dictated by any obvious countervailing threats. For example, the fact that nuclear weapons have not been used since 1945 cannot be accounted for just by the credible prospect of retaliation—that would leave out the possibility of using them in conflicts of nuclear powers against countries that do not possess a nuclear deterrent. [43]

The failure to explain the globalized world is a direct consequence of realism's disregard for the importance of the rules of the game—or "institutions." If there is a common theme to conservative, classical liberal, libertarian, or "neoliberal" thinking about social organization, it is its emphasis on the existing institutional setup as the main driver of economic and social outcomes. In fact, one influential stream of center-right thinking on the European continent, associated with the name of the Lippmann Colloquium attendee Wilhelm Röpke, calls itself *Ordoliberalism*, to emphasize the critical role that rules play in fostering beneficial social and economic outcomes. [44]

Most social scientists agree that good institutions, sustaining competitive markets, and accountable government lead to good outcomes whereas bad, exploitative institutions condemn societies to poverty and possibly violence. [45] It takes a special kind of blindness to accept the importance of institutions in the domestic setting while deciding to disregard them in the international realm. After all, even if interactions between states are anarchic, as realists argue, they are still structured by institutions. Similarly, anarchic interactions between individuals that occur in different institutional settings will have dramatically different outcomes.

Yet this institutions-free perspective on international affairs has long been popular among US libertarians—perhaps because it has led to largely non-interventionist prescriptions for America's defense policy or because of the libertarians' characteristic cynicism about *any* government, democratic or otherwise. Until recently, both libertarian and realist thinking about international affairs was relegated to the fringes of policy debates in capitals of the Western world. The rise of populist nationalism, however, has given this tradition a new lease on life, as it provides a veneer of intellectual credibility to nationalist, protectionist, and isolationist impulses, which may be themselves driven by extrarational factors.

To be sure, this book's perspective on globalism is not Panglossian. It should not be read as an unqualified endorsement of *all* existing structures of international cooperation or their activities. Nor does it reflect the belief, still common in some circles, that multilateralism is intrinsically valuable, instead of being an institutional form that can be put to good or bad uses. In fact, one of the main observations motivating this book is that "globalism" or "global governance" are not one thing. Rather, international and transnational cooperation takes many different forms, encompassing a vast array of different institutions and organizational forms and addressing an incredibly diverse spectrum of policy subjects—with widely different results. Some of its manifestations have proven effective and enjoy wide popular support, others less so. Part of the challenge, at a time of an acute crisis of legitimacy for Western democratic politics, consists of reconstructing the international system so that it can deliver.

For good and ill, the task at hand is not to build a new international system from scratch but rather to slowly rebuild and update the structures that already exist. To make things more complicated, there is no single blueprint for how international cooperation should work. The sheer diversity of current problems and possible institutional responses precludes that, much to the chagrin of those who imagine that a truly global, centralized form of governance could one day replace the nation-state. This book can be seen as a manifesto for institutional diversity and trial and error as necessary components of successful governance in the globalized economy of the twenty-first century, rather than for any particular manifestation of "global governance"—say the UN system or the European Union.

The current populist backlash against globalism has to do with the often-correct perception that the existing system has systematically overpromised and underdelivered. But if the performance of many currently existing international institutions leaves a lot to be desired, it does not follow that retreating into the cocoon of the nation-state would in any way be an improvement. Quite the contrary. Populist nationalism is bound to fail because of the mismatch between the institutional solutions that they propose—namely nation-state-centric governance—and the real challenges posed by the "flat" world that we inhabit.

The prediction that the current populist surge will fail does not reflect a naive, Whiggish triumphalism about the supposed direction of history. Rather, it reflects the belief that over the long run, some version of a political Coase theorem applies in free, self-governing societies. In its original version, the Coase theorem states that, if the costs of transacting are low, people will be incentivized to conduct efficiency-enhancing bargains around existing rules.[46] As a result, the theorem concludes, the initial assignment of rights would not affect the final use of resources. Of course, we know that the rules of the game do affect economic and social outcomes since the ability of humans to strike such bargains is limited. That is true of the private economy—and even more so of the political "market."

However, one of the most significant appeals of self-governing societies is that political accountability, a competition of ideas, and continual contestation allow such adjustments to be made, however clumsily and slowly. Such adjustments result from political and intellectual entrepreneurship by individuals who can mentally step outside of the existing constraints and imagine different political configurations, different institutions, and different policies. Those alternatives might be feasible or not, daring or only marginally different from those currently in existence. And just like in the case of economic entrepreneurship, it takes a process of trial and error to see whether the proposed alternatives work and are in fact an improvement over the status quo. Good new ideas are rare, both in politics and in business, and their success requires correct execution, leadership, and fortuitous timing.

This book is meant to be a resource for likeminded political and intellectual entrepreneurs on the center-right, both in the United States and in Europe. Not all conservatives and classical liberals have made their peace with the populist nationalism that has captured large swathes of the political right on both sides of the Atlantic. Those who want to fight back need to have good answers to the charges leveled both by the nationalists and conservatives enamored with the nation-state. Hopefully, the following chapters provide at least some.

The next chapter quickly sketches the intellectual and geopolitical history of "globalism" and outlines the diversity of its manifestations around the world. Chapter 3, in turn, introduces *polycentrism*—an analytical approach developed by the late Nobel laureate in economics Elinor Ostrom and her husband, Vincent, with the explicit purpose of accounting for existing institutional diversity. Polycentrism is also a source of design principles that help organize governance in settings involving multiple centers of decision-making—a condition that characterizes the international system.

In chapter 4, the focus is on historical examples of polycentric governance spanning across national borders, aiming to dispel the myth that the unitary nation-state is somehow a natural or preordained condition of human affairs. The three examples discussed are the Holy Roman Empire, a loose federal structure that governed a large part of Europe for almost a millennium; the Hanseatic League, an association of cities that dominated trade across the Baltic Sea throughout much of the early modern period; and the classical gold standard, which traditionally tied together the finances of central banks and national governments.

Chapter 5, in turn, studies the depth of trade liberalization achieved in the postwar era and the governance structures that have facilitated it. In addition to multilateral efforts, economic opening up has been driven by the mushrooming of regional preferential trade agreements and various forms of regulatory cooperation—making it more resilient to sudden spurts of protectionism than the trading system that existed in the interwar period.

Questions of national sovereignty, self-governance, and effective national control over policies are discussed in chapter 6. That international cooperation imposes constraints on governments is a feature, not a bug. There may be legitimate questions about how international cooperation might be reconciled with constitutional systems existing in different countries—particularly in the United States—but unless one adheres to a Jacobinic version of crude majoritarianism, it is hard to see "globalism" as a threat to self-governance. And effective national control, either over policies or over policy outcomes, is largely a mirage in the era of instantaneous capital flows and costless global communication. If anything, effective cooperation can boost control over outcomes that would otherwise be out of reach for national governments.

Chapter 7 offers thoughts about the ethics of nationalism and cosmopolitanism. The thrust of the argument does not seek to deny the reality of nationhood or of existing political allegiances. Those, however, cannot be taken as fixed parameters but as historical contingencies, subject to evolution and change. As a result, though membership in particular political communities bestows certain privileges and duties, there is nothing special about them—rather they are simple consequences of the fact that the world is divided into different polities.

Finally, in chapter 8 possible avenues toward a reconstruction of the existing international order along polycentric lines are discussed. An application of Elinor Ostrom's design principles for decentralized governance yields a number of practical lessons for reforms of existing institutional arrangements. One is that international organizations and other forms of governance need clear and limited mandates and boundaries so that they do not interfere with the autonomy of their constituent parts—an idea that actual forms of international cooperation have not always lived up to. A second is that international governance cannot be a one-way ratchet but needs to be a two-way street. That means that it needs mechanisms for unwinding organizations and rules that have outlived their purpose, and for effectively sanctioning actors that do not abide by their commitments. Yet another idea is that cooperation between free, self-governing, and democratic societies is fundamentally different from the one arising with the presence of autocracies at the table. That does not mean that no engagement is possible with unfree countries but rather that free societies are natural allies and that any forms of international or transnational governance ought to be constructed as an extension of already existing self-governing arrangements.

Chapter Two

What Slippery Slope?

At least 262 million people died at the hands of governments over the course of the twentieth century according to estimates by the late political scientist Rudolph Rummel of the University of Hawaii. That is almost seven times as many as all those killed in combat over the same period.[1] If arbitrary violence, murder, and genocide were essential characteristics of governments, then cooperation between them would not be an appealing proposition. Yet clearly not all governments were created equal in that regard. The horrors of the twentieth century did not come indiscriminately from the hands of *all* governments, nor from their random selection. Instead, they came invariably from totalitarian and authoritarian regimes, and from states suffering from various levels of dysfunction.

As a flipside to those government-orchestrated horrors, effective and accountable governments, limited in their powers yet able to provide essential public goods, seem to be a necessary condition for economic development.[2] Contrary to the claims made by many conservatives and libertarians, whether a government is prone to tyranny and murder or whether it is conducive to good economic and social outcomes is not inversely proportional to its fiscal and regulatory footprint, or to the largesse of its welfare assistance programs.[3] *Practically all* prosperous democratic societies feature governments that are fairly large in conventional fiscal and regulatory terms and involve also a substantial degree of income redistribution. Conversely, some of the most oppressive and dysfunctional regimes—think Afghanistan or the Central African Republic—have only modest fiscal resources at their disposal. The quality of government is not a function of its size but of the institutional constraints under which it operates—most important, rule of law and democratic accountability. Similar to rallying against government *in general* as something inherently sinister, blanket dismissals of international cooperation are not persuasive. Valid criticisms can be addressed at this or that treaty or international organization. Disagreements around "how" and "how much" are only natural since international cooperation, just like other areas of social life, offers no free lunches. Yet it is misleading to see globalism as a monolithic slippery slope leading to a tyrannical global rule by self-appointed bureaucrats.

The past has seen attempts at global rule. Some were driven by totalitarian ideologies, such as communism; others came from supposedly universal polities in Europe or China.[4] In the cases of large continental empires, their "universality" was often a corollary of their isolation. In other situations, such as the Holy Roman Empire, which spanned across much of the European continent for more than a millennium, the nominally universal nature was not matched by effective political authority, which remained radically *decentralized* throughout the Middle Ages and the Early Modern period. The distinctly utopian idea of a world united under one political authority also makes frequent appearances in the history of political thought, culminating with some segments of the twentieth-century progressive left.

Yet, the reality of "global governance" has little to do with seeking to abolish the nation-state or democratic governance. "Supra-nationalism," in the sense of irrevocably transferring decision-making authority from national government to international bodies, is largely a bogeyman. The most consequential attempts at international cooperation have not been global and top-down but have instead arisen as responses of free societies to common challenges. Most importantly, the emergence of international institutions built by Western democracies after the Second World War—most notably by the United States—has coincided with an unprecedented expansion of individual freedom, economic openness, and prosperity around the world.

DREAMERS, CLASSICAL LIBERALS, AND WORLD FEDERALISTS

The idea of governance spanning across national borders is nothing new in Western political thought. Federalist thinking has mirrored Europe's political reality as a continent trying to reconcile its extraordinary diversity with its shared Classical and Judeo-Christian heritage. As a result, many medieval and early modern thinkers, including the Dominican theologian and philosopher Francisco de Vitoria (1492–1546) of the heavily pro-market School of Salamanca,[5] entertained the idea of a global government.[6] Writing against the background of Europe's religious conflicts and witnessing the emergence of the first successful federal states in Switzerland and the Low Countries, the Calvinist thinker Johannes Althusius (1557–1638) formulated a vision of a composite, consensus-based political order based on the associative free will of the individual and of their natural, social, and political communities, which earned him the title of "the first federalist" in the eyes of some.[7]

However, Immanuel Kant, in 1795, offered probably the first modern and compelling formulation of the possibility of the world's states forming a polity in order to prevent recurrent warfare:

> The practicability (objective reality) of this idea of federation, which should gradually spread to all states and thus lead to perpetual peace, can be proved. For if fortune directs that a powerful and enlightened people can make itself a republic, which by its nature must be inclined to perpetual peace, this gives a fulcrum to the federation with other states so that they may adhere to it and thus secure freedom under the idea of the law of nations. By more and more such associations, the federation may be gradually extended.[8]

Similarly to international federalists of the twentieth century, Kant's vision was not of a unitary world state, much less of one that would eschew political accountability, but of an *association* that would bind "republics," as opposed to the absolutist monarchies of the time, in a rules-based system. Others approached the subject in a less rigorous, yet no less passionate way. Queen Victoria's poet laureate Alfred Tennyson (1809–1892) wrote in his poem "Locksley Hall":

> For I dipt into the future, far as human eye could see,
> Saw the Vision of the world, and all the wonder that would be;
> . . .
> Till the war-drum throbb'd no longer, and the battle-flags were furl'd
> In the Parliament of man, the Federation of the world.
> There the common sense of most shall hold a fretful realm in awe,
> And the kindly earth shall slumber, lapt in universal law.[9]

In the nineteenth century, characterized by immense economic progress, political turmoil, and recurrent conflicts, the idea of a governance structure spanning across national borders gained currency across the political spectrum. Even the communist vision of a classless society was global in its outlook. The bloodshed of the First World War, brought about by a concatenation of aggressive nationalisms, lent further credibility to the notion that the world needed international rules. The interwar period was thus not only an era of growing political radicalism, amplified by the Great Depression, instability, and conflicts, but also of the Paneuropean Movement, the League of Nations, and efforts at taming the nation-state.

To observers of the era, the 1930s in particular must have appeared as a global train wreck in slow motion. And for many prominent classical liberal authors of the era—such as the attendees of the Lippmann Colloquium in Paris in 1938—international federalism provided a natural answer to the destructive, conflict- and protectionism-prone nature of nationalism. Its aim was not just to facilitate cooperation between states but also to constrain their actions to ensure that their behavior was structured by rules. The gradual embrace of international federalism reflected a broader intellectual realignment that was underway in the West, most importantly in the United States, where the Republican right started moving away from its traditional isolationist stance over the course of the Second World War.

In 1943, in *One World*, a best-selling book written by President Franklin D. Roosevelt's Republican opponent, Wendell Willkie, argued the United States had to lead the efforts to "unify the peoples of the earth in the human quest for freedom and justice."[10] Another famous book, *The Anatomy of Peace*, written by the Hungarian émigré and activist Emery Reves and published in 1945, made an explicit case for global federalism and an end to the nation-state.[11] Many leading figures on the Republican right, such as Michigan Senator Arthur Vandenberg, who had initially opposed US involvement in the war and any open-ended "entangling alliances," came to the similar conclusions as Willkie and Reves and firmly embraced the internationalist agenda.[12]

As the contours of new international organizations such as the United Nations were becoming apparent, the United World Federalists were formed in 1947 to push for the creation of an international federal government, tasked with keeping the world at peace. Even Albert Einstein lent support to the cause, on the grounds of the danger posed by modern weapons of mass destruction:

> A world government must be created which is able to solve conflicts between nations by judicial decision. This government must be based on a clear-cut constitution which is approved by the governments and nations and which gives it the sole disposition of offensive weapons.[13]

In contrast to the hesitation prevailing today, few doubted in the decades after the war that further cooperation was the way of the future. The US commitment to the security of Europe and its global leadership in the fight against communism was a matter of bipartisan consensus and was rarely questioned outside of political fringes. In Europe, the emerging project of the continent's political integration was endorsed alike by the conservative Christian democratic right, social democrats, and free-market liberals such as Röpke. That is not to downplay differences in how various streams of Western political thought approached questions of international cooperation. However, throughout much of the postwar era, an agreement over its basic parameters existed, captured in Margaret Thatcher's speech ahead of the United Kingdom's 1975 referendum about membership in the European Economic Community. "[A]lmost every major nation," she argued "has been obliged . . . to pool significant areas of sovereignty so as to create more effective political units."[14]

In line with the proliferation of different forms of international coopera-tion and global governance, the advocacy and scholarship on the subject have exploded. Yet, in contrast to the alarmist picture painted by some conserva-tives, one would be hard pressed to find influential voices arguing for the creation of a genuinely global government superseding the nation-state. Even the most enthusiastic supporters of global governance see its mechanisms merely as complementary to those of democratic governance at the national level. As Anne-Marie Slaughter, one of the prominent progressive voices for global governance, puts it:

> The new networks thus coexist alongside a much more traditional world order, structured by both the threat and use of "hard" power. In that old world order, states still jealously guard their sovereignty and undertake commitments to one another with considerable caution. Still, it is possible to glimpse the outlines of a very different kind of world order in the growing system of government networks. In this system, political power will remain primarily in the hands of national government officials, but will be supplemented by a select group of supranational institutions far more effective than those we know today.[15]

GLOBALISM AND THE NATION-STATE

The fact that nation-states remain indispensable parts of the global order would have disappointed Albert Einstein and others who once advocated the creation of a genuine global government, as would the fact that the experi-ence of international cooperation has often fallen short of its ambitions. But that does not mean such cooperation has been inconsequential.

Besides military alliances, early attempts at formalized international cooperation dealt frequently with trade issues (more on those in chapter 6), postal services (the International Postal Union was founded in 1874), and health—the first International Sanitary Conference, with a focus on cholera, took place in 1851.[16] In 1889, French politician economist Frédéric Passy and the Brit Randal Cremer—both among the first recipients of the Nobel Peace Prize, in 1901 and 1903, respectively—founded the Inter-Parliamen-tary Union, which still exists. Initially, its members included individual par-liamentarians, but it has since become a platform for dialogue between na-tional parliaments themselves.

The turn of the century also saw multilateral efforts to create international rules to reduce conflicts and their lethality. The two Hague Conferences, in 1899 and 1907, led to the creation of the Permanent Court of Arbitration, which has since adjudicated disputes over territorial and maritime boundar-ies, sovereignty, human rights, and investment and trade. Just a few years before the outbreak of the First World War, the conferences produced a number of treaties and declarations, especially ones committing countries to reduce armaments and ban the use of asphyxiating gases in war—which of course saw their heyday only a few years later.

The First World War, which claimed over sixteen million human lives, gave a new sense of urgency to efforts to bind countries in a system of cooperation that could prevent similar disasters from happening in the future. One of the outcomes of the Paris Peace Conference was the creation of the League of Nations, whose inaugural General Assembly in 1920 concluded the proceedings of the conference. But the aspiration to make military conflicts disappear was not enough to overcome the challenges of the following two decades: crippling debt burdens, hyperinflation, the Great Depression, and the rising appeal of totalitarian ideologies throughout the 1920s and 1930s.

The League of Nations' mission was to "promote international co-operation and to achieve international peace and security."[17] This was the first major intergovernmental organization in the contemporary sense, built with the ambition of preventing global conflicts from recurring. At its peak, the League featured fifty-eight member countries but saw significant attrition in the late 1930s. Nazi Germany left in 1933, while the Soviet Union was expelled after its attack against Finland in 1939. With the outbreak of the Second World War, the League became largely irrelevant and what remained of it was absorbed into the emerging UN system in 1946.

Although US President Woodrow Wilson played a leading role in founding the organization, the US Senate refused to ratify the League's Covenant due to restrictions it was seen as placing, through Article 10, on Congress' ability to declare war.[18] The debate over US membership in the League was an initial salvo in a series of debates about the role that America should be playing in the world, which have continued until the present day. Earlier, Wilson excluded Republicans from the US delegation at the Paris Conference, adding fire to Republican opposition led by Senator Henry Cabot Lodge.

If not for Wilson's partisanship and his ideological agenda, the Republican position would have likely been different. Earlier in the war, the former President Theodore Roosevelt, a Republican, said that the time had come for "a great world agreement among all civilized military powers to back righteousness by force."[19] President William Howard Taft, another Republican, founded the League to Enforce Peace in 1915, with the stated purpose of advocating for the creation of a US-led international organization charged with ending interstate conflict. Even Lodge endorsed the goal when he said at a League to Enforce Peace meeting that he did not believe "that when Washington warned us against entangling alliances he meant for one moment that we should not join the other civilized nations of the world if a method could be found to diminish war and encourage peace."[20]

The League's decisions were taken by the Assembly of all member states and by its Council. A precursor of today's UN Security Council, the Council consisted of four permanent members (Great Britain, France, Italy, and Japan) and four temporary ones, elected by the Assembly for a three-year period. Some of the League's various offshoots, such as the International Labour Organization and the Health Organisation (later the World Health Organization), survive to the present day.

The League played several practical roles. First, it helped adjudicate territorial and other disputes between states. In the case of Upper Silesia, divided between Germany and Poland in 1922,[21] and in border disputes between Colombia and Peru, negotiations led to mutually agreeable settlements.[22] The League indirectly governed former colonies of Germany and the Ottoman Empire and other remote territories through its system of mandates. Those included large parts of the Middle East, as well as remote territories such as various Pacific islands. The stated purpose was to facilitate economic and political development until local leaders could assume the responsibilities of statehood.[23]

In several cases, such as Mussolini's invasion of Abyssinia, Japan's attack on China, the Spanish Civil War, Hitler's Anschluss of Austria, and the annexation of Sudetenland, the League was unable to make any difference to the outcomes. The League's failure to prevent the worst conflict in human history stood in contrast to the utopian thinking of the era, also manifested in the Kellogg-Briand Pact of 1928, which sought to outlaw war and ensure that "the settlement or solution of all disputes or conflicts . . . shall never be sought except by pacific means."[24]

The idealistic spirit that animated the League was not matched by the tools at its disposal. In order to secure world peace, the organization envisaged imposing sanctions against its aggressive members, but those never amounted to much. More fundamentally, the underlying rules, especially those geared toward a gradual reduction of armaments "to the lowest point consistent with national safety"[25] were not incentive-compatible. For one, the organization lacked any tools to curb the clearly offensive re-armament of nonmembers such as the German Reich. Meanwhile, countries such as France, Poland, and Czechoslovakia were building up their militaries primarily because they were concerned about the balance of power in their neighborhood after the rise of German Nazism. For obvious reasons, the League could not provide them with assurances against aggression from either Germany or the Soviet Union.

THE PROMISE OF THE UNITED NATIONS

The devastation, suffering, and industrial-scale killing that characterized the Second World War brought questions of international order and peace to the fore with a new salience. The advent of nuclear weapons added to the case for building a world system of governance to bring an end to armed conflicts, which could now mean the complete destruction of the planet. Adding to the anxieties was the subjugation of a large part of Europe by an aggressive communist Soviet Union, whose leadership did not hide its ambitions to conquer the world.

Some of the structures created after the war were global and universal in their aspirations, particularly the United Nations Organization. Its architecture, including the Security Council, was already the subject of discussions between the Allies during the war. In 1945, fifty-one nations joined as initial members. Unlike twenty-five years earlier, the Senate ratified the UN charter with a bipartisan majority of eighty-nine votes, reflecting a new internationalist consensus on US foreign policy.

Besides the General Assembly and the Security Council featuring five allied nations (China, France, the United Kingdom, the United States, and the Soviet Union—later Russia) as permanent members, the United Nations has ushered a large number of new agencies into existence. There was the Economic and Social Council to promote economic development and provide an umbrella for a long list of functional and regional commissions, specialized agencies, and other bodies; the International Court of Justice to settle disputes among member states; funds and programs under the auspices of the General Assembly, such as the International Children's Emergency Fund (today's UNICEF) originally created to help children in countries devastated by the war; the United Nations Development Programme; and many others.

However, the UN system has never grown into a world government in any sense of the term, nor has it shown any signs of moving in that direction during its seventy-year history. The UN Security Council comes the closest in the international realm to an international institution with genuine coercive powers, even though it relies on capabilities provided by individual countries. Accordingly, the benchmark for any coercive decision is very high, requiring unanimity of its five permanent members. The most important underlying rationale for such an institution is to serve as a backstop in instances of state failure leading to mass violence, murder, or genocide, as well as to prevent interstate conflicts.[26] And although its peacekeeping has played a helpful role, the United Nations lacks the capability to fulfill the most urgent mission that global federalists ascribed to it: curbing the proliferation of weapons of mass destruction. True, numerous arms-control agreements and conventions exist, together with the International Atomic Energy Agency in 1957 and later the Organisation for the Prohibition of Chemical Weapons. However, the existing agreements and nonproliferation agencies, as well as the United Nations itself, mostly lack the power to compel states to follow the rules.

In one important respect, the United Nations's design departs from the advice provided by theorists of international federalism from Kant to Hayek. Such thinkers envisaged that the international federation of the future would be formed by democracies—or republics of "enlightened peoples." In contrast, the one-country-one-vote principle and the permanent place of Russia (formerly of the Soviet Union) and China on the Security Council have meant that the world's tyrannies have been sitting as equals with free societies of the world.

While international politics requires bargaining between actors holding effective power, even if some of those might be totalitarian regimes, in the UN Security Council's case the result has often been dysfunction and paralysis. The Soviet Union and later Russia has been the most frequent user of the veto on the Security Council.[27] In August 1968, the Soviet veto prevented the Security Council from condemning the invasion of Czechoslovakia, for instance.[28] In more recent times, Russia has frequently exercised its veto against resolutions concerning the war in Syria. In April 2018, Russia even vetoed a proposal to establish a UN-led investigation into the chemical attacks against Syria's civilian population in the Douma area outside Damascus.[29]

Similarly, the UN Human Rights Council (replacing the UN Commission on Human Rights in 2006) has given an undue platform to tyrannical regimes. From its inception in 1946 until 2016, sixty-seven of its resolutions condemned Israel, compared to only sixty-one dedicated to human rights challenges in the rest of the world.[30] The council's current members (until 2020) include Angola (not free according to the 2018 *Freedom in the World* report), the Democratic Republic of Congo (not free), Nepal (partly free), Pakistan (partly free), and Qatar (not free).[31] In 2015, the Saudi ambassador to the United Nations in Geneva was elected chair of the council's panel appointing independent experts, notwithstanding the country's dismal record of human rights violations.[32] The world's most egregiously inhumane governments, including the Soviet Union, Ba'athist Syria, Central Africa ruled by "Emperor" Jean-Bédel Bokassa and later General André Kolingba, and many others have been parties to the United Nation's key legal instruments on human rights, including the 1966 International Covenant on Civil and Political Rights. Likewise, the 1948 UN Convention on the Prevention and Punishment of the Crime of Genocide[33] now has over 149 signatories. Those have prominently included countries that have since seen acts of genocide: Rwanda (a signatory since 1975), Yugoslavia (since 1950), Cambodia (since 1950), and Syria (since 1955).

Among the recent proposals to reform the UN system, the idea of a UN Parliamentary Assembly, put forward by a coalition of nongovernmental organizations,[34] would only compound these pathologies by requiring real parliamentarians from democratic societies to engage with "fake" ones, coming from regimes with no free elections. According to the 2018 edition of Freedom House's *Freedom in the World* report, only eighty-eight countries accounting for 39 percent of the world population qualify as free.[35] While that is not a reason to treat all the remaining ones as pariahs, pretending that a global democracy can be built with the assistance of undemocratic governments is thoroughly misguided.

PAX AMERICANA

It is no denigration of the United Nations to say that its creation was *not* the most consequential milestone of international cooperation of the postwar era. Instead, the threat of global communism to Western democracies was arguably the most important catalyst for cooperation between free societies. The North Atlantic Treaty Organization (NATO), founded in 1949, extended US security guarantees to Western European democracies. The stipulation that "an armed attack against one or more [members] in Europe or North America shall be considered an attack against them all"[36] in Article 5 of the North Atlantic Treaty, NATO's founding document, resembles Article 10 of the Covenant of the League of Nations. The fact that its ratification by the US Senate was uncontroversial reflected the intellectual shift already visible in the ratification of the UN Charter, as well as the immediacy of the Soviet threat.

Building a united military front against a common enemy with the ambition to bring the entire world under Soviet domination went hand in hand with efforts to revitalize Western Europe after the destruction of the Second World War and to prevent the recurrence of conflicts among European countries. The Marshall Plan, a US program of economic assistance, amounted to a modest 2 percent of GDP of recipient countries. As economists J. Bradford De Long and Barry Eichengreen showed,[37] the significance of the plan was often misunderstood. In itself, the amount of financial aid was far too small to provide a meaningful macroeconomic boost to Europe's economies. Additionally, its timing—the funds were disbursed after 1948—meant that it arrived only after much of Europe's ravaged infrastructure had already been repaired. However, the plan did facilitate political bargains over reforms "that left [Europe's] post–World War II 'mixed economies' with more 'market' and less 'controls' in the mix,"[38] setting the stage for the continent's extraordinary growth performance, which lasted until the 1970s.

The Marshall Plan came with its own organizational structures. In 1948, the intergovernmental Organisation for European Economic Cooperation (today the Organisation for Economic Co-operation and Development) was formed to administer the plan. Cooperation under US auspices soon gave way to the creation of distinctly European institutions establishing tighter economic and political ties between once-warring countries in the 1950s. First, the European Coal and Steel Community was created in 1951, followed by the European Atomic Energy Community (Euratom) and the European Economic Community in 1957, which comprised the foundation of the European Communities, later transformed into today's European Union.

International trade and finance have also been shaped by the rise of new global rules and organizations. The 1944 conference in Bretton Woods, with the participation of forty-four allied nations, established a system of adjustable fixed exchange rates built around the US dollar and two organizations that have played an influential role in the postwar world: the International Bank for Reconstruction and Development (today, the World Bank) and the International Monetary Fund (IMF). The Soviet Union took part in the proceedings but never ratified the agreement and never joined either institution. One underlying aim of the Bretton Woods system was to create an alternative mechanism for addressing macroeconomic imbalances, which during the Great Depression led countries to adopt protectionist policies, deepening the collapse of international trade and the economic contraction of the 1930s.

If the IMF's main role was to help stabilize the Bretton Woods system of fixed exchange rates, postwar governments also sought to set up formal structures that would ensure that international trade would be liberalized in a lasting manner. In 1947, the General Agreement on Tariffs and Trade (GATT) was set up among twenty-three countries and built around the idea of applying the principle of most favored nation in a nondiscriminatory manner, in order to prevent the reemergence of protectionist trading blocs. The agreement was the predecessor of today's World Trade Organization (WTO), which counted 164 members as of 2018. In nine rounds of multilateral negotiations, GATT proceeded with multilateral reductions of tariffs to the historic lows. Since the beginning of the Uruguay round in 1986, it has also made significant strides in reducing the nontariff barriers hindering international trade. Besides a mechanism that allowed countries to make mutual trade concessions in a collective way, GATT has set up fora for resolving trade disputes between governments.

It may be tempting to see these various institutions as neatly separable. In reality, they often come as parts of a common package. The elimination of power competition in Western Europe through the security guarantees extended to the continent through NATO went hand in hand with the process of economic integration. Economic openness, in other words, could not have been sustained for long without a shared commitment to peace. Conversely, as the Lippmann Colloquium attendees understood well, it is hard to imagine lasting peace in Europe if tools of economic protectionism had been still used by individual countries in the pursuit of narrow domestic goals. Today, the process of the United Kingdom's departure from the European Union illustrates just how difficult it is to "unscramble" the eggs of globalism without significant collateral damage: Even if it is in everybody's best interest that the United Kingdom remains involved in numerous facets of pan-European cooperation after Brexit (say, on security matters), the process of leaving has in itself proven to be a major distraction from such cooperation. More importantly, the acrimony created by Brexit has reduced the appetite for such cooperation in the years to come, leaving both the United Kingdom and the European Union weaker, more vulnerable, and poorer.

THE BEST OF TIMES?

Unquestionably, "the world that America made," to borrow the title of Robert Kagan's book,[39] has been extraordinarily kind to humankind. Violence, poverty, disease, and illiteracy have all declined, whereas democratic governance, economic openness, and life expectancy have risen substantially. With the fall of the Soviet Union, the global threat of totalitarian communism ended, and the United States emerged as an uncontested global superpower, shaping the world in its largely benign and democratic image.

Following the killing in the first half of the twentieth century, global deaths from both interstate and domestic conflicts have plummeted, as documented by authors including the Harvard University psychologist Steven Pinker,[40] University of Oxford economist Max Roser,[41] and the Cato Institute's Marian Tupy.[42] Furthermore, especially in the Western world, violence in general has been declining since at least the onset of modern times and has attained historically unprecedented low levels in the decades following the end of World War II.[43] Notwithstanding the recent resurgence of authoritarianism in countries including Russia, Turkey, and the Philippines and to a lesser extent in Poland and Hungary, democracy has been also spreading successfully around the world.[44] The two phenomena are not independent, as democratic countries are unlikely to engage in mutual warfare.[45]

The world has also become dramatically wealthier. Since the early postwar years, global GDP measured in real terms increased more than thirteenfold, as the global population quadrupled. In recent decades, the growth in global prosperity has been driven by the rise of previously underdeveloped regions of the world, including in Asia and sub-Saharan Africa. The embrace of markets and Schumpeterian creative destruction has gone hand in hand with a stronger emphasis on domestic institutions—rules guiding the business environment, rule of law, and reliability of the judiciary. On all such metrics, the world has seen dramatic progress. If current trends continue, extreme poverty (defined as subsistence on less than $1.25 per day) could be eliminated by 2030.[46]

The rising degree of economic openness has been instrumental to the postwar rise in economic prosperity.[47] Some of it is a result of domestic policy changes. An important part of it is an outcome of multilateral liberalization efforts under the GATT/WTO umbrella and also projects of regional economic integration. Average tariffs applied by advanced industrialized countries have fallen dramatically thanks to successive rounds of GATT negotiations. Traditional estimates of tariff barriers among the world's leading economies in the aftermath of World War II were about 40 percent,[48] whereas today's average tariff rates hover below 5 percent. New research suggests that the 1947 average tariff rate among the six main industrialized economies was closer to 22 percent, but the ensuing reductions were still significant. "Had [the postwar tariffs] remained in place," economists Chad Bown and Douglas Irwin argue, "these restrictions would have stifled the growth of world trade in the postwar period, and presumably slowed the economic recovery from the war."[49]

Although humankind faces many environmental challenges, not least that of climate change, which risk carrying substantial costs in the years to come, past decades have been also marked by improvements on a range of environmental indicators: Forest areas are growing in advanced countries, even in China, thanks to increasing yields; cropland erosion has declined; and greenhouse gases emitted by agriculture have fallen.[50] There have also been examples of indisputably successful large-scale international cooperation in protecting the environment—most prominently the case of phasing out chlorofluorocarbon emissions under the Montreal Protocol.[51]

It is, however, a grave mistake to see Pax Americana as an altruistic gift of Americans to the world. In a famous 2018 interview, the Fox News host Tucker Carlson asked President Trump: "Why should my son die for Montenegro?"[52] NATO's security guarantees and economic and trade liberalization facilitated by American leadership have been keenly in the US national interest. The sometimes demanding commitments that Americans make (e.g., to come to the defense of their small European allies) are made with the understanding that they boost America's security and other vital interests in the long run. A robust and credible NATO reduces the likelihood that US troops will die fighting in Europe, as hundreds of thousands of them did in the two world wars of the first half of the twentieth century. An open global economy sustained by institutions that the United States helped build has been a boon for America's innovators, entrepreneurs, and workers. And even if not everyone has benefited equally from the postwar era of globalism, wishing for its demise is extraordinarily shortsighted.

MOVING BEYOND STRAWMEN

For those hoping that the world would become a single polity replacing the nation-state, the postwar rise of international institutions must have been underwhelming. For one, the most effective forms of international cooperation are neither global nor have resulted in a dissolution of the nation-state. Instead of an evolution, for better and for worse, toward more unified governance structures, the reality of global governance has been characterized by diversity and fragmentation—in subject matters, institutional forms, and membership.

Today, international institutions cover a wide array of topics. There are organizations and legal instruments dealing with health issues (World Health Organization; Global Fund to Fight AIDS, Tuberculosis and Malaria), labor regulation (International Labour Organization), humanitarian assistance (UN Office for the Coordination of Humanitarian Affairs), protection of human rights (UN Human Rights Council), children (UNICEF, UN Convention on the Rights of the Child), prosecution of war crimes (International Criminal Court), the environment (UN Environment Programme, UN Framework Convention on Climate Change), agriculture (Food and Agriculture Organization), fisheries (Convention on Fishing and Conservation of Living Resources of the High Seas, Western and Central Pacific Fisheries Commission), security and arms control (Organisation for the Prohibition of Chemical Weapons, Mine Ban Treaty), telecommunications standards (International Telecommunication Union), trade (WTO), technical standards (International Organization for Standardization, International Electrotechnical Commission, CEN/CENELEC), food and food safety (Codex Alimentarius), financial stability (International Monetary Fund, Bank for International Settlements), economic development (World Bank Group, Inter-American Development Bank, Asian Development Bank, African Development Bank), and many others—as well as various combinations of the above on a regional basis (European Union, Association of Southeast Asian Nations, African Union).

Only a limited number of international institutions operate under the UN umbrella or claim to be universal in their character. Rather than "multilateral" in their operation (that is, involving *all* relevant actors—e.g., members of an international organization), many initiatives are increasingly plurilateral—that is, relying on small, voluntary subgroups of actors to cooperate. That is true even of the highly formal organizations such as the European Union, where especially during the eurozone and refugee crises different "coalitions of the willing" have emerged seeking to address different policy challenges.

Some international institutions are heavily bureaucratized and rules-based; others—such as G7 and G20—are informal while still exercising significant influence over world affairs. Many involve actors beyond national governments—the International Union of Local Authorities, an umbrella association of cities and local and regional governments, has been in existence since 1913. Standards and policies for air travel around the world are largely set by the International Air Transport Association, a trade association of air carriers from 117 countries around the globe. Technical standardization, both within Europe (CEN/CENELEC) and globally (International Organization for Standardization/International Electrotechnical Commission), has been spearheaded by the private sector in cooperation with national standardization bodies (public and private).[53] Responsible Care, representing chemical firms in sixty-seven countries and accounting for nearly 90 percent of global chemical production, sets voluntary safety standards for chemical products. Even some recent financing platforms in the area of health and humanitarian assistance, such as the Global Fund to Fight AIDS, Tuberculosis and Malaria, rely on private-sector participation as much as on national governments.[54]

Contrary to the common caricature of "out-of-touch" bureaucrats, international organizations can be effectively controlled by their "principals"—particularly by national governments. Of course, such control raises challenges but not impossible ones, nor fundamentally different from those existing within other organizations. Needless to say, international agencies have also become increasingly more open and responsive to civil society and other actors. Public consultations and outreach to the relevant stakeholders before making decisions is now commonplace.[55] That carries risks as well as opportunities because only a small subset of relevant actors can meaningfully engage with international organizations, not necessarily representative of everyone affected by their decisions.

Already in 1971, the influential German sociologist Niklas Luhmann predicted that global governance and particularly international law would experience a radical disintegration, driven not so much by differences between countries but by differences between "social sectors," policy areas, and the amounts of intellectual baggage and expectations behind each of them.[56] Today, some academics express their concern at the resulting "fragmentation" of international cooperation. "On balance, conflictive fragmentation of global governance architectures appears to bring more harm than positive effects," one study concludes, "and can generally be seen as a burden on the overall performance of the system."[57] But despairing that the reality of international cooperation is more multifaceted than a single coherent, top-down system of world government some would wish for is just as unhelpful as the alarmism, suggesting that the world might be just a few steps away from an unaccountable tyranny of international bureaucracies.

Not all forms of international cooperation are equally effective in achieving their stated ends. In particular, those with broad mandates and global membership often resemble large, expensive talking shops or employment programs for experts in the more obscure fields of international law and social sciences. At the same time, for example, the GATT/WTO system has clearly provided a critical anchor for open and nondiscriminatory trade policies. Its main contribution lies not only, or predominantly, in acting as an omnipotent global authority—the organization, after all, lacks any real coercive powers—but simply in holding governments to account by making their violations of common rules publicly known.[58] In contrast, the most effective environmental agreements comprise relative small numbers of countries and tend to be reached by countries that are similar in size.[59] As a general rule, design specifics matter a lot, such as the extent to which institutions mitigate cheating.[60] In trade, the nature of political regimes is extremely consequential: pairs of democracies are twice as likely to reach a trade agreement as pairs of a democracy and an autocratic regime, and four times as likely as pairs of autocracies.[61] In short, provided the diversity and the complex nature of international cooperation, anyone painting global governance with too broad a brush is likely to miss much of what makes this area of social life truly interesting.

There is a lot that conservatives and classical liberals can contribute to debates about international cooperation. But first, they need to stop forcing the world's reality into their Procrustean bed of simplistic dichotomies between the market and the state, or between national sovereignty and globalism. The next chapter shows how.

Chapter Three

The Anatomy of Globalism

International cooperation is not a monolith—quite the contrary. Writing about policies addressing climate change, political scientists Robert Keohane and David Victor noted a "Cambrian explosion" of different methods of international cooperation: "[A] wide array of diverse institutional forms emerges, and through selection and accident a few are chosen."[1] The resulting fragmentation may be unsettling. Yet many other social processes, including market competition, are characterized by their decentralized, seemingly chaotic operation. In fact, it has been long a hallmark of classical liberal and conservative scholarship to show why and how some of those mechanisms—involving trial and error, learning, and uncertainty—can produce socially desirable outcomes, which could not be replicated by top-down decision-making.

It is hardly a fruitful exercise to compare the complex, inevitably imperfect reality of existing international institutions with an unattainable utopia of fully coherent policy solutions to international problems, devised by a benevolent and omniscient social planner. In a world ridden with frictions, uncertainty, and incomplete information, coherence or perfection are rarely on the menu. Instead, the task of those seeking to understand globalism and improve on it is to tease out specific trade-offs that existing cooperation entails and to identify practices that are conducive to "good" results in real-world conditions. Such "goodness" is never an absolute. Social problems—related to the stability of the global economy, international peace, or environmental degradation—are rarely tractable problems with clear-cut solutions. Rather they involve gradual discovery, by fallible and possibly opportunistic individuals, of mechanisms that enable polities to exploit gains from cooperation. The quest for such solutions thus relies as much on learning by doing, trial and error, and on the *art* of politics and persuasion as it does on technical social science.

From the outset, it is important to make the distinction between international *institutions* and international *organizations*. Institutions, as social scientists understand the term, are rules of the game. Organizations, in contrast, are explicit associations of individuals or other actors, guided by rules (institutions) of one kind or another: government agencies, firms, political parties, business associations, foundations, or international organizations. Although essentially all international cooperation is *institutional* in character, only its subset involves the creation of specialized *organizations* featuring international agencies, secretariats, courts, and so on.

POLYCENTRICITY AND INTERNATIONAL ORDER

If there is one intellectual tradition built expressly to study the functioning of institutions in a range of different contexts, it is the Bloomington School of Political Economy, associated with the late Nobel laureate in economics Elinor Ostrom (1933–2012) and her husband, political scientist Vincent Ostrom (1919–2012). Instead of proceeding like most economists and political scientists—namely by setting up formal mathematical models and confronting their quantitative implications with existing data—the Ostroms pioneered the use of qualitative methods and fieldwork in both political science and economics. Elinor's initial focus was on the management of natural resources and local governance. She did her research "riding as an observer in a patrol car in the central district of a large American city,"[2] traveling to Nepal to study local irrigation systems,[3] watching forestry management in countries ranging from Switzerland to Japan, and investigating Pacific fisheries and lobster harvesting in Maine.[4]

The key insight of the Bloomington School is that the traditional dichotomy between markets and the state often fails to reflect the diversity of arrangements that people create to structure their affairs.[5] In the management of natural resources, as well as in other instances of local public goods provision, one observes numerous intermediate forms of organization—combining market-like characteristics, such as competition between different suppliers, with a lack of conventional private property rights and market prices.

Messy, hard-to-pin-down organizational forms tend to arise for good reasons, and it is hard to improve on them through deliberate policy reforms. For example, using evidence about residents' self-reported satisfaction, Elinor Ostrom famously argued against the consolidation of local and municipal governance and police districts in the 1960s and the 1970s. Overlapping and duplicitous arrangements existing in urban areas were actually cheaper and were associated with higher levels of citizen satisfaction than the more rational, consolidated structures proposed by the era's progressives.[6] The Ostroms' conjecture was that since "overlapping service areas and duplicate facilities [were] necessary conditions for the maintenance of competition in a market economy," similar forces were operating in the public sphere as well.[7]

The main concept deployed by the Ostroms is that of polycentricity, coined originally by the polymath Michael Polanyi—who happened to be present at the 1938 Lippmann Colloquium—to describe the operation of the scientific community.[8] Unlike monocentric forms of governance, where the proverbial buck stops with one decision-making node, polycentricity requires the existence of "many centers of decision-making which are formally independent of each other,"[9] constantly adjusting to each other's actions within a shared system of rules. Polycentric orders can be found in a variety of contexts. What they share is their basic nature as "open systems that manifest enough spontaneity to be self-organizing and self-governing. But the maintenance of such orders depends upon a sufficient level of intelligent deliberation to correct errors and reform themselves."[10]

This emphasis on deliberation and bargaining sets the Ostroms' intellectual agenda apart from the highly technical areas of modern social sciences. Concepts such as leadership, persuasion, and political entrepreneurship are difficult to operationalize in formal, quantifiable terms and yet they play an important role in most accounts of polycentric governance. The emphasis on those concepts distinguishes polycentric orders from a different but related concept developed by classical liberal economists, most notably by Friedrich von Hayek: that of *spontaneous order*.[11] Both rely on the existence of rules and involve many different nodes of decision-making instead of a single authority. One distinguishing characteristic of spontaneous order is a lack of agreement on common goals: a competitive market economy is able to produce socially beneficial outcomes while participants pursue their individual goals. In most polycentric orders, in contrast, an agreement on a common goal (preventing a common-pool resource from being depleted, for example) will be necessary.

Similar to spontaneous orders, polycentric governance too carries descriptive, explanatory, and normative connotations. Those are not always easy to disentangle in the Ostroms' work. On the descriptive and explanatory side, the no-nonsense research philosophy of the Bloomington School can be summarized by the idea that an institution "that works in practice can work in theory."[12] The Ostroms' approach is minimalistic in its theoretical apparatus, seeking to understand seemingly arcane arrangements on their own terms and thus uncover the logic and incentive structures behind them. "Elinor Ostrom's great contribution to human understanding was to document in detail how imaginative human beings are finding ways to turn social conflicts into opportunities for social cooperation," write the economists Peter Boettke, Liya Payagashvili, and Jayme Lemke. "Communities demonstrate a great ability to devise rules that align incentives among the various parties so that resource depletion and violent conflict are avoided and groups can reasonably manage common-pool resources and organize their collective choice in a self-governing manner."[13]

The normative dimension of the Bloomington School's research project is twofold. Firstly, based on the rich array of case studies of more and less successful instances of polycentric governance, general design principles can be teased out to help policymakers identify appropriate institutional structures to deal with particular international problems. Such principles include most prominently the existence of binding, enforceable rules; the ability of participants to change those rules in an orderly way; access to mechanisms of dispute resolution; freedom of entry and exit; and the decision-making autonomy of participants.

Secondly, and perhaps more controversially, free, democratic, and self-governing societies *ought to* display attributes of polycentricity, instead of being top-down hierarchies that one associates with unitary nation-states. A covenantal, federalist form of government is a natural response to the pluralist nature of a free society, allowing for a variety of beliefs, lifestyles, and values. According to Vincent Ostrom, self-governing societies are thus "richly nested assemblages of associations that include the diverse forms of association developed within and among units of government."[14] That is a holistic vision, which starts from the level of the individual and extends beyond the individual countries to international order. And although, as Vincent puts it, "the American way . . . is not the only way to achieve polycentric systems of order,"[15] true international order is possible only among self-governing, free societies. "The world cannot remain half free and half in servitude. Each is a threat to the other."[16]

The Ostroms' intellectual agenda is definitely not value-free. Rather, it is as an extension of the intellectual tradition of American federalism for which democratic politics is primarily about self-governance among equal and free individuals. For Vincent in particular, polycentricity provides a direct application of the logic behind Madison's *Federalist No. 51* and de Tocqueville's idea of "a society [that] governs itself for itself."[17] In other words, it is necessary to "grapple with the problem of constituting systems of government that operate with the consent of the governed."[18]

This is a tradition that naturally resonates with both conservatives and classical liberals, or libertarians, for whom the proper role of government is limited and derived from the consent of the governed. Very much like several connected streams of scholarship—public choice theory or new institutional economics—the Bloomington School provides an effective antidote against one-size-fits-all solutions, utopias, and panaceas for social problems. For

European conservatives, in turn, it is worth noting the parallels existing between the Ostroms' intellectual project and the distinctly continental tradition of personalism.[19] Embedded in Catholic social teaching and illustrated by figures such as Emmanuel Mounier (1905–1950) and Denis de Rougemont (1906–1985), personalism was the key source of intellectual inspiration behind the rise of Europe's center-right Christian Democracy after the Second World War. Using a holistic approach that starts from the individual as a member of a variety of organic communities, personalism takes a much more skeptical view of the nation-state than conservative thinkers do today, seeing it as an entity that is needlessly centralized and monolithic, and which can also become oppressive and Jacobinic. As a result, continental conservative thinkers have long proposed a reconstruction of existing nation-states along federal lines and "cooperation between independent decision-making centers and restructuring of the whole of society, both based on freely entered into contracts."[20] A covenantal, federalist approach was a means of decentralizing states and integrating self-governing communities in a common political order extending through the European continent.

Like personalism, the logic of polycentric governance extends to international problems. "[T]he substantive nature of many local and global problems is similar," wrote Elinor Ostrom and Michael McGinnis in their 1992 paper on "global commons." "Despite vast differences in the scale involved in local and global commons, the underlying logical configuration of the [common pool resource] situation at these levels is fundamentally similar. Thus, the theoretical principles underlying successful cooperation at both levels are also similar."[21] "If [a polycentric] system is to be extended literally 'through the whole system of human affairs,'" Vincent wrote, "it is necessary to explore the application of polycentricity to the realm of international affairs as well."[22]

Similar to the local level, one of the Bloomington School's key insights is that a simplistic dichotomy between the nation-state and global governance—or between "nationalist" and "imperialist" political projects, to borrow terms from Hazony's recent book[23]—is inadequate in accounting for the observed reality of international cooperation. More importantly, Vincent wrote after the fall of communism in Eastern Europe:

> Nation-states need not be viewed as the ultimate achievement in the organization of human societies. If patterns of associated relationships are to transcend national boundaries, rich networks of voluntary associations need to be complemented by rules that take account of communities of relationships that are multinational in character. It is federalism that provides the alternative to empire and opens opportunities in the light of 1989, for building upon and amplifying people's capacity for self-government.[24]

A rich, applied scholarship drawing on the lessons and methods of the Bloomington School has already emerged in response to the observed "fragmentation" of international cooperation. The empirical work has focused on the polycentric governance of international sporting events,[25] international shipping,[26] European Union,[27] climate change,[28] cyberattacks,[29] and financial regulation,[30] among other subjects.[31] The conclusions of much of this research are far from Panglossian. The existence of multiple centers of decision-making and the presence of both public and private actors raise questions of efficiency (especially when compared to first-best policy regimes imposed by a benevolent social planner) and also of accountability. As Elinor Ostrom herself expressly recognizes, "not all self-organized resource governance systems will be organized democratically or rely on the input of most appropriators. Some will be dominated by a local leader or a power elite who only change rules that they think will advantage them still further."[32]

However, in a world that lacks a central authority holding an ultimate monopoly over the legitimate use of coercion which could be invoked to uphold rules of the game, international cooperation is by necessity polycentric. No matter how lofty they appear, global governance arrangements invariably arise from the bottom up and involve independent nodes of decision-making. Of course, there is no reason why boundaries of policy problems, whether they have to do with public goods provision, mitigating externalities, or other issues, should coincide with national borders—just like they do not necessarily coincide at lower levels of government where an "[i]nformal arrangement between public organizations may create a political community large enough deal with any particular public's problem."[33]

DILEMMAS OF COLLECTIVE ACTION

The existence of actors independent of each other gives rise to problems of strategic interaction, or collective action. Such problems arise whenever decisions made by one actor (e.g., government, corporation, or international organization) affect other actors who face decisions of their own. In social sciences, such situations—in which the rational course of action requires one to provide the "best" response to what the other side does—are typically modeled using the tools of game theory, which encompasses a variety of different situations. Those range from situations where the interests of actors diverge and cooperation is difficult, though not necessarily impossible to sustain (a prisoner's dilemma, for example) to those in which cooperation occurs naturally (a coordination game). The following are some of the best-known examples that are relevant to the international arena, summarized more formally in Table 3.1.

All strategic interactions share several characteristics. First, the outcomes of such situations for every actor depend not only on their decisions but also on those taken by others. Payoffs and strategies are defined in terms of responses to what the other player does. Second, there is a continuum along which individual preferences are either increasingly in harmony or conflict: from a coordination game to a battle of the sexes and a prisoner's dilemma to a game of chicken. Mutually beneficial responses to such problems, in the forms of agreements and other cooperative mechanisms, must be adapted to characteristics of those situations.

The most immediately recognizable example of interactions encountered in the international sphere is a *prisoner's dilemma*, or a public good problem.

Table 3.1. Common Forms of Strategic Interaction

Prisoner's Dilemma		Actor 2	
		Cooperates	Defects
Actor 1	Cooperates	5,5	0,7
	Defects	7,0	2,2

Stag Hunt		Actor 2	
		Cooperates	Defects
Actor 1	Cooperates	5,5	0,4
	Defects	4,0	2,2

Coordination Problem		Actor 2	
		Strategy 1	Strategy 2
Actor 1	Strategy 1	5,5	0,0
	Strategy 2	0,0	5,5

Battle of the Sexes		Actor 2	
		Strategy 1	Strategy 2
Actor 1	Strategy 1	7,3	0,0
	Strategy 2	0,0	3,7

Game of Chicken		Actor 2	
		Aggressive	Accommodating
Actor 1	Aggressive	0,0	6,1
	Accommodating	1,6	5,5

In a basic public good setting, regardless of what the other party does, the incentives for each player are stacked in favor of not cooperating. Both actors find themselves trapped in a situation in which a common good is not supplied—even if both recognize that sustained cooperation would make them better off.

In economic textbooks, the mere existence of public goods is often cited as a rationale for their centralized provision by government. Likewise, for some defenders of global governance, the existence of *global* public problems is an argument for the creation of a single world government. However, cooperation in prisoner's dilemmas occurs in a decentralized fashion as well—most notably when the interaction takes places in "future's shadow"—that is, if the game is being repeated. Alternatively, players can use different mechanisms to tie their hands and commit to cooperation—that is, through explicit rules or delegation. Some of those can be self-enforcing, whereas others can rely on the presence of a third party to monitor and sanction defection.

A pure public good is characterized by nonexcludability and nonrivalry of its consumption. The former characteristic means that it is very hard to exclude those who do not cooperate from enjoying the good once it is produced. The latter one implies that the enjoyment that one derives from the good does not detract from the enjoyment of others. But the world does not offer many examples of goods that would satisfy both of those characteristics fully and unconditionally. Instead, excludability and rivalry each exist on a spectrum and can vary for the same physical good or resource depending on the number of users, technology, and existing institutions. Apart from private goods, which are rivalrous *and* excludable, others may be rivalrous but nonexcludable (common-pool resources, such as a common land used by a community for grazing). Others are excludable but nonrivalrous until a critical number of users is reached (club goods, such as a noncongested swimming pool or a golf course).

It is worth stressing that the "good" in question does not have to be a tangible commodity, resource, or service. In the international arena, governments *refraining* from certain activities (imposing discriminatory tariffs, for example) can also be understood as a public good, providing a compelling rationale for international cooperation. Already in 1939, Hayek's essay on international federalism made the point that "the federation will have to possess the negative power of preventing individual states from interfering with economic activity in certain ways, although it may not have the positive power of acting in their stead."[34] The idea of international institutions as self-imposed constraints on policymaking extends beyond questions of economic policy and the narrow category of international public goods. International cooperation provides an important safeguard against state failure in different contexts—for example, through effective peacekeeping and willingness of governments to stop, including by coercive action, acts of state-sponsored mass violence.[35]

A *coordination game* is another instance of strategic interaction with numerous practical applications in the international context. There, the actors' payoffs depend simply on whether they are all able to follow the same strategy. Following the same course of action, irrespective of what it is, brings greater rewards than divergence. Examples include technical standards, such as the layout of keyboards (QWERTY versus Dvorak) or driving on the left or right side of the road. There are strong incentives to converge on a single standard. As long as communication channels are open and participants are not already locked into incompatible strategies, the game settles easily on one of the available equilibria, without the need for elaborate enforcement mechanisms. However, getting every technical minutia aligned correctly matters a lot, especially for private business. The proliferation of voluntary technical standards, set by agencies funded and organized largely by the private sector, such as International Organization for Standardization, International Electrotechnical Commission, or CEN-CENELEC illustrates the solutions that arise to highly complicated coordination problems.

A hybrid between a coordination game and a prisoner's dilemma is known as a *stag hunt game*. Similar to a simple coordination game, it features two equilibria—but one of them is unambiguously better for everyone concerned. When two hunters pool their efforts to hunt down a stag, their rewards will be greater than when they both decide to hunt for hares. Because hunting down a stag requires a collective effort, the worst decision a hunter can make is to embark on a stag hunt while his partner chases hares. *Unlike* in a prisoner's dilemma (and similarly to a coordination game), players face no temptation to deviate from the high-reward effort to hunt down a stag as long as they believe that the other players are following the same strategy.

An important question is whether most real-life situations involving the provision of public goods on an international scale resemble prisoner's dilemma or a stag hunt games. But what is equally, if not more, important is how institutions can transform strategic situations so that they "lead to outcomes other than remorseless tragedies."[36] When complemented with mild sanctions for noncooperation, a prisoner's dilemma can be transformed into a stag hunt game in which cooperation will be self-enforcing. Alternatively, cooperation can arise through repeated, open-ended interactions.

The details of these strategic interactions matter for institutional design. In a simple coordination game, for instance, players do not care what particular strategy they want to play. All they want is to align their actions with those of other players. However, it is also possible to imagine a setting under which governments or other actors have an incentive to coordinate with others while holding different views over the desired outcomes of such coordination. Such a game is known as a *battle of the sexes*, based on the textbook parable of a couple that seeks to spend an evening together. True to gender stereotypes, the male partner wants to see a boxing match, whereas the woman wants to have a romantic candlelit dinner. Both, however, prefer each other's company over pursuing either of those activities alone. In technical parlance, both going to the dinner together and going to the boxing match together constitutes a Nash equilibrium.

To sustain cooperation, the two partners will likely have to come up with a mechanism for either alternating between different evening activities or compensating each other through other means (e.g., by monetary transfers). Unlike in a prisoner's dilemma, the future's shadow is of little help here. Rather than seeking to lock into one equilibrium (say insisting on going to a boxing match every evening), cooperation is enhanced by flexibility and availability of avenues for regular renegotiation.

Practical examples abound in the international context. Sometimes the different preferences over outcomes reflect purely material or economic considerations. At other times, they correspond to deep-seated cultural or ideological divides. The European Union, for example, is expected to act in areas in which member countries disagree vehemently, such as migration and asylum. Voters in some countries (e.g., Spain and Germany) have so far tolerated more lenient asylum policies than in others (e.g., Poland or Hungary), for whom the arrival of large numbers of asylum seekers from culturally distant societies is unacceptable. Alternating between a "high-immigration" and a "low-immigration" scenario—as between going to dinners and boxing matches—is not practicable. Although compensatory payments to states accepting a higher number of migrants or asylum seekers have been proposed in the form of tradable refugee quotas,[37] this mechanism has not yet been translated into policy practice.

One cannot take for granted that in such situations cooperation will always be sustainable or even desirable. The key question is whether the gains created by cooperating outweigh the costs of making cooperation viable. Such costs involve bargaining, transacting, and possibly dividing the surplus through some compensation scheme. But if those costs are too high, then *not cooperating* might very well be more desirable[38] —even if it means foregoing real gains from cooperation.

In settings in which actors' preferences are diametrically opposed, one actor's gain can become another's loss. Governments might make simultaneous claims to a single scarce resource or piece of territory. In such situations, an overtly aggressive move—say, military aggression—by one makes it rational for the other to back off, and vice versa. Such situations of conflict are often likened to a *game of chicken*, involving two teenagers driving cars on a collision course toward each other, or a *hawk-dove* game.

But even in a game of chicken, overall gains from cooperation might exist. That is, the overall size of the pie may be larger when confrontation is avoided. Furthermore, cooperative efforts, especially collective security, play an important role in deterring prospective adversaries from pursuing aggressive strategies. Deterrence consists of signaling, in a believable way, that if one's opponent plays an aggressive game, one is determined to respond with aggression—*even if* that brings about the least desired outcome for both. Effective deterrent threats can involve the prospect of using nuclear weapons, or they can involve alliances with larger and more powerful countries. By itself, Estonia cannot threaten Russia with overwhelming force should the Kremlin decide to invade. However, as long as NATO remains a credible organization, potential Russian aggression is deterred by the prospect of NATO allies, including the United States, coming to Estonia's help. Of course, the alliance's credibility itself is a public good problem as the member states of the alliance may be individually incentivized to shirk their responsibilities.

Using toy models to draw practical policy recommendations is fraught with difficulties. Unlike in elementary game theory, real-world situations in local and international contexts are complex and uncertain and involve different actors facing different information. As a result, such situations are rarely reducible to formal game theoretical models. The assumptions made by game theorists about rationality and shared knowledge of the structure of the game, too, might be detached from the reality of problems arising in the international arena, especially considering that states hide sensitive information from their adversaries. The structure of the game itself is rarely set in stone. The relevant payoffs reflect not only the limiting realities of the physical world (scarcity of resources, environmental damage associated with different types of pollution, etc.) but also prevailing beliefs, technology, available institutions, and business models. New military technologies, such as nuclear weapons, provide new sources of deterrence. First, absent international rules, organizations can provide devices for sanctioning uncooperative behavior, and so forth.

Applying the tools of game theory to the real world requires a careful understanding of the true motivations of the actors involved. Such understanding can be relatively straightforward in the case of private companies, which seek to maximize shareholder value, as well as in the case of nongovernmental organizations or lobbies with known agendas. Especially in the case of firms operating in a highly competitive marketplace, profit maximization is thus an emergent outcome of market filters that weeds out companies straying too far from efficiency, rather than an explicit objective of individual chief executives and entrepreneurs.[39] Most fundamentally, agents in game-theoretic settings are rarely expected to be also *architects* of situations that they find themselves in. Yet it is precisely that condition that characterizes international cooperation and other forms of polycentric governance. In other words, the strategic situations facing governments and other actors can be changed *by actors themselves*, through institutional design.

In contrast, self-described realists[40] see international cooperation and its effects on the structure of strategic situations facing governments as irrelevant. Moreover, realism assumes the existence of well-defined national interests, which tend to be *identical* regardless of the characteristics of the government or the country in question and can be reduced to the pursuit of power. "[R]ealism does not distinguish between 'good' states and 'bad' states," writes University of Chicago's John Mearsheimer, "but essentially treats them like billiard balls of varying size."[41] But the decision-making of governments is less straightforward than that of firms facing fierce competition. Competition in the international arena is much weaker compared to a marketplace with free entry. The world, after all, has seen numerous failed and dysfunctional states and polities that have nonetheless persisted for a long time. Different states behave very differently on the international scene when faced with similar decision-making problems. That is not surprising. Social choice theorists demonstrated a long time ago that there was no direct link between individual preferences and those of collective bodies. As a result, it is impossible to see states and their motives as simple aggregations of preferences and motives of their inhabitants.[42]

Furthermore, most social scientists agree that institutions (rules of the political, economic, or social game) play a fundamental role in shaping societies, including the quality of their governance and long-term economic and social outcomes.[43] National governments that rely on the consent of the governed face different political incentives than those that thrive on predation or rely on large revenues from natural resources and can be expected to pursue different aims in the international arena as well. Because of their numerous veto points, significant foreign policy commitments undertaken by democracies often reflect a broader political consensus, not just the whims of a narrow governing elite. In contrast, promises made by authoritarian regimes carry a much weaker degree of credibility as they can be reversed more easily. More generally, however, it would be a mistake to presume that the world of international cooperation and conflict is populated by actors guided by symmetrical, or even broadly comparable, motivations.

THE DOs AND DON'Ts OF POLYCENTRICITY

How does polycentric governance solve collective action problems? By creating explicit rules and delegating decision-making authority, governments may find it easier to stick with socially beneficial policies, such as free trade, and to curb conflict inherent in prisoner's dilemmas and games of chicken. "Nested" governance helps address free riding directly as well.[44]

Overcoming a prisoner's dilemma faced by an extremely large group, say the entire population of Europe, might be impossible. However, if Europe's nation-states are nested within a system of international cooperation, such as the European Union, the problem can be broken down into a number of prisoner's dilemmas occurring *within* individual European countries, and one facing EU member states as a group as well. Assuming that national governments are each in a position to tackle such collective action problems through appropriate domestic policy—a Pigouvian tax or a better definition of property rights—all that remains is to overcome the collective action problem existing *among* European countries. That can still be challenging but is likely more easily achieved than cooperation across the entire European population. In coordination problems, common platforms for communication between governments or other actors provide focal points that help countries select among the available equilibria. If there are diverging preferences over available equilibria, a common layer of governance helps devise compensation schemes or other ways of sharing the surplus created by cooperation.

The aim of international cooperation is not to come up with ready-made solutions to policy problems. Rather, it is to structure interactions between governments and other actors through rules or institutions, while allowing individual decision-makers to pursue their own interests subject to agreed-upon rules.[45] Contrary to what critics allege, international institutions are not arbitrary impositions. Instead, the existing ecosystem of institutions, agencies, treaties, and conventions, with their idiosyncrasies, successes, and failures, is a result of choices, negotiations, and bargaining of governments and various nonstate entities, with the aim of solving real or perceived problems.

Many decisions have to be made about any efforts at international cooperation. First, what structures, if any, should be built? Should there be international agreements? Platforms for regular engagement between governments on a given policy topic? Agencies with autonomous decision-making powers? Should membership be exclusive, open to any country (or perhaps to nonstate actors), or defined regionally? What is the substantive scope of the new mechanisms of cooperation? Often, single-issue institutions change or expand their focus under political pressures and changing social realities. Unlike in the past, for example, trade agreements often delve into questions of labor standards and regulation. Who is liable to comply with the rules set by the institution? States? Corporations? Private individuals? Who will monitor compliance and what will the sanctions regime look like? What tools will be available for changing the institution once it is set up?

For cooperation to be successful, the actors' institutional choices must correspond to the characteristics of the problem under consideration, including the strategic nature of the situation (prisoner's dilemma, coordination game, etc.). The number of actors, their symmetry and like-mindedness, or lack thereof affect the costs of reaching an agreement, as does uncertainty about the actors' behavior and motivations—or indeed, about the underlying state of the world.[46]

Studying the links between international institutions and such characteristics is not easy. More often than not, institutions are *sui generis* and not easily reducible to a small number of measurable dimensions. More fundamentally, there is nothing mechanical about their construction. Instead, they are results of decisions made by actors who are fallible, faced with incomplete information, and influenced by prevailing intellectual orthodoxies of their time. Unlike a Hayekian spontaneous order, a polycentric form of cooperation requires intelligent deliberation about the underlying rules and "sophistication about rule-ordered relationships."[47] A self-governing society needs active citizens to generate rules, solve problems, and push against encroachments of power. One challenge of international cooperation is to extend the same ethos of self-governance, contestation, and responsiveness into the international realm in order to solve problems of collective action that cross national borders.

In their 1992 paper, McGinnis and Ostrom investigate the extent to which the conclusions arrived at by the study of polycentric governance in local settings can be scaled up to inform decisions over the design of structures governing the "global commons."[48] The design principles that they propose are not derived from first principles but are informed by decades of fieldwork and case studies of polycentric governance taking place in different contexts, both large and small.

Actors face strategic settings limited by their *boundaries*. The polycentric literature on common-pool resources emphasizes a clear definition of boundaries that enable participants to exclude outsiders from accessing the resource in question. In the international domain, an equivalent mechanism consists of producing *club* goods for those who participate in certain international arrangements—the North Atlantic Treaty Organization's (NATO's) security guarantees or the European Union's single market are good examples. But very often, such arrangements produce substantial positive externalities that spill over onto other actors. In other situations, the challenge is global in nature, erasing the significance of boundaries altogether. Yet what is true for all governance arrangements is the importance of clearly defined mandates, focused on challenges that span across national borders—instead of wishy-washy aspirations at improving the human condition.

Rules are at the heart of any system of governance. The rules have to be congruent with the underlying strategic situation that the mechanism is aiming to tackle. In a polycentric order—unlike under simple top-down impositions—those who are affected by the rules ought to be able to participate in modifying them.[49] The exercise of *voice* (having a say in the content of rules) can be structured in different ways. In real-world international organizations, we can observe a variety of voting rules ranging from unanimity to simple majority voting. As a classic work by Buchanan and Tullock shows, an "optimal" voting rule will balance two types of costs: *decision-making costs*, which involve the time and effort required to reach a collective decision, which rises as the majority needed for passage of proposals increases; and *external costs*, or the expected losses to those who are overruled by collective decisions. Those fall as the required majority gets larger—all the way to zero in the case of unanimity.[50] Both types of costs depend on the subject matter and other characteristics of the organization, especially its membership—all of which vary dramatically in the real world. In some contexts, it may furthermore be reasonable to assign different weights to different actors (governments, for example), based on the population they represent or the financial contribution that they make to the functioning of the organization. A polycentric order also gives participants the option of leaving the arrangement, especially if it does not live up to their needs and preferences. Voice and *exit* are complementary forces that enable the governance structures to adapt—or to allow sorting into multiple different cooperative arrangements responding to each participants' needs.[51]

Compliance with the rules needs to be *monitored*, either by participants themselves or by an entity accountable to those participants. Violations of rules would lead to "*graduated sanctions*" by "other participants, by officials accountable to these participants, or by both."[52] It is of little value when mechanisms of international governance are used not to guide behavior that has important cross-border effects but simply to assert general aspirations without ambition or means to translate them into reality. Examples from the international realm include numerous human rights conventions, oftentimes signed by the most egregious of authoritarian regimes.[53]

The use of monitoring and sanctions has to reflect the character of the situation. In some settings, especially in simple coordination games, there is little need for explicit enforcement. Instead, actors voluntarily converge on a solution as long as they can overcome informational barriers. By contrast, in prisoner's dilemmas (such as maintaining a free and undiscriminating global trading system) defections need to be systematically punished in order to sustain cooperation. But in all polycentric settings, "participants and their officials have rapid access to low-cost, local *arenas to resolve conflict* among participants or between [the] participants and officials."[54]

Finally, in order to qualify as polycentric, a system of governance also needs to preserve the organizational and decision-making *autonomy* of participants. In the international context, that means that the various mechanisms of governance—including treaties and international organizations—cannot reduce states and other actors to simple units of a bigger whole but instead "nest" them into mechanisms of international cooperation *while* preserving their ability to govern themselves independently. The same reasoning applies to the "nesting" that occurs within smaller units, all the way down to the individual. The emphasis on the political order as a self-organizing structure built from the level of the individual up and with the explicit intention of preserving individual autonomy distinguishes the polycentric approach from its more ambitious alternatives.[55]

AGAINST PANACEAS

In both its explanatory and prescriptive forms, polycentrism provides an antidote to utopian thinking, whether it takes the form of romanticizing national sovereignty as if international problems did not exist, or a utopian vision of global governance—capable of fixing all that is ailing humankind. There are no one-size-fits-all solutions to social problems, and neither does the existence of global problems imply the need for unified global solutions.[56]

Quite the contrary, "institutional diversity may be as important as biological diversity for our long-term survival," as Elinor Ostrom wrote with her coauthors in a 1999 article in *Science*.[57] Such diversity is not incompatible with international cooperation. In fact, if diversity is going to generate desirable outcomes, it has to be embedded in an overarching international system of rules that facilitate self-governance, contestation, and adaptation—instead of existing in a state of Hobbesian anarchy. "Societies that place substantial reliance upon polycentric patterns of order present contestable options that must necessarily challenge systems organized on autocratic principles," writes Vincent Ostrom.[58]

The key lessons that the Bloomington School offers to foreign policy practitioners are simultaneously simple and powerful. First, international instruments should only be used to tackle international problems: conflict and terrorism, trade, investment, movement of people, environmental challenges with substantial cross-border effects, common-pool resources, and so forth. Policymakers should not be relying on international instruments to get their way on domestic policy questions that appear too difficult to address through normal political and legislative processes. International institutions have to preserve the internal autonomy of states and other actors, structure interaction between them, and give participants the possibility of exit. That alone distinguishes mechanisms of international governance from state and state-like entities, which claim monopolies on the legitimate use of coercion.

Second, successful instances of international governance rest on rules, which are designed to accommodate strategic situations spanning across borders. Such rules are not immutable but can be changed by relevant participants so that governance arrangements may adapt. The decision-making and organizational autonomy of actors—most frequently of governments, but also of various state and nonstate entities including regulators, corporations, chambers of commerce, and so forth—must be preserved in a nested governance structure, without international decisions sidelining or suffocating their normal operation.

Finally, successful governance efforts require a common understanding of the underlying strategic situation and trust reflecting a shared, sincere intention to realize the gains presented by cooperation. That is where questions of political leadership, bargaining, and persuasion come into play, making polycentric governance more than just a technical exercise. As anyone who has attended a meeting of their homeowners' association will attest, a high degree of like-mindedness is not necessarily present at the local level either, which is why the Ostroms' work emphasizes the role of human agency and leadership in the context of local governance.

Arguably, achieving such like-mindedness is even harder in international contexts. But that makes the elusive questions of leadership and persuasion all the more important. The United States, for example, played a critical role after the Second World War by not only stopping the Soviet expansion in Europe and elsewhere in the world through its sheer military might but also by providing various international public goods, which in turn made other countries in the noncommunist camp more eager to cooperate.[59] Finally, America's soft power and its attraction as "the shining city on the hill" provided an indispensable focal point and a compass without which the post-1989 transitions to market economies and democracies in Eastern Europe would not have been possible.

The same considerations underlie the importance of the question of *who* is cooperating. Transnational associations of private individuals, firms, or organizations united by a shared set of goals, or governance structures set by governments that are accountable to their electorates, operate fundamentally different from those that unite different actors around one table as equals. There might still be a case for, say, democracies and authoritarian regimes sharing channels of communication or having access to a multilateral bargaining forum. However, one should be under no illusion about the willingness of autocracies to use the tools of multilateral cooperation—many of them devised to service free, democratic societies—to their own advantage.

Furthermore, the fact that mechanisms of governance arise from the bottom up is not in itself a guarantee of good outcomes. Challenges arise particularly when polycentric governance involves different categories of actors with different motivations—democracies and authoritarian regimes, or governments and the private sector—or when the institutional setup is not constructed adequately to tackle the underlying strategic situations, or when policymakers overreach to use tools of international cooperation to address domestic issues. But contrary to claims made by those who have been sounding the alarm about global governance, the main risk of such failures is *not* the emergence of unaccountable, tyrannical structures destroying democratic accountability but rather dysfunction, waste, and ultimately a populist back-lash of the kind that we are seeing in the Western world today. Relatedly, the risk lies in the possibility that in the absence of clear-headed Western leader-ship—the adversaries of freedom and self-governance will seize these instru-ments and use them against us.

Chapter Four

The West's Globalist History

If the critics and defenders of globalism make one common mistake, it is the idea that transnational and international governance structures are simply a recent add-on to an age-old political structure: the nation-state. That view is deeply flawed. "History does not repeat itself," as the famous saying attributed to Mark Twain goes, "but it rhymes." Although different in both scope and style, governance across state borders was no stranger to the West's past, particularly in Europe.

For one, the nation-state, usually taken as the baseline for any conversation about these topics, is *far* from a historical norm. Rather, it became fully fledged only in the second half of the nineteenth century and followed a period of romantic nationalism and efforts at self-emancipation among different European ethnic groups living in political units, which had existed for far longer than the modern nation-state and had borne little resemblance to it. Furthermore, the track record of the nation-state in its sovereign heyday, from the mid-nineteenth century to the Second World War, is decidedly mixed. The era was one of recurrent conflicts and destructive economic policy, including protectionism, financial instability, and episodes of hyperinflation.

Second, even the age of the nation-state was not free of international cooperation. At the turn of the twentieth century, much of the Western world was tied up in a cobweb of bilateral trade agreements[1] and was also part of the same monetary regime: the gold standard. Neither of those systems, however, proved to be robust to the turbulences that lay ahead. More significantly, perhaps because of the excesses of disruptive nationalism of the time, the era of modern nation-states was also marked by a growing interest in questions of international cooperation.

In short, globalism is *nothing new*. The real question is not so much whether global governance is desirable, but rather *what form* it should take. *Institutions* have long shaped interactions between various polities. The past, like the present, witnessed a proliferation of shared institutions, joint decision-making, and common, polycentric governance. Their quality and effectiveness varied widely, as did their longevity. However, it would be a mistake to dismiss the relevance of past examples of "international" governance on the grounds that they have not survived to the present day. Many lasted for much longer than either present-day nation-states or today's international organizations, and as was the case of the Holy Roman Empire, they lingered for over a *millennium*.

What makes Europe's history a particularly useful reference point for today's conversations about international cooperation is that it combined a high degree of political and institutional diversity within a relatively small geographical space that shared many, though not necessarily all, of its cultural and intellectual reference points. According to the economic historian Joel Mokyr, it was precisely this combination of diversity and unity that provided a space for local experimentation in science and technology, business models, and policy, combined with a shared European marketplace of ideas, and that was responsible for the West's economic rise in the Industrial Revolution.[2]

At the same time, political fragmentation on a relatively crowded continent meant frequent collective action problems, frictions, and conflicts. The rest of the world offered coherent, consolidated models of societal organization—the great empires of China, the Mughals, and the Ottomans, for example. But those existed in relative isolation and displayed a high degree of political centralization, eschewing the challenges that come with the existence of numerous independent centers of decision-making.

With a large number of states and state-like entities crammed onto a densely populated continent that shared the common anchors of Christianity and classical thought, medieval and early modern Europe were in some ways microcosms of today's globalized world. As a result, some describe the present as a "new medievalism," due to the parallels between overlapping sources of political authority, their sometimes universalistic claims, and multiple and fuzzy political loyalties.[3]

Today, many highly diverse countries coexist in a world that seems "flat" thanks to deeper economic integration, improving communication and transport, global consumer patterns, shared business culture, and English as the world's *lingua franca*. During the Middle Ages and the early Modern Period, the same effect was exercised by Europe's geography, the presence of many different sources of authority, and the ubiquity of Latin.

The Roman Empire was a true exercise in *global* governance. Romans did not recognize other state-like entities and sought to assert their *imperium* indiscriminately over the entire known world. The idea of such a universal jurisdiction did not disappear entirely with Rome's fall but it had to accommodate the dramatic decentralization of Europe into myriad different polities—kingdoms, duchies, free cities, and fiefdoms. A vast majority of those, however, were tied together by diverse feudal relations, alliances, and institutional structures built to facilitate commerce. Furthermore, similarly to the Roman legal tradition—itself influenced by stoicism—the Catholic Church saw the whole of human society as a single ethical and moral community and therefore subject to the same "natural law."[4]

Three distinctly polycentric "international" institutions from those periods help illustrate the ubiquity of governance across national borders in Europe's past: the Holy Roman Empire, a loose federation that spanned a large portion of Europe's territory for over a thousand years; the Hanseatic League; and the classical gold standard, a de facto currency union spanning across most of the Western world in the second half of the nineteenth century.

Although none of these three examples was short-lived, they suggest that there is nothing permanent about the specific forms that polycentric governance spanning across jurisdictions takes. Yet the existence of externalities, collective action problems, and other challenges across the borders of political units is a recurring theme throughout history—as are the collective efforts to address such problems. The forms of governance discussed here all displayed strong polycentric characteristics. They featured nodes of decision-making that were autonomous from each other instead of being organized into a hierarchical system with decisions taken at the top. All were based on common rules, in which participants had a say. Noncompliance led to sanctions and the arrangements offered the possibility of exit. Finally, all of them hinged on a common understanding of the underlying strategic situations. When some of these attributes disappeared, either suddenly or gradually, the governance system came under strain, often irreparably. But, most importantly, all three of these examples clearly pierce through the illusion of the sovereign nation-state as a somehow primitive fact of human (or European) history.

THE HOLY ROMAN EMPIRE

For more than a millennium after the fall of the Roman Empire, Europe was a smorgasbord of state-like entities. These were not sovereign nation-states in the modern sense. Due to a limited understanding of geography, jurisdiction was not even defined in territorial terms until the modern era. What is more, the polities themselves were linked together by feudal relations. Much of Europe's society was bound together by Christendom. Until the Reformation, the pope's jurisdiction was seen as universal, not limited to any particular territory, including even the right to award lands in *terra incognita*.[5]

To be sure, notional papal jurisdiction did not always go hand in hand with effective political control. Throughout the medieval period, the pope's claim to universal jurisdiction had a secular counterpart: the emperor of the Holy Roman Empire, which styled itself the successor to Ancient Rome. The Holy Roman Empire, which lasted from Charlemagne's coronation in 800 until 1806, was a highly decentralized elective monarchy that encompassed hundreds of different state-like entities: kingdoms, principalities, duchies, and self-governing cities, with different degrees of representation in the three-tier Imperial Diet, which included at its top the electors, followed by other princes, bishops, and city representatives. At its peak, around three hundred different states and state-like entities, including very small ones, were part of the empire.

Though its underlying rules changed over time, at no point could the empire be seen as a unitary state or a federation with a clearly identifiable central government. Perhaps the most contentious rules were those that concerned elections of the emperor. In the Golden Bull of 1356, Emperor Charles IV limited the number of electors to seven, and during the Thirty Years' War, two additional ones were included. The Hussite Wars, the Reformation, and the Thirty Years' War made the association between the Holy Roman Empire and the Catholic Church unsustainable, leading to an increasing degree of devolution as a solution to the problem of religious toleration.[6]

The empire had no standing army. Its own economic resources were limited to those of the *Reichsgut*—territories in direct imperial possession. But those yielded revenues that were increasingly insufficient, and the elected emperors, especially the Habsburgs, were forced to rely on their own resources. The hybrid character of the empire—more than a personal union but less than a federation—has given rise to lively debates about its nature among legal scholars, including Jean Bodin and Samuel Pufendorf, who called the Holy Roman Empire a "mis-shapen monster."[7] Because of its claims to continuity with Ancient Rome, many scholars tried to apply mechanically Roman legal concepts to the empire, seeing the emperor as *summa potestas* (highest authority), princes as *praesides provinciarum* (officials exercising delegated authority over provinces), and Imperial Diets as a version of *senatus*.[8] Because of the visible mismatch between the empire's reality and those concepts, Pufendorf—one of the most important legal scholars of the era—saw the empire not as a federal state (and much less as an extension of Ancient Rome's unitary imperium) but rather as an ill-formed alliance of states.

Neither Roman law nor a simplistic view of the empire as an ad hoc alliance does justice to its real functioning or explains why and how it survived for a millennium. There was never a clear-cut settlement to the question of who held ultimate legal authority, which was a source of constant tensions. To scholars of polycentric orders, particularly to Vincent Ostrom, that tension was not necessarily a weakness:

> The constitution of the Holy Roman Empire evolved over a period of nearly a thousand years through processes of oath taking mediated through the Church amid struggles for papal and imperial supremacy. The rituals of investiture in both ecclesiastical and secular offices involved the acknowledgment of obligations to others. Struggles over authority relationships were sustained both within the ecclesiastical realm, and within the secular realm as well as between these two realms. . . . Wars persisted; but the presumptions of God's peace interposed limits against violating churches as places of refuge, of assembly, and of worship, and in establishing the presumption that rules of war applied among knights as the warriors of Western Christendom.[9]

Unlike entities more loosely connected to the empire, such as the Netherlands' United Provinces or the Swiss Confederation, imperial states *were* subject to the emperor's decisions and those of the Imperial Diet and the empire's courts. However, the constituent states also controlled much of their domestic policy, particularly on questions of religion and foreign policy. At the Westphalia negotiations, the empire's Protestant delegates assembled first with the Swedes in Osnabrück, whereas the Catholics met in Münster under the French leadership. The two groups convened only after common positions were reached along confessional lines.

The peace treaties of Westphalia concluded at Münster and Osnabrück provided a new legal backbone to the empire. Contrary to the popular interpretation, the treaties implied little in terms of "Westphalian sovereignty" and did not herald the beginning of the era of independent nation-states.[10] Instead, the treaties of Westphalia provided the empire with a constitution, superseding the previous reliance on customary law and several fundamental laws, such as the Golden Bull, which set the rules of the election process, defined the privileges of princes and bishops, regulated the mining of metals and salts, and outlawed associations of cities and lords that posed a threat to the emperor's authority.[11] Critical among the earlier fundamental laws was the Peace of Augsburg of 1555, which sought to reconcile the Catholic universalism of the empire with the rise of Lutheranism within its territories. It codified the *ius reformandi* ("right of reform") exercised mainly by Protestant princes in determining the faith of their subjects and the legal rules associated with religion.

Augsburg did not provide a lasting solution to religious conflicts. *Ius reformandi* opened the way toward the secularization of the church's property in Protestant lands. The principle did little to resolve situations in religiously mixed territories, nor did it address questions of migration. In contrast, Westphalia's institutional innovation consisted of a secular constitutional framework, which phased out the power of princes to regulate religious life altogether. It gave legal protections to subjects of different faiths with regards to their local authorities and "froze" the status of church property based on the status quo in 1624.[12]

Before and after Westphalia, the empire featured little in terms of a central government other than the emperor and the Imperial Diets. However, the polity always shared legal rules and a regime of sanctions for violations of such rules. For instance, the Golden Bull stipulated that "privileges or charters concerning any rights, favors, immunities, customs or other things," as well as feudal possessions, could be revoked from anyone who "in any way invades his lords . . . or disturbs them, or brings harm upon them, or furnishes counsel, aid or favor to those doing this."[13]

The empire had also a system of judicial review, featuring two supreme courts: the Imperial Cameral Tribunal and the Imperial Aulic Council. The Peace of Westphalia posited that half of the judges of the former had to be Protestant. The members of the latter were directly appointed and paid by the emperor and represented the nobility, the knights, and "scholars." Both courts acted as appellate courts in civil and criminal cases but also in disputes against the estates of the empire. Only the emperor enjoyed immunity. Furthermore, the Aulic Council exercised, at least in theory, a degree of control over the finances of local territories. Princes and free cities were required to have major loans authorized by the council. In cases of insolvency, the council temporarily suspended the authority of the prince and appointed a commission to take over the local government until such creditors were paid off.[14]

The empire offered the possibility of exit for its constituent states. During the late Middle Ages, the Swiss cantons in particular asserted themselves as de facto autonomous within the empire, gaining immunity from the rulings of Imperial Courts, with the exception of the Basel canton.

The empire's extraordinary longevity reflected the extent to which its covenantal nature fostered peace among its constituent units. That was no small feat—yet, in an era of geopolitical turbulences, the empire's decentralized operation proved less effective at defending itself against aggressive and increasingly powerful neighbors, especially France. Most ecclesiastic principalities, free cities, and other small polities in the empire disappeared after 1803 as a result of territorial losses to France and the expansion of leading German states. This raised the question of how the dispossessed nobles and bishops should be compensated by the cash-strapped empire. The gradual political consolidation eliminated the principal beneficiaries of the legal and security umbrella provided by the Holy Roman Empire, which was declared dissolved in 1806, following Napoleon's victory at Austerlitz.

HANSEATIC LEAGUE

In the Middle Ages, self-ruling cities often formed alliances with shared mechanisms of governance over trade or monetary questions. The many examples include the Lombard League[15] and the two Rhineland alliances of the thirteenth and fourteenth centuries.[16] However, one city association stands out for its longevity, sophistication, and distinctly polycentric features: the Hanseatic League. The Hanse (sometimes also spelled Hansa), which experienced its heyday during the fourteenth and fifteenth centuries, started as an informal trading network of self-employed merchants operating across the Baltic Sea, before developing into a formal political structure among the cities themselves, with explicit rules and decision-making structures. The league's influence—which included around seventy larger and 130 smaller cities and towns—started to wane by the end of the fifteenth century, and the organization had de facto ceased to exist by the outbreak of the Thirty Years' War.

For an extended period, however, Hanseatic traders came to dominate, if not completely monopolize, commercial activities in Northern Europe. This success occurred despite their small amounts of initial capital and relatively simple trading structures—a far cry from the bourgeoning financial innovation and complicated cashless schemes seen in Italy over the same period. The most common Hanseatic arrangement was a *commenda*-like depositary partnership[17] through which a merchant in one city would entrust their goods for sale to another merchant headed to a different city. Thanks to reputation, repeated interaction, and reciprocity, such arrangements managed to curb opportunistic behavior that would naturally arise in one-off, single-deal interactions. The key to Hanse's success, much like in the well-known case of Maghribi traders of the eleventh century,[18] was trust and reciprocity that developed alongside kinship-based commercial networks.[19] The shared culture and alignment of preferences over desired social norms and practices provided the basis for a social contract that gave birth to formal political institutions shared across the cities of the Hanseatic League.[20]

As cities started to offer Hanseatic traders privileges and commercial activity intensified, formal institutions were developed to complement the existing informal practices. Those lowered transaction costs by giving traders access to new contractual and enforcement mechanisms. First, *Kontore* (trading posts) were founded initially in Bruges, London, Bergen, and Novgorod, where traders enjoyed various trading privileges.[21] *Kontore* actively lobbied to protect Hanseatic privileges, adjudicated disputes, and featured a cashier and a seal necessary for legal acts.

In the middle of the fourteenth century, the *Kontore* were complemented by meetings of the Hanseatic Diet (*Hansetag*). The first meeting took place in 1356 with the purpose of creating a platform for making common decisions on behalf of the Hanseatic League as a whole. The *Hansetag* made decisions about internal matters as well as foreign relations with other powers and feudal lords of the era. A tabulation of the 205 questions addressed by *Hansetag* between 1265 and 1418 suggests that around 37 percent of the decisions dealt with "international" questions.[22] Those revolved around the defense of privileges that had been granted to Hanseatic traders by various rulers of the era. Internal matters, in turn, included detailed regulations on shipping and freight, money exchange, and measurement standards.

Hanse's relations with England were particularly complicated.[23] One contentious point was the league's notorious protectionism. To protect its position in Bergen, for instance, the league almost ousted Norwegian traders.[24] Faced with Hanseatic traders who enjoyed privileges granted by the English crown, English traders demanded reciprocal arrangements in Hanseatic towns. A 1375 petition of English merchants identified the monopolistic nature of the league as a force behind price increases of Baltic goods. Richard II concurred and awarded new trading privileges to English businesses, resulting in even higher prices for goods coming from the Baltic region.[25] The league retaliated with sanctions before reaching a settlement in 1380. However, that was not the end of tensions, as the Hanse-friendly Teutonic Knights continued to harass English traders in the Baltic. A more lasting solution was found only in the Treaty of 1437, which granted the English the right to enter Prussia and settle there, tax free. Yet that was not enough to overcome the declining interest of the English in the Baltic region, who were driven out by English domestic problems, particularly by the War of the Roses.

Besides questions of trade, the league took efforts to provide security for its cities and trade routes by forming alliances with bishops and other feudal lords in the neighboring regions. In Saxony, for example, Hanse cities collectively sought the protection of the bishop of Halberstadt, the count of Hessen, and the dukes of Brunswick-Lüneberg. As late as 1468, the Hanse organized a naval blockade of England, demonstrating that the commercial alliance was also a military force to be reckoned with.[26]

The Hanseatic League had strong polycentric features.[27] Of course, the *Kontore* relied on the services of numerous bureaucrats and technical experts. Yet the league itself had neither a central political authority other than the *Hansetag* nor any permanent central staff. By providing a formal underpinning and political clout to previously existing informal trading networks, the league was supplying valuable club goods to its members, albeit sometimes those clashed with commercial interests of businesses outside the Hanse. In practice, convergence on a single set of standards and a form of legal "harmonization" consisted of an increasing reliance on Lübeck law, which was the leading city of the league. Other Hanse cities explicitly adopted large parts of Lübeck's legal code. With some exceptions, disputes could be referred to Lübeck courts whenever interpretation of Lübeck law was in question.[28]

The rules of the Hanseatic League involved sanctions for noncompliance. After one member of the league, Cologne, sided with the English in recurring trade disputes and the naval war between the Hanse and the English crown, temporary sanctions were imposed on the city following the Treaty of Utrecht in 1474. Those effectively excluded, for a period of time, the city from the league. It was also possible to exit the league: Berlin and Frankfurt an der Oder did so with other Brandenburg cities after the league had failed to protect them against a hostile takeover by Elector Frederick II in 1442.[29] Later, Krakow stopped paying membership fees and sending its representatives to *Hansetag*, thus ceasing to be a member around 1500.

Because the league was an outgrowth of an informal network of trading arrangements, its functioning relied on a shared commercial culture and increasingly on common legal traditions embodied in Lübeck law. Ultimately, the alignment of interests was contingent on economic and political reality. Due to the changing nature of Baltic trade, the interests of cities in the league diverged in the late Middle Ages. As a result, the value of cooperation within the Hanse declined for both traders and cities alike. Although some formal Hanseatic arrangements remained in force until much later, from the sixteenth century onward, the league found itself increasingly irrelevant and died out peacefully as its purpose was no longer of value to its members.

THE GOLD STANDARD

Control over monetary policy is usually seen as an essential prerogative of sovereign nation-states. From that perspective, projects such as the euro, which has replaced national currencies in much of Europe with one currency and a single central bank, appear to be anomalies. Even scholars who are generally sympathetic to the idea of European integration are often skeptical about the euro. Kathleen McNamara, director of Georgetown University's Mortara Center for International Studies and an acclaimed expert on the European Union's politics, called the common currency "a unique experiment in monetary governance without a government."[30]

Yet that view is almost the exact opposite of historic reality. The combination of fiat money controlled by nation-states and floating exchange rates, which has dominated the world since the collapse of the Bretton-Woods system, are a deviation from the historic norm—for better and for worse.

To be sure, there is a lively scholarly debate about the euro, as well as a large literature that assesses preconditions under which it is advisable for countries to join currency unions.[31] The latter is built around the idea of "optimal currency areas" developed by the Nobel Prize–winning economist

Robert Mundell.[32] But regardless of whether monetary unions and fixed exchange rate mechanisms are desirable and under what circumstances, it is wrong to claim that they are somehow anomalous.

True, governments have been long involved in controlling money supply, first directly and later through central banks, which were set up initially to provide governments with credit. However, until the twentieth century, their ability to do so was limited, as the value of major world currencies was almost always invariably defined in terms of precious metals, most frequently gold and silver. Because the supply of such metals was limited, so was the ability of governments to expand the supply of money and use it to finance public debt or conduct macroeconomic stabilization policies.

That did not necessarily mean the absence of any monetary policy, because the growth of money supply and inflation are also shaped by the behavior of the banking sector, legal requirements to hold reserves, and so forth. Wherever they initially existed, central banks were used, even under commodity standards, to monetize public debt. Italian city-states, for example, led the way in debasing their coins and inventing new denominations in order to finance wars.[33] Still, under such a standard, the leeway enjoyed by governments and central banks was greatly restricted compared to what is now taken for granted. It is not a surprise, therefore, that the most dramatic instances of hyperinflation in history occurred in the twentieth century—in Weimar-era Germany, the former Yugoslavia, and Zimbabwe—in settings in which governments did not guarantee the convertibility of money into any commodity.

In some cases, particularly in the United States before 1913 as well as in Canada and Scotland at various points in their history, the gold standard operated in a completely decentralized manner, without the presence of any central banks whatsoever. For instance, between 1792 and 1913, both gold and silver were freely coined in the United States, and private banks would also issue banknotes redeemable in one of the two metals.[34] Obviously, under any commodity standard, the total issuance of banknotes was not necessarily equal to the amount of the commodity in the bank's vaults. Still, the system operated smoothly as long as the banks were able to redeem those who demanded it. Individual banks faced incentives to avoid overissuing banknotes because that led to an outflow of gold from their reserves, potentially eroding confidence about the bank's ability to redeem all of its bank notes.

Decentralized gold or silver standards operating without the presence of any central bank constituted polycentric orders.[35] Some of the same polycentric features were also present *internationally* under the "classical" gold standard of the late nineteenth century, which overwhelmingly featured central banks (the United States was a prominent exception). That arrangement was characterized by an absence of restrictions on the mobility of international capital. If a central bank relaxed its monetary policy, an outflow of gold and capital from the country would ensue, creating strong incentives for bankers and "regulators" to change course quickly. As long as central banks were determined to maintain gold convertibility, the international monetary system was capable of rebalancing itself and delivering a nontrivial degree of financial and economic stability.[36]

What matters is not so much how the operation of the gold standard compares to modern central banking but rather that international commodity standards, accompanied by a high degree of capital mobility, acted as effective monetary unions or fixed exchange rate mechanisms. Upon closer inspection, the world of yesteryear—particularly the gold standard—resembles the operation of the eurozone much more than the juxtaposition of myriad national currencies with floating exchange rates that form the baseline of today's monetary system, and are therefore taken for granted in most policy conversations.

Fixed exchange rates and capital mobility were the defining features in a world characterized by a hitherto unseen degree of economic integration. Economist John Maynard Keynes wrote:

> The inhabitant of London could order by telephone, sipping his morning tea in bed, the various products of the whole earth, in such quantity as he might see fit, and reasonably expect their early delivery upon his doorstep; he could at the same moment and by the same means adventure his wealth in the natural resources and new enterprises of any quarter of the world, and share, without exertion or even trouble, in their prospective fruits and advantages; or he could decide to couple the security of his fortunes with the good faith of the towns-people of any substantial municipality in any continent that fancy or information might recommend.[37]

The classical gold standard relied on two very simple rules: gold convertibility and free capital flows. No explicit enforcement, other than the market-based capital flows, were necessary to sustain the discipline. Countries also had the option of exiting and abandoning either the gold parity or free movement of capital. As a matter of fact, many did in the interwar period, especially during the Great Depression, particularly as they arrived at the conclusion that the macroeconomic costs of sustaining the gold parity were not justified. Those central banks that were determined to uphold their currencies' ties to gold were often unable to provide sufficient liquidity to avoid deflationary pressures of the 1930s, which in turn led to high levels of unemployment. In contrast, those economies that left the gold standard early in the Great Depression experienced more vigorous recoveries than those that remained in "golden fetters" for longer.[38]

In its "classical" form, the gold standard rested on a shared understanding—or a lack thereof, depending on one's perspective—of the macroeconomic role of government, which was dramatically different from the one prevailing today. In particular, few saw a significant upside in active management of interest rates or credit by the government. If anything, the prevailing orthodoxy leaned toward the idea that such efforts would be destabilizing.[39] That view was later challenged not only within the economic profession but also after the Great Depression, as the general public came to expect macroeconomic management as a part of the government's purview. Still, even after the Second World War, Western leaders decided to forego free capital mobility, not a fixed exchange rate. What resulted was a system of managed exchange rates in which the Federal Reserve committed to guaranteeing the convertibility of the US dollar to gold, but only to other central banks. That, jointly with restrictions on capital flows, effectively ended the self-balancing mechanism of the gold standard in favor of a system by which countries could maintain significant external imbalances as a result of their autonomous monetary policies.

* * *

The three examples—the Holy Roman Empire, the Hanseatic League, and the gold standard—illustrate just how ahistoric the idea of nation-states as islands unto themselves is. The history of the Western world is a history of international institutions and governance spanning across national borders. Ideologically driven efforts to rewrite it into a history of politically autarchic nation-states are thus bound to be exposed, sooner or later, for what they are.

All three examples discussed in this chapter also displayed strong polycentric features. They involved autonomous actors—medieval polities, cities, and central banks—independent in their own spheres of decision-making. The governance mechanisms sought to respond to commonly perceived challenges: external threats, mutual commercial interests, lowering of transaction costs, and so on. They relied on rules, shaped by the actors themselves, and on graduated sanctions for noncompliance. All of them provided, explicitly or de facto, the option of exit to their participants. This alignment of ideas and motivations was essential and once it disappeared—as a result of territorial consolidations of states within the Holy Roman Empire, transformation of Baltic trade, or effects of the Great Depression, alongside with changes in ideas—the viability of such systems of governance quickly faded.

There is a lesson to be drawn from the fact that none of the three historical examples survived to the present day, despite their significant longevity. Nothing is permanent in social affairs, and the withering away or pruning of obsolete institutional arrangements is not inherently bad. Needless to say, today's world of global governance offers many examples of agencies, treaties, and norms that have outlived their purposes. But the question of how such institutions disappear, what replaces them, and who makes that determination are all critically important. Even if the ongoing backlash against globalization is driven by justified grievances, it risks destroying institutions that are definitely *not* obsolete and still fulfill important roles. Defending them and making the case for their renewal is one of the key challenges of our time.

Chapter Five

Free Trade and Its Discontents

"If there were an Economist's Creed," Paul Krugman wrote in 1987, "it would surely contain the affirmations 'I understand the Principle of Comparative Advantage' and 'I advocate Free Trade.'"[1] Although Krugman, who won the Nobel Prize in economics in 2008, has become one of the leading voices of America's intellectual left, he has never revisited his broad commitment to free trade. A 2012 University of Chicago poll of leading academic economists showed their practically unanimous agreement with the statement that "freer trade improves productive efficiency and offers consumers better choices, and in the long run these gains are much larger than any effects on employment."[2] Somewhat surprisingly, the public shares economists' enthusiasm. In a recent poll, 82 percent of Americans stated that free trade was good for the US economy.[3] And for all of Europe's protectionist reputation, 73 percent of polled EU citizens believe that free trade is a good thing, according to a Eurobarometer survey.[4]

Yet, judging by the politics of the moment, free trade seems also under unprecedented attack. Ahead of the 2016 presidential election in the United States, Hillary Clinton joined Donald Trump in rejecting the Trans Pacific Partnership,[5] a comprehensive trade agreement that would have joined twelve American and Pacific countries in ambitious trading arrangements. Once in office, President Trump appointed Peter Navarro as the White House's Director of Trade and Industrial Policy. Navarro's views,[6] especially on trade with China, fall far outside the mainstream of the economic profession, similarly to Trump's own emphasis on bilateral trade deficits.

President Trump has halted the negotiations between the United States and the European Union over the equally ambitious Transatlantic Trade and Investment Partnership (TTIP) and introduced, or threatened to introduce, a number of new tariffs in the hope of reducing the US trade deficit. In Europe,

TTIP stirred controversy too, along with the European Union's trade agreement with Canada, hardly a haven of unregulated Dickensian capitalism. Numerous activists and politicians claimed that the two agreements would erode Europe's high standards of food safety and consumer protection and "endanger citizens' rights to basic services like water and health."[7]

The increasingly tense interplay between trade and politics should not blind us to the fact that the postwar liberalization of trade worldwide has been a resounding success and remains one of globalism's most significant achievements, if not *the* most important achievement, period. This opening up did not happen spontaneously in an institutional vacuum. Instead, the current degree of economic openness and the resulting prosperity are results of a combination of multilateral trade negotiations under the auspices of the General Agreement on Tariffs and Trade (GATT) and later the World Trade Organization (WTO), underwritten largely by the United States, as well as a variety of regional initiatives.

The existing platforms for trade liberalization—WTO, regional trade blocs, and other preferential trade agreements (PTAs)—have their weaknesses. One is that the low hanging fruit of slashing tariffs and quotas has been mostly picked. The remaining trade barriers revolve around politically thorny issues related to technical and regulatory questions, intellectual property, and distorted agricultural markets. In addition, the one-way nature of WTO membership has been subject to abuse by state-capitalist economies, particularly China, which has gained access to Western markets while jealously shielding its incumbent firms from foreign competition.

However, giving up on the institutions underpinning the current trade regime would be extremely unwise. Without the creation of the WTO and PTAs, nothing would stop politicians from reverting back to trade policies that cater to special interests while distributing the costs over the wider public. As the example of the Great Depression showed, danger would be imminent in bad economic times when the temptation to impose discriminatory trade barriers would be strong and doing so would amplify the size of adverse economic shocks. And, as the attendees of the Lippmann Colloquium witnessed during the 1930s, a zero- or negative-sum economic environment provides fuel for extremist ideologies, militarism, and war.

WHY FREE TRADE?

Given the prominence of voices skeptical of free trade, such as Harvard's Dani Rodrik[8] and Cambridge University's Ha-Joon Chang,[9] it is easy to exaggerate the disagreements existing among economists. Skeptics typically claim that industrialization is essential to modern economic growth. And because processes of industrialization often took place under a substantial degree of economic protection, as in late eighteenth-century England, nineteenth-century United States, and East Asian economies after the Second World War, they argue that the canonical advice given to developing countries to simply open up their markets to trade is misguided.

Apart from the fact that for every instance of seemingly successful industrial policy that relied on protection against imports one can find several examples of its failure, the link between protectionism and manufacturing is dubious. Although important trade barriers existed in the eighteenth century, few economic historians argue that those account for the Industrial Revolution in England. Likewise, in the highly protectionist late nineteenth-century United States, economic growth was driven by the rise of population and capital accumulation, not by trade policy. In fact, as a study of US growth by Douglas Irwin shows, "tariffs may have discouraged capital accumulation by raising the price of imported capital goods" and the observed productivity growth also seemed the strongest in sectors that were not affected by the tariffs, such as utilities and services.[10] Furthermore, industrialization is not the only path to high incomes. The economic rise of Hong Kong, South Korea, and Singapore, for example, revolved around exports of labor-intensive manufactures rather than through conventionally conceived industrialization. New Zealand, Australia, and Ireland also eschewed conventional forms of industrialization and maintained an extreme degree of economic openness during their respective economic takeoffs.

The case for free trade relies on a number of arguments, from the classical concepts of division of labor and comparative advantage, developed respectively by Adam Smith and David Ricardo,[11] through ample empirical evidence that links trade openness and economic performance,[12] to new insights developed under the umbrella of the so-called New Trade Theory. The latter uses realistic assumptions about product differentiation and economies of scale to explain the richness of real-world trade flows.[13] To be sure, the case for trade under New Trade Theory is more complex than in earlier settings and not without qualifications. Still, a vast majority of the economic profession would agree that for the complicating factors existing in the real world, free trade constitutes a desirable baseline policy regime.

The main challenge to free trade is thus not intellectual, but political. Political leaders under all regimes face temptations to provide concentrated benefits to well-organized interest groups in exchange for support, while dispersing the costs of such policies across the wider population. Tariffs, quotas, and other protectionist measures are perfect examples. The benefits for domestic producers tend to be sizable, whereas the destroyed gains from trade between domestic consumers and foreign producers are many, although individually small. In his famous essay "What Is Seen and What Is Not Seen," the nineteenth-century economist and journalist Frédéric Bastiat famously points out that the gains from protectionist policies tend to be visible, while their costs (i.e., foregone opportunities) are not. [14]

As a result, the challenges of trade liberalization are primarily *domestic* in nature: one of keeping the influence of well-organized interest groups at bay. Or, as Krugman puts it, the "reason we have international trade agreements . . . [is] not to protect us from unfair trade practices by other countries. The real goal, instead, is to protect us from ourselves: to limit the special interest politics and outright corruption that used to reign in trade policy." [15] The domestic political economy is thus the main reason why a unilateral policy of no tariffs is a poor policy prescription, even if it is economically justified. [16] Unilateral free trade assumes away the domestic problem of sustaining a regime of unilateral free trade politically in an environment where partner countries might well engage in discriminatory protectionism. The only way such a regime could thrive is through a sudden enlightenment of policymakers worldwide regarding their resilience to domestic clamoring for protection from foreign competition.

Individually, governments face the choice of whether to provide their producers with protection against foreign competition, while imposing an overall burden on the rest of the economy. Depending on the specifics of the situation, this choice can be understood as a prisoner's dilemma or as a stag hunt game. Either way, the presence of such collective action problems provides a strong rationale for *international institutions* to sustain trade openness politically.

HISTORY OF TRADE, FREE AND UNFREE

Free trade is not the historic norm. In his landmark 1776 work, *An Inquiry into the Nature and Causes of the Wealth of Nations*, Smith wrote that "[t]o expect that the freedom of trade should ever be entirely restored in Great Britain, is as absurd as to expect that an Oceania or Utopia should ever be established in it." [17] Britain and the Western world—and indeed humankind as a whole—has since then come a long way. Smith did not foresee that his teachings, alongside those of other classical economists, would soon inspire a wave of political activism. The campaign to open up trade led to the repeal of the Corn Laws in 1846, which had been introduced to keep domestic grain prices up (as well as rents accruing to landowners). Europe then saw a wave of trade liberalization, most of which occurred through bilateral trade agreements between countries. [18] The Cobden-Chevalier trade treaty concluded between Britain and France in 1860 provided a model for many other governments. Prohibitions on French imports were removed and replaced by duties not exceeding 30 percent. Britain dramatically reduced wine tariffs and started admitting many French products duty-free. [19] The Cobden-Chevalier Treaty triggered a wave of similarly structured bilateral trade agreements throughout the continent, many featuring "most favored nation" (MFN) clauses—ushering in a period of unprecedented trade liberalization, as other countries emulated the example.[20] MFN clauses obliged countries to apply indiscriminately the same terms that they had made available to any other country. Trade liberalization even eventually reached the once-insular empires of Japan and China, which concluded trade agreements with major Western economies—in the case of Japan[21]—or were forced to allow their trade regime to be set by foreign powers—as in the case of China after the Opium Wars.[22]

Yet the open trade regime did not survive for very long. By the time existing trade agreements were due for renewal, the economic and political climate in Europe had changed. Furthermore, protectionist ideas came back into prominence, especially through the work of the German Historical School[23] and the salience of its "infant industry" argument in European countries undergoing belated industrialization. Presaging arguments made by today's trade skeptics, the German Historical School rejected the cosmopolitanism implicit in arguments of classical political economists such as Adam Smith and Jean-Baptiste Say in favor of free trade.[24] Instead, it embraced a parochial, nation-centric perspective on economic development that naturally resonated during the consolidation of Europe's nation-states, especially the German Reich and Italy.

After Germany's victory over France in 1871, Chancellor Bismarck imposed a sizable war indemnity on France. After France's early repayment, the German economy plunged into a crisis triggered by the Panic of 1873. The hardship amplified the voices of German producers clamoring for tariff protection. The government was also looking for new sources of revenue to make up for the shortfall created by France's early repayment. In 1879, Bismarck introduced the Iron and Rye tariff, imposing import duties on various agricultural and industrial goods: grains, meat, pigs, textiles, machinery, and also various semi-manufactured products. In 1882, France experienced a severe banking crisis that threw the country's economy into a recession lasting for the remainder of the decade, which was exacerbated by falling commodity prices. In the second half of the 1880s, those generated enough political pressure to reintroduce trade barriers, including in industries that had traditionally been export-oriented. In 1892, a new system of tariffs was introduced, named after its leading advocate, Jules Méline.

A series of trade conflicts and a gradual retaliatory rise in tariffs preceded the outbreak of the First World War. To be sure, global trade continued to expand during what later became known as the "First Age of Globalization," though without approaching the current levels of economic integration existing around the world. The growth of trade during this period was primarily a result of the falling costs of transport and the integrated financial system, underpinned by the gold standard. When the war came, the effects on trade were devastating. Governments introduced new tariffs, foreign exchange controls, and other restrictions and sought to reorient their economies toward war production. Physical infrastructure needed for trade—roads, railroads, and ports—was being destroyed, and warring sides engaged in frequent blockades and U-boat campaigns in order to bring each other's trade flows to a halt.

Sadly, the peace of 1918 did not stop the tide of protectionism. With the exception of a temporary tariff truce between 1927 and 1928, average tariff rates continued to climb during the 1920s and then exploded with the arrival of the Great Depression—particularly after the United States turned its back on free trade with the introduction of the Smoot-Hawley Tariff Act of 1930.[25] As a result, the volume of international trade contracted by some 40 percent between the Depression's onset and the early 1930s, returning international trade to its pre–World War I levels.[26]

The rush to protectionism was particularly pronounced in countries tied to the gold standard, which could not respond to economic shocks by monetary policy.[27] Yet the main reason for the failure to maintain a free trade regime was political. The cobweb of bilateral trade agreements with MFN clauses created a problem of collective action. Instead of engaging in trade liberalization, governments waited for others to do the political heavy lifting of trade negotiations, hoping to reap the benefits through the MFN clauses. The United Kingdom's introduction of a preferential tariff system for Commonwealth countries in 1932 marked an effective breakdown of the nondiscriminatory trade system,[28] followed by the emergence of warring trade blocs that persisted long after the war.

In contrast, the progress achieved since 1945 has been astounding. The average tariff rate applied by leading industrialized economies in the late 1940s was around 20 percent, with some earlier estimates running as high 40 percent.[29] Today, after seven decades of continual trade liberalization, that rate is firmly below 5 percent. That decline has been a result of multilateral tariff reductions under the auspices of the GATT and WTO, as well as the proliferation of preferential, mostly regionally organized trade arrangements.

The GATT/WTO negotiations proceeded in a series of rounds. The most recent one, the Doha Round, was launched in 2001 and has been effectively dead since the ministerial meeting in Nairobi in 2015. While the initial rounds included several dozen countries, took months, and involved only tariff concessions, 159 countries are participating in the current Doha Round—which has focused overwhelmingly on the complicated issues of regulatory and nontariff barriers. To an extent, the WTO system has been a victim of its own success. With most tariffs and quotas out of the way, what remains are the hard cases of politically sensitive sectors (e.g., agriculture), the diversity of regulatory regimes, questions of intellectual property, and so forth. As the acrimony of ever-longer and inconclusive negotiations suggests, a common forum involving most of the world's governments and insisting on negotiations in the form of a "single undertaking" (requiring an agreement on everything or nothing) might no longer be the most suitable venue for achieving further progress.

Yet it is a mistake to see the WTO only through the prism of the now-stalled multilateral negotiations. Its main contribution is the idea of nondiscrimination, which has become a basic principle of trade policy applied globally. Nondiscrimination refers to two distinct concepts. First, nondiscrimination means that governments afford the same legal and regulatory treatment to domestic and foreign goods (or investors) alike. Second, nondiscrimination entails the idea of MFN: countries are not allowed to legally discriminate between imports (or investments) from different countries and have to apply the best treatment that they extend to imports from any country to all countries. That principle is not absolute—if it were, then trade liberalization outside of WTO would be impossible. Under Article XXIV of GATT, PTAs are allowed as long as they do not increase trade barriers facing other countries, liberalize all trade (in order to avoid distortions), and are duly reported to the WTO.[30] The organization thus allows countries to agree on trade obligations that go beyond what has been agreed multilaterally.

> An option provided by the WTO treaty is to pursue new trade obligations *plurilaterally* through negotiations among a self-selected subset of WTO members seeking the perceived economic advantages of agreements within the WTO rules framework that are "WTO-plus," which add to existing obligations and afford additional benefits to those members that choose to accept the obligations by becoming parties to the agreements.[31]

The global trading system built around the WTO also offers numerous venues where conflicts can be resolved, inviting countries (and sometimes firms) to "shop" for appropriate venues to settle their disputes.[32] The easy problems are typically resolved bilaterally, whereas the more difficult ones are addressed multilaterally, at the WTO level.[33] The WTO features a two-stage system of panels and the Appellate Body, created in 1995, for resolving disagreements *between states*.

WTO skeptics sometimes point out that member states do not trade more than countries outside the organization.[34] However, that only shows the benefits that nondiscrimination confers even on nonmembers.[35] In a rules-based global environment, PTAs can proceed effectively by complementing the multilateral system, not undermining it—as they did in the 1930s.[36] That matters because even on theoretical grounds PTAs are viewed by economists with a degree of suspicion. Under the economic theory of "second-best,"[37] removing trade barriers in a selective way can create new distortions. As a result, the amount of trade *destroyed* by partial trade liberalization can outweigh the welfare gains from trade that is *created*. Even a heavy dose of protectionism, as long as it is nondiscriminatory, does not necessarily change relative prices. Yet a selective removal of tariffs on imports from a small number of countries can intensify trade with those economies, at the expense of others. If the resulting distortion in trade flows goes too far beyond what would be justified by underlying economic fundamentals, it can result in a less efficient overall outcome.

Unlike the warring trade blocs of the past, often built by competing colonial powers, the PTAs of today do not produce such perverse results.[38] Besides the fact that these occur in an international environment shaped by the WTO, such agreements tend to arise organically between countries that are already natural trading partners, either geographically or due to other underlying connections, such as common history, language, or past economic and business ties.

Integral to PTAs are state-to-state dispute settlement mechanisms, complementing those existing at the WTO level. Furthermore, the postwar era has also seen the emergence of dispute resolution mechanisms *between investors and states*, known as investor-state dispute settlements (ISDSs). Some three thousand are currently in existence,[39] commonly part of modern-day trade agreements in addition to bilateral investment treaties. Those allow foreign companies to seek remedies against domestic governments at an international court or ad hoc arbitration body. The original rationale for ISDSs comes from the instability of economic policy in postcolonial developing countries, where foreign investors often faced the threat of expropriation. In order to mitigate such concerns, governments commit to abide by the decisions of such bodies. Over time, that original rationale has become weaker—perhaps because of ISDSs' proliferation and their success—yet, with the resurgence of economic nationalism around the world, including in European countries such as Hungary and Poland, it is hard to argue that ISDSs are obsolete.

ISDSs go beyond the WTO's nondiscrimination rules requiring "fair and equitable" treatment of foreign investors. Some fear that ISDSs give unfair privileges to foreign corporations not available to domestic ones. Yet winning an ISDS dispute is not straightforward: a recent study of ISDS filings shows that governments win 37.7 percent of the time, investors 29.1 percent, and a settlement is reached in 33.1 percent of cases. And even when companies win, they only recover 30 to 40 percent of their initial claims.[40]

MORE THAN TARIFFS

With tariff barriers at historic lows, further trade and investment liberalization is a function of domestic reforms, many of which are impervious to change. During TTIP talks, European and US negotiators sought agreement on the qualifications of architects, engineers, and auditors; animal welfare and food safety standards; and intellectual property.[41] While differences in legal and regulatory standards in each of those areas cause trade frictions, there may also be compelling reasons for their existence. Attempts at compromises in these areas, especially when reached behind closed doors, risk provoking backlashes, further catalyzed by exaggeration and hyperbole characteristic of the internet age.

Intellectual property issues within TTIP, for example, encompass the question of geographical indications. Those reflect a genuine divide running across the Atlantic, with Europeans being much more strongly wedded to the idea of terroir than Americans. To the French, Italians, or Greeks, the notion that Champagne wine, Prosciutto di Parma, or Feta could be made by producers in other countries is heresy. Likewise, in the United Kingdom, the prospect of opening up public procurement to US competition prompted largely unfounded but entirely predictable fears of "privatizing" the National Health Service,[42] alongside widely mediatized fearmongering over coming imports of "chlorinated chicken" from the United States.

The existence of differences in domestic policies goes a long way toward explaining why, despite the falling tariffs and the increasing "flatness" of the world, geography still matters. Similarly to Newton's model of gravity, the volume of trade between any two economies around the world can be estimated quite precisely by simply knowing their size and proximity. A 2002 paper by economists Jonathan Eaton and Samuel Kortum studies a hypothetical model of trade in which such "gravity" does not exist. In such an imaginary world, five times as much world trade would exist as what is observed in reality.[43] Another study estimated the size of trade frictions in developed countries as equivalent to a whopping 170 percent tax—and even more so in the case of developing countries.[44]

Distance matters less than in the past but what makes its continuing relevance so striking is the fact that transport costs have fallen so dramatically over the second half of the twentieth century that many economists simply equate those to be zero for convenience.[45] To be sure, some of the remaining barriers to trade are likely impervious both to technology and to public policy. Language barriers, for example, reflect not only the ease of direct communication (a problem that could be conceivably solved by technology) but also trust and the existence of a shared business culture.[46] Much has been written, for example, about the trade networks created by the Chinese diaspora across Southeast Asia[47] or about the role played by differences in corporate management practices.[48] In other words, the binding constraint on economic integration today is the costs of transporting *ideas*, as the economist Richard Baldwin puts it.[49]

A part of such frictions stems from differences in legal rules. Because complying with regulations is costly, the more different sets of rules a business needs to follow, the higher its compliance costs. At one point, such costs will deter firms from entering markets where they could otherwise be profitable. There is some evidence that such technical and regulatory barriers have grown in importance just as tariff barriers disappeared,[50] suggesting that governments actively sought new tools to keep foreign competition out.

In services, the burden of regulatory barriers has been estimated as equivalent to tariffs ranging between 20 and 75 percent.[51] In manufacturing, complying with different sets of standards requires costly redesigns. In a case cited by the Alliance of Automobile Manufacturers, for instance, a US company that sought to export a popular model of light truck to Europe had to create one hundred unique parts, spending an additional $42 million on design and development, and perform rigorous tests of thirty-three different vehicle systems—"without any performance differences in terms of safety or emissions."[52]

The World Bank's *Technical Barriers to Trade Survey* summarized one-time fixed costs incurred by firms from sixteen countries in Eastern Europe, Latin America, the Middle East, South Asia, and sub-Saharan Africa and found a variation from $357 to $12.3 million, averaging at $425,000, or 4.7 percent of annual value added.[53] In addition, regulatory compliance raises additional costs as new employees or services are necessary to manage testing and certification. Overall, the costs are much more of a barrier for small businesses than they are for large, established firms with large legal and compliance departments.

Under the rules in WTO's agreements on Technical Barriers to Trade[54] and Sanitary and Phytosanitary Measures,[55] member countries promise that their regulations, standards, and conformity assessment procedures are non-discriminatory and do not create unnecessary obstacles to trade. Needless to say, the protectionist design of regulations is rarely put on open display. And even when such WTO litigations succeed, governments are often reluctant to remove the challenged measures, instead making only minor adjustments or facing the financial penalties. More fundamentally, the absence of overt regulatory discrimination does not in itself eliminate compliance costs. It is the multiplicity of legal regimes that makes certain exchanges too costly to perform—even if such differences arise for perfectly benign reasons.

To completely eliminate regulatory barriers, the world would have to be governed by one set of legal rules, just like national markets. Short of that, the question is how frictions created by different regulatory regimes can be reduced in a world of many different polities. Clearly, not all regulations are going to carry the same weight in such efforts. In many sectors, such as services that require the simultaneity of provision and consumption or a common language (haircuts are often invoked as a canonical example of such "nontradeables"), the potential for any cross-border trade is limited, weakening the rationale for efforts to reduce the costs of compliance.

The tools for reducing regulatory barriers are multiple, overlapping, and mostly decentralized. Governments themselves could allow for more stringent scrutiny of the effects of new legislation on trade. Reviews of the economic effects of new legal rules, known as regulatory impact assessments (RIAs) are already quite common—in the United States, for example, federal agencies proposing new regulation are required to demonstrate that the economic benefits it generates exceed the costs and also that the measure appears favorable relative to its alternatives, including doing nothing.

Only occasionally, however, do such assessments focus explicitly on trade effects created by regulation.[56] As a result, the Organisation for Economic Co-operation and Development (OECD) reports,

> [d]omestic RIAs are by design and purpose a tool to maximize national welfare. To that end, RIAs usually assess and model the impacts of a regulatory proposal at the domestic level. They rarely assess impacts that transcend national borders, and, even more fundamentally, they often do not assess regulatory proposals against similar regulations in other jurisdictions.[57]

Furthermore, whereas RIAs are built to evaluate single regulatory proposals, traders are typically concerned with the overall impact of the regulatory environment (i.e., the sum of regulations, standards, and laws in a given sector) on trade.[58]

The private sector has reduced some of the compliance costs through international standards, which cover a number of different industries, from electrical appliances to food processing, where a comprehensive, globally adhered-to Codex Alimentarius has been produced jointly by the United Nation's Food and Agriculture Organization and the World Health Organization. Technical standardization is voluntary, designed to ensure compliance with higher-level, and legally binding, regulations existing in different countries. To make trade easier, standards must not only exist but have to be also acknowledged by national regulations as a sufficient condition for compliance. Firms are free to rely on such standards or to ignore them and comply directly with legal rules applicable in every country, which is often much more expensive.

Do technical standards make a difference? Diffusion of the International Organization for Standardization (ISO) 9000 standard has had a large positive effect on exports from developing countries.[59] A 2010 OECD report studied domestic electrical appliances, natural gas, and telephone handsets in five OECD members (Canada, the European Union, Korea, Mexico, and the United States) and found evidence of substantial recognition of technical standards by national regulators,[60] especially on questions of safety risks posed by electromagnetic fields and regulation of electromagnetic compatibility, which all reflect International Electrotechnical Commission standards. While that suggests that the presence of standards does indeed facilitate trade, it also serves as a reminder that governments rarely recognize a variety of different standards, thus precluding competition between them and entrenching standardization bodies as de facto monopolists.

Two main formal tools available to governments to reduce regulatory barriers to trade are harmonization (and the related idea of alignment) and mutual recognition. Harmonization requires governments to agree on common, uniformly applied rules across their jurisdictions. Alignment involves a *gradual* approximation of foreign or international norms by the domestic regulatory system. Finally, the idea of mutual recognition can apply either to conformity assessments or, more ambitiously, to legal rules themselves. Both harmonization and mutual recognition arise in different contexts but often are built into PTAs. However, in principle, either phenomenon can occur unilaterally, with a government deciding on its own to either recognize other countries' standards or to align its legislation with that existing elsewhere.

In addition to facilitating trade,[61] mutual recognition has the added advantage of preserving the diversity of different regulatory norms and fostering healthy competition between them. Harmonization, in contrast, can easily become heavy-handed and counterproductive. In the 1980s, for example, the European Union was often ridiculed for its approach to dismantling trade barriers, which involved regulating product markets in great technical detail. With the advent of its New Regulatory Policy in 1985, that problem has been reduced, with European legislation indicating only broad contours of public policy goals with the details then being typically left to voluntary technical standards.[62] Alternatively, within the broad parameters set by EU law, member states are able to legislate themselves, though they "cannot apply certain specific details of national regulation to intra-European Communities imports of goods, if the objective or effect of the relevant law in other member states is equivalent to that of the importing country."[63]

Mutual recognition and harmonization are not discrete, exclusive choices. Rather they reinforce each other. For example, the European Union's single market, which is built on the principle of mutual recognition, would not be politically sustainable without a layer of common European rules. In fact, in sectors where there are important differences in how member states regulate, particularly in services, the European Union's markets remain fragmented. Very few examples of successful mutual recognition arrangements exist between jurisdictions abiding by vastly different sets of rules. For instance, in 1998 a mutual recognition agreement was concluded between the United States and the European Union, covering telecoms equipment, electromagnetic compatibility, electrical safety, recreational crafts, pharmaceutical manufacturing, and medical devices. However, in practice, the usefulness of the agreement has proven limited because regulatory practices continued to diverge on both sides of the Atlantic.[64]

Other than the European Union's single market, the Trans-Tasman Mutual Recognition Arrangement provides perhaps the only other example of mutual recognition of *rules* regarding goods. Its key principle is the same as in the case of the European Union's single market:

> a good that may be legally sold in the jurisdiction of any Australian party may be sold in New Zealand and a good that may be legally sold in New Zealand may be sold in the jurisdiction of any Australian party. Goods need only comply with the standards or regulations applying in the jurisdiction in which they are produced or through which they are imported.[65]

Although some exceptions exist, the arrangement starts from the presumption of essentially unconditional mutual recognition. But Australia and New Zealand are in a unique situation. Unlike other trading blocs that would seek to replicate such an arrangement, both countries share legal and political traditions, find themselves at comparable levels of economic development, face no language or cultural barriers, and foster active contacts between their regulators.

Mutual recognition works best when underlying regulations are already close—or when it is applied to lightly regulated economic sectors. But then the economic benefits of mutual recognition are also going to be modest. In contrast, when mutual recognition is forced on dramatically different regulatory regimes, it tends to break down or create pressures toward harmonization.[66]

Yet regulatory heterogeneity is not just a cost to be minimized. There are usually perfectly benign reasons for different regulatory norms and practices—most importantly different policy preferences. This diversity also creates natural experiments that help scholars and policymakers learn about what works and what does not. In contrast, global regulatory monocultures can be sources of unexpected vulnerabilities, just like during the financial crisis of 2008.[67]

THE PERILOUS POLITICS OF TRADE

In his recent book, Dani Rodrik discusses a thought experiment that he conducted with his class of students. Suppose Rodrik were "capable of making $200 disappear from Nicholas' [one of his students] bank account—poof!—while adding $300 to John's [another student]. This feat of social engineering would leave the class as a whole better off by $100."[68] Unsurprisingly, such an arbitrary redistribution of income, even if it makes society as a whole better off, would rub against the grain of most people's moral intuitions. The key question is *how* that change occurred. If Nicholas and John ran competitive businesses and John worked harder, invested more, and were more innovative, few would mind that Nicholas suffered a loss of $200 and were driven out of business. But "[s]uppose John had driven Nicholas out of business by importing higher-quality inputs from Germany? By outsourcing to China, where labor rights are not well protected? By hiring child workers in Indonesia? Support [in the class] for the proposed change dropped with each one of these alternatives."[69]

Of course, that does not mean such outsourcing is undesirable but simply that it can set in motion political dynamics that are difficult to control. The deeper integration of China to the world economy, including its WTO accession in 2001, is a particularly poignant example. The economic reforms undertaken during Deng Xiaoping's rule in the 1980s set China on a path of extremely rapid economic growth, albeit from a low base. Although Chinese living standards went up spectacularly as a result, the result has not been, as many hoped, the emergence of a competitive market economy and an increase in political accountability. Rather, a hybrid form of state capitalism under a totalitarian political rule appeared, relying on modern technologies for surveillance and social and economic sanctions to stamp out internal dissent.

Make no mistake—the rise of Chinese export-oriented manufacturing has generated large benefits both to low-wage workers in developing countries and to low-income consumers in poor countries. Walmart's business model, which relies heavily on Chinese manufacturing, has played an important role in reducing poverty in the United States throughout the 2000s.[70] According to one study, "China's WTO entry drove down the U.S. price index of manufactured goods by 7.6 percent, averaging around one percent annually between 2000 and 2006."[71]

Together with automation, however, Chinese exports created a downward pressure on US wages and manufacturing employment[72]—with perhaps as many as 2.4 million US jobs being destroyed between 1999 and 2011. While that pressure was more than outweighed by the growth of US service exports, leading to a net rise in labor demand,[73] it did not lead to a simple transition of workers from manufacturing to services—rather, it left behind significant swaths of America's working-age population.

That outcome was not solely a result of China's inherent cost advantage or of the astuteness of its entrepreneurs. Because of implicit and explicit subsidies and various privileges extended to Chinese state-owned and state-connected companies, it is often impossible for Western companies to compete in Chinese markets. And the forms of support used by China—including the generous credit policies of state-run banks, through the fact that failed enterprises do not go bankrupt but are merged with other state-owned entities, the provision of privileged access to state-owned land, and the widespread violations of intellectual property rules—are not easily challenged under the narrow WTO rules.

Committed free traders may shrug off such criticisms. Indeed, if the Chinese government wants to distort the country's economy, why should Americans care? But voters see things differently. A 2017 study finds that in a series of congressional and presidential elections, "trade-exposed districts with an initial majority white population or initially in Republican hands became substantially more likely to elect a conservative Republican, while trade-exposed districts with an initial majority-minority population or initially in Democratic hands also become more likely to elect a liberal Democrat," thus replacing more moderate candidates.[74] Not only have trade issues returned to the electoral limelight because of Chinese competition,[75] but, more disturbingly, economic shocks generated by Chinese imports "[drove] negative attitudes towards immigrants and minorities."[76]

The main lesson of these developments has less to do with China and more to do with the importance of keeping the public on board at times of consequential and potentially disruptive changes to the economic environment. Nurturing a basic sense of fairness—and transparency—within existing institutions underpinning international trade is also critical. There is no reason, for example, why ISDSs should not be open to other actors beyond foreign corporations to include domestic firms, consumers, or organized labor. Furthermore, far-reaching trade agreements that cover large areas of domestic policy cannot be approached as purely technical exercises to which the public is expected to silently acquiesce. But, more importantly, maintaining public support for free trade requires better domestic policies to ensure no one is "left behind." That includes, most prominently, generous social safety nets to both compensate the losers of trade (or from competition by intelligent machines, for that matter) and help them rebuild their professional lives.

There is no question about the extraordinary economic benefits provided to humankind by the opening up of global markets since the end of the Second World War. That opening was without historic precedent[77] and resulted from the setting up of formal institutions, especially the multilateral system of GATT, the WTO, and the projects of regional economic integration. Under continuing pressure, the existing system has so far proven resilient—including to genuinely stupid policies, such as those advocated by the current occupant of the White House. Unlike past surges of protectionism—particularly those of the 1930s—which reduced international trade flows to a shadow of their former selves, the Trump administration is only scratching the surface of international trade flows with its occasional tariff measures. That is a testament to just how resilient the underlying institutions of international trade have been—at least for now.

Chapter Six

The Mirage of Sovereignty

In April 2018, it was reported that the Museum of Sovereignty would open in Lincoln, England, to celebrate the British euroskeptic movement, starting with the far-left opponents of the European project of the 1970s, continuing through the Maastricht Rebels of the 1990s to the leading figures of the 2016 campaign.[1] To date, the plan appears to have resulted in nothing more than a website,[2] but the earnestness and enthusiasm behind the project should not surprise anyone. In the eyes of euroskeptics, the 2016 referendum was not just a dispassionate assessment of the costs and benefits of EU membership. It was a historic opportunity to retake democratic control of the United Kingdom after decades of foreign domination—a British version of the "Flight 93 election," requiring one to "charge to cockpit or . . . die."[3] Unsurprisingly, in a 2017 YouGov poll, 61 percent of those who had voted to leave agreed that "significant damage to the British economy [was] a price worth paying for bringing Britain out of the European Union."[4] "This isn't about pounds and pence, this is about our democracy," Arron Banks, the founder of Leave.EU, told a House of Commons select committee. "I would pay almost any price to be away from [the European Union]," he added.[5] "[O]ur membership of the EU stops us being able to choose who makes critical decisions which affect all our lives," said Michael Gove, then the United Kingdom's Justice Secretary.[6]

Taken seriously, the idea that leaving the European Union is necessary to save British democracy, whatever the cost, amounts to a rather damning indictment of the European project—and essentially of any form of international cooperation. Indeed, the European Union does tie the hands of elected British politicians in various ways, and so do many other treaties, organizations, and covenants to which the United Kingdom is a party. But does that mean that such arrangements are by necessity detrimental to democratic self-governance and that countries cannot be truly sovereign as long as they keep participating in them?

Before answering that question, it is worth examining the idea of sovereignty in greater detail. Common dictionary entries of this somewhat nebulous term include "unlimited power over a country" and "a country's independent authority and the right to govern itself."[7] One could find others, but all of them tend to suggest two basic dimensions of sovereignty. First and foremost, there is its role as an *international* institution structuring interactions between states as between autonomous equals.[8] Second, sovereignty can be understood through *domestic* lenses as the ability of a society to govern itself and the control that voters and their elected representatives have over laws, policies, and social and economic outcomes.

SOVEREIGNTY, WITH QUALIFICATIONS

Clearly, sovereignty as an international institution—frequently misnamed as "Westphalian"—is not an absolute imperative. In fact, the idea easily finds itself at odds with other important values. Since at least the Nuremberg trials, it has been an established and uncontroversial norm of international life that governments that fail to meet minimal standards of human rights (*jus cogens*) cannot make a compelling claim to be recognized as sovereign by other countries—or to expect the rest of the world to just sit idly by as atrocities go on within their territory.[9] As the late Senator Jesse Helms (hardly a proponent of globalism in any form) wrote, "nations derive their sovereignty—their legitimacy—from the consent of the governed. Thus, Slobodan Milosevic can hardly claim sovereignty over Kosovo when he has murdered Kosovars and piled their bodies into mass graves. Nor can Fidel Castro or Saddam Hussein hide behind phony claims of sovereignty while they oppress their peoples."[10] Now, as the Western world has learned in Iraq and Afghanistan, military interventions that seek to unseat genocidal or tyrannical governments are not always advisable or practical. However, in and by themselves, appeals to sovereignty are not compelling reasons for why the world's governments and international organizations should have stood idly by as the Rwandan genocide, the massacre in Srebrenica, or Bashar al-Assad's bombing of civilians unfolded.

In that respect, it is hardly surprising that both Russia and China frequently invoke their sovereignty in response to criticisms of their human rights records.[11] Paradoxically, it is also such regimes—not intrusive international organizations or treaties—that have been guilty of the most flagrant violations of this principle. Examples include the continuing occupation of Abkhazia and South Ossetia, the annexation of Crimea, the war in the Donetsk and Luhansk "People's Republics," and the fomenting of instability in Transnistria. The Soviet Union justified its open interference in the internal affairs of other countries—most famously the 1968 invasion of Czechoslovakia—which with what became known as the Brezhnev Doctrine. "[W]hen . . . forces hostile to socialism try to turn the development of a given socialist country in the direction of restoration of the capitalist system," Brezhnev said, "this is no longer merely a problem for that country's people, but a common problem, the concern of all socialist countries."[12] Scrap the veneer of Marxist rhetoric, and Brezhnev's idea of limited sovereignty is alive and kicking in the Kremlin.

Whatever one thinks of the United Nations or the European Union, comparing either of them to the totalitarian yoke of the USSR is a grotesque hyperbole. By acting voluntarily in concert within the European Union or by participating in various UN fora, countries do not become any less sovereign international actors—if only because they are always free to leave such platforms, unlike under the Brezhnev Doctrine. The only feature of the existing international legal architecture that is genuinely nonnegotiable and can give grounds to genuine coercion by the United Nations and other actors is *jus cogens*, or the failure of national governments to protect basic human rights. However, as the examples of the Rwandan genocide, Srebrenica, and the atrocities committed by the Syrian government show, *jus cogens* alongside the United Nations' design raise the bar for effective coercive intervention extremely high. The problem is thus not excessive and arbitrary interventionism by the "international community"—rather, it is its absence in situations that need it.

In the abstract, of course, one can imagine arrangements between countries through which states *would* forego their sovereignty in an irrevocable way, similar to the "merger" of thirteen American colonies into the United States. It cannot be excluded that sooner or later the European Union will arrive at a similar point of no return. Yet that is emphatically not the reality of today's Europe, much less of other international institutions.

WHO IS IN CHARGE?

Has globalism destroyed the ability of nations to govern themselves? The UN Charter explicitly prohibits the United Nations from "intervening in matters which are essentially within the domestic jurisdiction of any state."[13] Even President Wilson's messianic internationalism, instrumental to the creation of the League of Nations and a natural starting point for many of the more utopian streams of globalist thinking, was based on the idea of national self-determination, albeit in his case limited to advanced European societies.[14]

True, international commitments place real constraints on political decision-making. But that is hardly an indictment. Within individual states too, decision-making authority is shaped by rules and divided between different nodes of decision-making—just think of constitutional rules, independent judiciaries, and delegation to central banks or independent regulators. At both the national and international levels, such constraints are almost never absolute and irrevocable. With the exception of the narrow *jus cogens* "backstop" (an equivalent of sorts of the basic rules of constitutional order), international institutions invariably offer the possibility of exit, either formally or de facto. More importantly, democratic self-governance is not an exercise in *unbounded* discretion, either by elected political leaders or by popular majorities. Although self-governance rests on the consent of citizens, it is embedded within a constitutional order that structures legitimate political action and places limits on its scope. In the British case, for example, the ultimate authority resides with the Crown and Parliament, within a framework of unwritten constitutional rules. In the United States, on the other hand, sovereignty rests with "'We the People' who 'ordain' the Constitution and may change it, but only by procedures prescribed in the Constitution itself,"[15] as the legal scholar Jeremy Rabkin puts it.

One would expect conservative thinkers would be at the forefront of pointing out the difference between democratic self-governance and crude majoritarianism, which finds its roots in Rousseau's proto-totalitarian notion of a general will (*volonté générale*). Applied consistently, such majoritarianism treats people as a homogenous mass and knows no constraints on its power.[16] Alas, many on the right have eschewed this distinction. In British conservative circles, the result of the 2016 plebiscite has been elevated to the status of an almost religious dogma. The three judges who ruled in November 2016 that the UK government would require the consent of Parliament to give notice of Brexit, complicating thus the path out of the European Union, were branded as "enemies of the people" by the influential tabloid *The Daily Mail.*[17] In January 2019, Jacob Rees-Mogg, the arch-euroskeptic Conservative Member of Parliament, suggested that the government should close Parliament temporarily to prevent it from voting to stop a no-deal Brexit.[18] In the United States, too, President Trump has labeled critical media outlets as an "Enemy of the People."[19] The implication is not only that he sees himself as the rightful representative of that homogenous mass, but also that the plurality of values, views, and opinions that characterizes free societies is irrelevant.

The populist affinity for majoritarianism is not accidental. By definition, populist politicians claim to speak on behalf of "the people." But at a deeper level, the demand for such a brand of politics reflects a yearning among some voters for a less complex and less intractable world, which would be more amenable to effective political control. The exit from the European Union was presented by the Leave campaign as "a once-in-a-lifetime opportunity to *take back control*,"[20] and nearly half (49 percent) of leave voters said the single biggest reason for wanting to leave the European Union was "the principle that decisions about the UK should be taken in the UK."[21] Focus group research conducted by the British think tank Demos in the United Kingdom, France, and Germany suggests that the demand for populist politics—which often involved a severing of international ties and a scaling back of European integration—reflected "nostalgic narratives, some of which have gained renewed salience" as Europe confronted a multitude of different crises, from the financial one in the eurozone to the uncontrolled wave of refugees and migrants that swept across the continent in 2015.

In all three countries, antiestablishment leaders have actively encouraged nostalgia for a simpler past and promised to reverse the decades of political and economic change through unspecified policy decisions: "Those who benefit from citizens' anxieties about change are those peddling the promise of 'control.'"[22] Likewise, in the 2016 Republican primary race, for example, the strongest predictor of voting for Donald Trump as the first-choice nominee was the agreement with the idea that "people like me don't have any say about what the government does," dwarfing in its predictive power "any preferences based on respondent gender, age, race/ethnicity, employment status, educational attainment, household income, attitudes towards Muslims, attitudes towards illegal immigrants, or attitudes towards Hispanics."[23]

The desire for control is a powerful political force, rooted in human psychology. In a famous early experiment, a group of students that included some who were suffering from depression were told that pressing a button *might* turn on a green light. For each appearance of a green light, a small financial reward was offered. Although pressing the button had no effect on the light, nondepressed students were more likely to believe that their actions brought about the desired outcome,[24] suggesting that the sense of being in control is associated with a healthy, nondepressed outlook. A different experiment instructed forty students to react to small six-second-long electric shocks. After ten iterations, half of the subjects were told, untruthfully, that if they reacted more rapidly, the shock duration would be reduced. In the second half of the experiment, all participants received shorter, three-second shocks. However, those who mistakenly believed to be in control of their length perceived the shocks as shorter and less painful.[25]

Yet effective control of social and economic outcomes either by national governments or by voters themselves does not amount to a meaningful political goal. For one, popular majorities are almost never a coherent source of answers to public policy questions. The purpose of elections and plebiscites is not to extract what "the people" collectively think—there is no such thing. And from an individual's perspective, the ability of a voter to "control" policies is miniscule, as any given vote carries a negligible chance of being pivotal in an election or a referendum.

More importantly, neither voters nor their elected representatives exercise effective "control" over economic and social outcomes. The list of reasons is a long one, starting with the fact that such control is limited by state power. The ability of, say, Estonia—a country of 1.3 million people—to control its policies hinges on the geopolitical environment in which it finds itself, especially on the aggressiveness of its neighbor to the east. Small countries have rarely had significant sway over international institutions in which they choose to participate. And when they decide not to participate, they continue to be affected—much like Iceland is reduced to the role of rule-taker relative to the European Union. Unfair though it may be, a country's size and international clout will always constrain the ability of its voters and their elected representatives to directly "control" its policies, not to speak of relevant social and economic outcomes.

Obviously, the United States, with its gargantuan internal market and unrivaled military, finds itself in a different position than Estonia or Iceland. But not even America is an island unto itself, and the federal government is never in full control of economic, social, or geopolitical processes unfolding on US territory. If it had been, then problems of poverty, gun crime, and illegal immigration—to cite only a few examples—would have been solved a long time ago. Even for a world leader such as the United States, it can make utmost sense to pool its decision-making with other countries in search of solutions to problems that transcend national borders. Not only that, unlike smaller countries, the United States is in a unique position to shape regional and global institutions in its own image and to use them to project its influence around the world. Arguably, it has been this projection of US influence that has shaped the postwar world in uniquely beneficial ways—and has also benefited the United States itself.

The most fundamental reason for why populist promises of control are illusory is the world's complexity. As the Scottish moral philosopher Adam Ferguson famously observed, "[e]very step and every movement of the multitude, even in what are termed enlightened ages, are made with equal blindness to the future; and nations stumble upon establishments, which are indeed the result of human action, but not the execution of any human design."[26] This theme was later developed by classical liberal thinkers, most notably by the Nobel Prize–winning economist Friedrich Hayek, who argued that the successful functioning of a modern society relies on the use of local knowledge that is not available to anybody in its entirety but is instead dispersed among many actors and impossible to convey to any single center of decision-making. "The knowledge of the circumstances of which we must make use never exists in concentrated or integrated form, but solely as the dispersed bits of incomplete and frequently contradictory knowledge which all the separate individuals possess."[27] Throughout his work, Hayek warns against the attempts to replace the functioning of decentralized and spontaneous coordination mechanisms, especially market prices, by political fiat or planning. Such attempts, he argued, are bound to produce unintended consequences. Instead of searching for top-down solutions, social arrangements should encourage the decentralized discovery of responses to problems arising in human cooperation.

Hayek's insights are an antidote to political overreach of any kind, including by international organizations[28] and by those who believe that globalization necessarily needs centralized control and management. Yet they also show that the yearning for control that animates current debates in the West leads to wrongheaded policies. Since nobody, much less governments of individual nation-states, is *in control* of the world's complex globalized economy, populists are able to offer at best an *illusion* of control.[29] Consider President Trump's preoccupation with trade deficits. He sees those as evidence of the United States "losing" in trade. Tariffs imposed by his administration in response to the observed imbalances carry economic costs, borne largely by US consumers and businesses. But, barring extreme scenarios, tariffs and similar trade measures are unlikely to change the underlying factors driving the trade imbalance: the voracious appetite of foreign investors for US-denominated assets.

If control is an elusive objective, it does not follow that chaos is the inevitable or perhaps desirable alternative. The challenge of public policy is about structuring decentralized and spontaneous processes, often spanning across national borders, toward desirable and politically sustainable outcomes. As Vincent Ostrom put it, governance has to combine the spontaneity and trial and error inherent to competitive markets with a degree of "deliberateness in their creation, operation, and maintenance over time,"[30] in order to provide conditions for "contestation, innovation, and convergence towards mutually productive arrangements." That is equally true of domestic affairs as it is of international ones.

HAS GLOBALISM UNDERMINED AMERICA'S CONSTITUTIONAL ORDER?

The degree of veneration for constitutional documents is an interesting dividing line separating the United States from Europe. On the old continent, national constitutions rarely pose serious obstacles to international cooperation—most prominently to European integration. Germany's Basic Law, for example, has been amended multiple times to accommodate the country's European aspirations—something that would be difficult to imagine in the United States. In 1954, changes were made to the originally pacifist document to ensure that Germany's participation in the European Defense Community was legally possible. Several amendments were made also in 1993 and 1994 to make Germany's legal framework compatible with the requirements of the Maastricht Treaty. The changes involved the transfer of authority from the German Federal Bank to the European Central Bank, without which the common European currency would have been impossible. The constitutional amendment also allowed EU citizens to vote in German local elections, reversing an earlier ruling of the Federal Constitutional Court.

In contrast, international cooperation is commonly perceived as raising a number of challenges in US constitutional law. Those are often invoked as evidence of America's exceptionalism that is supposedly under threat whenever the US government decides to participate in certain international agreements and organizations. Upon closer inspection, however, it is hard to see such concerns as putting international cooperation into serious intellectual jeopardy.

One point of contention revolves around the question of whether ratified treaties are directly enforceable in US courts or whether they only constitute promises made by the US government, without legal weight in the United States. The question is salient because treaties may contradict the established status quo, yet their ratification is not subjected to the same procedural rigors as new legislation. The risk that some conservative critics see is that direct enforceability ("self-execution") of international treaties opens the door to changing domestic policy through the means of making international commitments, not through normal democratic deliberation in both chambers of Congress.

That is not an unreasonable concern. However, the antidotes are not judicial but political. Unlike in the British constitutional system, under which international treaties are non-self-executing unless "implemented" by Parliament, the US Constitution's Supremacy Clause makes it quite clear that "treaties made under [the] authority [of federal law], constitute the supreme law of the land."[31] And, as Chief Justice Marshall put it in 1829, a treaty is "to be regarded in courts of justice as equivalent to an Act of the Legislature, whenever it operates without the act of any legislative provision."[32] The Supremacy Clause was the framers' answer to the frequent failure of the United States to ensure compliance with the Treaty of Paris, which ended the Revolutionary War, under the Articles of Confederation.[33] It was no coincidence that Alexander Hamilton argued in a famous case, which predated the Constitution, that the Trespass Act adopted by the New York legislature to strip British loyalists of their property violated that treaty and needed to be struck down. In his ruling, Chief Justice James Duane concurred and wrote that "no state in this union [could] alter or abridge, in a single point, the federal articles or the treaty."[34]

In his 1995 article, Georgetown University's Carlos Vázquez finds four exceptions to the doctrine of self-execution: (1) explicit intent expressed in the treaty that additional legislation is necessary, (2) "precatoriness" and "vagueness" of provisions that would make their judicial enforcement impossible, (3) constitutionality (e.g., trying to accomplish a policy objective that is within the exclusive lawmaking power of Congress), and (4) the absence of a private right of action.[35]

To be sure, legal scholars may disagree over how broad those four categories are,[36] but the weight of the opinion of the legal profession, together with the text of the Supremacy Clause itself, leans heavily in the direction of self-execution as the default applied to most treaties, with a relatively narrow space left for exceptions falling in one of the four categories. For better or worse, the Constitution has granted broad powers to the federal government, especially to the executive branch, to pursue foreign policy.

The risk that such powers will be used—and perhaps abused—to change domestic policy without relying on normal channels of legislative action and congressional deliberation is real. But that is no reason for sweeping judicial revisionism or for indulging the naive hope that progressive political agendas can be defeated in courts instead of the polls. It is also worth remembering the role of the Senate in ratifying treaties. Over the years, the US upper house frequently conditioned its acceptance of treaties on reservations, understandings, and declarations that rendered those treaties effectively non-self-enforcing.[37] If self-governance in the United States has been coming under attack in recent years, the real reasons have more to do with Congress's abdication of its responsibilities[38] than with international cooperation in any of its forms.

Another concern revolves around the delegation of decision-making authority to international organizations. According to Rabkin, "[i]n the United States, at least, the traditional view was that the Constitution prohibits delegations of governing authority to foreign bodies and therefore also to international bodies."[39] The reason has to do with the fact that the US Constitution delegates powers to different branches of government "in trust." As a mere agent of "We the People," the government is not allowed to delegate those powers any further.[40]

However, an unqualified injunction against all delegation seems at odds with the generous nature of the powers granted to the executive branch in the area of foreign policy, including by prominent rulings such as *United States v. Curtiss-Wright*.[41] The case involved violations of President Franklin D. Roosevelt's embargo on arms shipments to some Latin American countries. In an argument that the court dismissed, the defendant argued that the president used unconstitutional authority to impose the embargo, violating the doctrine of nondelegation. In domestic practice, too, Congress has successfully delegated rulemaking authority to agencies within the executive branch, and most legal scholars see that power as extending easily to international delegation as well.[42] Such delegation does not mean that the United States foregoes influence over the substantive content of decisions made by international agencies—quite the contrary. Overwhelmingly, international bodies involve both *voice* and *exit*, and given its status as a global superpower, the United States has invariably been the most influential member of practically all such organizations.

Unsurprisingly, the alarmist rhetoric is rarely matched by compelling examples of ongoing or prospective assaults on US sovereignty with a potential for slippery slopes. More often than not, the cited examples are arcane and not even relevant to the United States at all: the 1993 Chemical Weapons Convention, the 1997 Anti-Personnel Mine Ban Convention (not signed by the United States), or the International Criminal Court (the United States withdrew from its founding document in 2002).

A separate source of concerns has to do with American federalism. Decentralization is an important element of the American (and also British[43]) idea of self-governance. Although the US federal government is the most important conduit through which the United States engages with the outside world, the country is not a unitary state. As a result, the states are not mere administrative units but enjoy "residuary and inviolable sovereignty," as the Supreme Court ruled in *New York v. United States*,[44] citing Federalist No. 39.[45] The ruling pushed against the efforts of the federal government to force states to participate in its scheme of low-level radioactive waste disposal. The court affirmed that the federal government could not simply compel the states into pursuing its own regulatory or policy objectives. Without a doubt, its logic places constraints on the types of international arrangements that the United States can enter into without interfering with the division of power between the federal and state levels.

But this is far from being a blanket argument against international cooperation. Quite the contrary—as an exercise in *divided* political authority, federalism provides a rationale for assigning decision-making power to a variety of actors. Those can include, as a matter of principle, transnational and international actors. Furthermore, taking federalism seriously requires accepting that subnational units of government (e.g., US states) are international actors in their own right in areas not explicitly claimed by the central government. That results in a richer, polycentric ecosystem of international cooperation. Already today, this decentralized form of globalism has provided a counterweight to President Trump's efforts to disentangle the United States from its international commitments.

State governors already enter into agreements with foreign governments, even if such agreements do not have the legal status of international treaties. Following the US withdrawal from the Paris climate accord, an alliance of US states and cities have stepped forward to reduce their carbon emissions to help the United States meet its target even in the absence of a firm commitment from the federal government.[46] The Great Lakes Charter binds Illinois, Indiana, Michigan, Minnesota, New York, Ohio, Pennsylvania, and Wisconsin—together with the Canadian provinces of Ontario and Québec—in an agreement concerning water management and environmental protection. Likewise, the implementation of various international commitments not ratified by Congress has been left in the hands of state governments, including the Hague Convention on the Conflicts of Laws Relating to the Form of Testamentary Dispositions.[47]

Finally, there are concerns over the status of customary international law in US courts—as well as the weight attributed to foreign statutes and rulings of foreign courts. The controversy around customary international law has to do with the fact that during the Founding, it was widely agreed upon that the United States needed to recognize the traditional rights of foreign sovereigns. In some interpretations, customary international law still carries the same weight as federal common law, even though its substantive content is much broader than that which was applied at the time of the Founding Fathers.[48] For its critics, customary international law becomes relevant only insofar as it is translated into domestic US legislation.[49] The latter position can be illustrated by Justice Antonin Scalia's dissent in *Roper v. Simmons* in which he famously deplored the Supreme Court's "[purporting] to take guidance from the views of foreign courts and legislatures."[50] While reasonable people can disagree about the extent to which domestic courts should pay attention to rulings and legislation in countries with similar legal systems and political traditions, how realistic is it to expect courts to ignore them altogether?

For all its uniqueness, the United States has never been—nor should it try to become—an island unto itself, unmoored from political and legal debates taking place around the globe. At its founding, the nation synthesized the key lessons of both the Scottish and Continental Enlightenment and created a hitherto unseen federal system of governance. Its abolitionist movement in the nineteenth century drew inspiration from previous efforts in England, led by the likes of William Wilberforce.[51] None of America's great advances—moral, intellectual, political, or economic—were a result of splendid isolation but rather of successful leveraging of human talent and intellectual influences from around the world. The idea that the work of government, including that of the judiciary, should be shaped uniquely by explicit domestic legislation betrays a narrowly statist and positivist outlook,[52] which is sharply at odds with America's political tradition of self-governance.

Moreover, the alarmism over the creeping corruption of America's jurisprudence by alien ideas would be more convincing if the critics could point to different examples of nefarious foreign influences. In *Roper v. Simmons*, the Supreme Court ruled against imposing the death penalty on individuals who committed crimes as minors by pointing to "the evolving standards of decency that mark the progress of a maturing society."[53] Other examples of a supposedly dangerous reliance on foreign precedents undermining Americans' ability to govern themselves include a case that struck down as unconstitutional the execution of an intellectually disabled defendant[54] and one that ended a state law criminalizing homosexual "sodomy."[55] Even if one believes that questions of such a nature ought to be decided primarily by democratic deliberation and not by judicial fiat, a case for American exceptionalism built around the states' right to criminalize homosexuality and inflict capital punishment on teenagers and the intellectually disabled is hardly a compelling one.

BEYOND THE DEMOCRATIC DEFICIT

Global and international organizations are often seen as suffering from a lack of democratic accountability, particularly at moments when they are tasked with making political decisions. During the eurozone crisis, the technocrats of the Troika—International Monetary Fund, European Commission (EC), and European Central Bank—were directly shaping policy decisions in countries on the eurozone's periphery without much local ownership. Likewise, the EC's proposal, at the peak of the refugee crisis of 2015, to introduce quotas of asylum seekers allocated to member countries provoked a backlash across the European Union, especially in Eastern Europe.

However, in the European Union's case, the problem of bureaucratic discretion somehow suffocating national politics is largely imaginary. If anything, fiscal governance in the eurozone suffers from the fact that the existing rules are ignored, rather than from the Troika's diktat. Needless to say, the EC's idea of refugee quotas has been scrapped following the pushback from national capitals. More generally, even if the EC may claim a monopoly on drafting and proposing new legislation, it is able to act independently only in a small number of areas set out expressly by member countries—such as enforcing rules of the single market and of competition policy. The co-decision procedure for adopting new legislation requires both the consent of member states (accountable to their domestic electorates) and of the European Parliament, elected by EU citizens. When the EC intrudes where it is not welcome—as in the case of asylum policy—the member states take matters into their hands.

Furthermore, if the European Union were a jail of nations, many others would be following the United Kingdom's example. Although we find ourselves at a time of a backlash against the European project, very few political leaders, populist or not, openly advocate dismantling the European edifice. At the peak of the eurozone crisis in Greece, the far-left Syriza party decided against leaving the common European currency, despite the considerable economic hardships that the country was undergoing. Notwithstanding Italy's poor economic performance and the fact that Italy is bearing a large part of the cost of policing Europe's borders, the populist Italian government formed in May 2018 has made no indication of considering leaving the European Union. Even Marine Le Pen switched from her initial demand to leave the eurozone to instead a vague promise to "open a debate" about the common European currency ahead of the 2017 parliamentary election in France.[56] Meanwhile, the public's perceptions of European integration remain very favorable in most member states, even if Europeans often disagree with particular EU policies. The proportion of EU citizens who hold a positive image of the European Union (40 percent in March 2018) has consistently exceeded the percentage having a negative image of the bloc (21 percent).[57]

This is not to argue that the European Union's institutional setup, or that of other international institutions, is beyond reproach. For example, all organizations have to solve the principal-agent problem,[58] or the motivational and informational disconnect between those acting (e.g., experts of international agencies) and the principals on whose behalf such actions are taken (e.g., national governments and other members of international organizations). Unlike in the context of corporate governance, international cooperation does not always generate direct benefits to such principals but rather to a variety of other actors. The principal-agent problem is also multilayered. In democratic societies at least, national governments are agents of their citizens. In contrast, autocratic rulers are primarily accountable to themselves and perhaps to a narrow coalition of actors who help keep them in power. Finally, in most international organizations, there are *many* principals, each pursuing a variety of goals, creating a collective-action problem in the monitoring and adaptation of international agencies. Yet these challenges are not intractable, and little evidence suggests that international agencies are faring dramatically worse than national and local bureaucracies. There is, for example, only a limited amount of slack in the World Trade Organization and World Health Organization, and the seeming autonomy of organizations such as the International Monetary Fund is usually a result of conscious decisions of governments to provide their international "agents" with leeway.[59]

As a general rule, the accountability and openness of international institutions closely tracks the domestic democratic standards of governments that are their members.[60] Needless to say, nation-states themselves long operated without democratically accountable institutions or a coherent body of public opinion, often seen as a prerequisite for democracy. Whether it is France, Italy, or Germany, modern European nations are results of political projects that sought to fit a complicated multiethnic, regionalist reality into the mold of a common polity and democratized only later on. Even today, because of the many imperfections of democratic politics—from the role played by interest groups, dispersed costs and concentrated benefits, and rational ignorance—democratic politics in nation-states fall short of the idealized vision of democratic politics in civic education textbooks.

Furthermore, a significant part of the democratic deficit in real-life democracies and at the level of international institutions is a result of conscious choices by democratically elected, accountable policymakers. Whether it is central banking, antitrust policy, or regulation of public utilities, there are solid reasons for removing such subjects from day-to-day political discretion and placing them in the hands of agencies insulated from immediate political pressures. The delegation of decisions to international agencies is no different. It is thus generally a fool's errand to try to reshape international organizations to make them resemble national democratic polities—much as it would seem silly, if not dangerous, to seek to "democratize" independent judiciaries or central banks.

If "global democracy" is a pipe dream, then the questions of formal standards of decision-making within international organizations and their openness to various stakeholders are at best auxiliary ones. What is much more consequential is the question of the *appropriate scope* for international institutions. That question can be answered with the idea of subsidiarity. Subsidiarity is integral to federalism and polycentric governance because it reflects the fact that different collective-action challenges have to and can be addressed through different institutional channels, always as close as possible to the relevant actors. Subsidiarity can be boiled down to the prescription that "a central authority should have a subsidiary function, performing only those tasks which cannot be performed at a more local level."[61] The idea was initially developed in the context of Catholic social thought in the nineteenth century[62] before making its way into broader legal and political thought and ultimately also into European treaties,[63] where it serves the purpose of defining the legitimate scope of policymaking by the European Union, as opposed to its member states.

Both the growth of the centralized administrative state at home and the delegation of distinctly local policy decisions to international authorities reflect a failure to translate subsidiarity into policy practice. That is not an easy task because identifying cross-border effects that merit a coordinated policy response is as much a political exercise as one of social scientific analysis. Accordingly, the idea of subsidiarity may be integral to European treaties, but its application does not have much bite. Article 5(3) of the Treaty on European Union (Maastricht Treaty) states that

> [u]nder the principle of subsidiarity, in areas which do not fall within its exclusive competence, the Union shall act only if and in so far as the objectives of the proposed action cannot be sufficiently achieved by the Member States, either at central level or at regional and local level, but can rather, by

reason of the scale or effects of the proposed action, be better achieved at Union level.[64]

Article 5(4) states the related principle of proportionality, which stipulates that "the content and form of Union action shall not exceed what is necessary to achieve the objectives of the Treaties."[65] Yet those are not binding legal principles comparable to the concept of enumerated powers of the US Constitution—after all, there has not been a single successful legal challenge to EU legislation *on subsidiarity grounds*. Instead, the principle only provides guidance on how the European Union should act in areas where the European Union and member states *already share* competencies—without asking why such competencies are shared as opposed to being exercised exclusively by either the European Union or its member states.

This oddity of the European Union's constitutional design reflects the bloc's supposed evolution toward "an ever closer union." The outcomes have not only defied subsidiarity, as conventionally understood, but also produced significant dysfunction, manifested during both the eurozone crisis and the refugee crisis of 2015. A well-known study by economists Alberto Alesina, Ignazio Angeloni, and Ludger Schuknecht assessed the European Union's policy scope through the prism of two basic criteria: the presence of external effects and the alignment of preferences.[66] The larger the external, cross-border effects of policies and the more alike the views of citizens in member states are, the stronger the case for common action is. Yet the European Union also plays large roles in areas such as social protection, where such externalities are small and where large differences of opinion exist. Simultaneously, the European Union has not built a sufficiently effective platform for common policymaking on questions of security or environmental policy, where external effects are significant and where consensus on common policies could be found much more easily.

If the current nationalist surge were guided by the principle of subsidiarity, it could provide a useful corrective to previous instances of overreach. However, populist and nationalist politicians are just as heavy-handed in their stated ambitions to repatriate power as the most naive advocates of global governance who seek to do the opposite. The logical outcomes of policy nationalism put into practice—a balkanized system of international trade, a weakened North Atlantic Treaty Organization, and a European Union fraying around its edges—carry dramatic price tags. Even when guided by the best intentions, national politics in isolation do not provide effective responses to challenges of economic, environmental, and social interdependence. The world is more integrated than ever, more people migrate than at any point in history, and the awareness of common challenges spanning across borders—from fish stock management to human trafficking to international terrorism—is at an all-time high.

As a result, it is a safe bet that over a longer period of time international cooperation will not only survive but continue to deepen. The lesson from the present era is to develop a better understanding of the relevant trade-offs. Not every form of international cooperation, regardless of area or institutional setup, is desirable or politically and legally defensible. When applied as a guide for designing international cooperation, polycentrism and subsidiarity can help charter an alternative both to the uncritical embrace of global governance and to the current fetishization of national sovereignty in conservative circles.

Globalism should be seen not as a technocratic exercise but rather as a novel instance of self-governance. Such an approach opens avenues for discovering what works and what does not—and also what voters are willing to accept. Guided by subsidiarity and principles of polycentric governance, international cooperation can avoid most of the pitfalls that its conservative critics have identified, starting with its supposed intrusion into democratic decision-making at the national level.

Chapter Seven

Citizens of Nowhere, Unite!

Forget left and right, and liberalism versus conservatism. The new dividing line in politics splits proponents of an "open" versus "closed" society, "globalism" and "patriotism"—or the "anywhere" and the "somewhere," as the British author David Goodhart put it in his best-selling book[1]—into irreconcilable tribes, leaving no place for ambiguity, hesitation, or nuance. "America is governed by Americans," President Donald Trump told the UN General Assembly in September 2018. "We reject the ideology of globalism, and we embrace the doctrine of patriotism."[2] Similarly, the United Kingdom's Prime Minister Theresa May told the Conservative Party Conference in Birmingham in 2016 that "if you believe you are a citizen of the world, you are a citizen of nowhere. You don't understand what citizenship means."[3]

Yet the choice between patriotism and globalism is a false one. Extensive international cooperation and pooling of sovereignty do not need to entail utopian visions of some postnational kumbaya. Instead, the goal is to address policy challenges that cannot be addressed adequately by the autonomous, independent action of national governments or other local actors. The umbrella of globalism also includes a vast range of institutional forms and arrangements. While simplistic dichotomies are rhetorically powerful, they do little to advance our understanding of international institutions, much less to improve their functioning.

Because democracy does not exist independently of political communities bound by shared values, some jump to the conclusion that international institutions are fundamentally arbitrary and illegitimate. Indeed, democracy needs a "demos"—a likeminded political community. As the British conservative philosopher Roger Scruton puts it,

[P]eople bound by a national "we" have no difficulty in accepting a government whose opinions and decisions they disagree with; they have no difficulty
in accepting the legitimacy of opposition, or the free expression of outrageous-
seeming views. In short, they are able to live with democracy, and to express
their political aspirations through the ballot box.[4]

A degree of moral likemindedness is necessary for democratic governance because of the importance of shared informal norms and patterns of
behavior. Unlike the spontaneous order of the marketplace, which for its
operation relies largely on the profit motive and presence of strong formal
institutions (property rights, contract law, effective judiciary), there is nothing automatic about the ability of communities to govern themselves. As
Vincent Ostrom notes, self-governance requires citizens with a degree of
"sophistication about rule-ordered relationships,"[5] similar to that of children
when they learn how to shoot marbles or play ball. Because self-governance
is polycentric, it is not enough for such sophistication and the ability to
reflect on the content of rules to come from just one node of decision-
making. Rather, it has to be a feature of the entire social ecosystem, relying
on a critical mass of engaged individuals across the community. Voting, for
example, is not an instrumentally rational activity as individual votes have a
miniscule chance of impacting the outcome of any election. Yet the functioning of a democratic society relies fundamentally on the willingness of citizens to vote—and moreover to vote in an informed, thoughtful manner.

Self-governance needs a culture of active civic participation and responsibility for the maintenance and repair of the existing legal and institutional
orders. But such culture is not binary. It can exist in various degrees in
different contexts and at different levels of government, layered over one
another. The existence of different sources of political authority and the
possibility of multiple political loyalties manifesting themselves in different
contexts is an important part of the appeal of federalism. To assert, in
contrast, that this culture is tied uniquely to the institution of the nation-state
is at best a failure of imagination. Worse yet, its application risks tying
Western democracies to a Procrustean bed of social organization increasingly
out of sync with reality.

COSMOPOLITANISM AND
ETHICS OF CITIZENSHIP

Ties existing within political communities have ethical implications. As
President Trump bluntly said in his 2018 speech to the United Nations, he
was "not the president of the globe." Although the decisions taken by a US
president are of monumental importance, not just for Americans but also for

billions of people around the globe, the US president is elected by American voters to serve *them*, not other people.

Accepting that governments' primary set of duties is toward their own citizens and not toward foreigners is not tantamount to an intellectual capitulation of Trump's "doctrine of patriotism." After all, even the most dedicated cosmopolites would be reluctant to suggest that wealthy Western European countries should extend their welfare nets indiscriminately to all noncitizens—or that anybody in the world in the world should be given the right to vote in the US presidential election. The question is not simply one of the special privileges that are conferred to citizens by national legal systems, while being simultaneously denied to noncitizens. A more accurate characterization is that the existence of states by necessity assigns different sets of duties to their citizens and noncitizens. That assignment can sometimes favor noncitizens. It is generally accepted, for example, that noncitizens enjoy negative rights that they would lose by virtue of citizenship: foreigners cannot be conscripted or, if they reside abroad, be taxed on their foreign income.

The existence of such distinct sets of duties among citizens and foreigners does not make either group special in any way. It is simply an artifact of a world that is divided into multiple polities, as opposed to existing under one global source of political authority. "At root," the philosopher Richard Goodin writes, "they are merely the general duties that everyone has toward everyone else worldwide. National boundaries simply visit upon those particular state agents special responsibility for discharging those general obligation vis-à-vis those individuals who happen to be their own citizens."[6] The situation can be compared, Goodin argues, to the matching of doctors and patients in hospitals: It is far more efficient to assign a particular doctor to one patient each than to have every doctor spend a fraction of their time treating each patient at the hospital. Assigning tasks this way says nothing about the patients themselves, similarly as citizenship does not single out its holders as particularly morally deserving or noteworthy in other ways.

What distinguishes this approach grounded in political theory from that of self-identified nationalists of political theory is its universalism—or "analytical egalitarianism." In short, such theorizing treats people as fundamentally equal, irrespective of their nationality, ethnicity, social status, or expertise. Analytical egalitarianism goes back a long way in the Western intellectual tradition and encompasses the roots of the economic profession and classical liberalism. Adam Smith wrote eloquently that "[t]he difference between the most dissimilar characters, between a philosopher and a common street porter, for example, seems to arise not so much from nature as from habit, custom, and education" to push against the idea that certain classes or ethnicities were naturally suited to rule over others. Similar considerations led other classical economists, most notably James Mill and Richard Whately, to oppose slavery in British colonies.[7]

The classical liberals who gathered at the Lippmann Colloquium in 1938 shared this broad outlook. Mises wrote in 1927,

> Liberal thinking always has the whole of humanity in view and not just parts. It does not stop at limited groups; it does not end at the border of the village, of the province, of the nation, or of the continent. Its thinking is cosmopolitan and ecumenical: it takes in all men and the whole world. Liberalism is, in this sense, humanism; and the liberal, a citizen of the world, a cosmopolite.[8]

Notwithstanding claims to the contrary, this outlook can be reconciled with the reality of belonging to a variety of political communities, including nation-states. In fact, one can even go one step further and assert that patriotism can play a helpful role in raising collective aspirations and encouraging economic dynamism, innovation, and good economic and social outcomes more generally. "To encourage economic growth, it does help to have a state that is able to coordinate and fund vital infrastructure," writes Victoria Bateman, an economic historian at the University of Cambridge. "This requires a wide enough tax base of citizens who are happy to sacrifice some hard-earned cash, and politicians and civil servants who feel a responsibility to the wider country as much—or more—than they do to themselves."[9]

Western history is in fact replete with examples of how the quest for national prestige encouraged economic dynamism, competition, and diffusion of new ideas and technologies, including the Industrial Revolution and the economic and technological breakthroughs driven by the Cold War. Globalism, properly understood, does not seek to eradicate patriotic sentiments but rather to channel them toward beneficial uses. It also recognizes that loyalty to a national political community is only one among many different allegiances that people carry with themselves, including ties to their families, religious groups, local communities, professions, regions, and so on. There is no inherent reason to assume that one *always* trumps the others. Rather, it is a task of political institutions and also political and intellectual leadership to facilitate their harmonious coexistence.

Because democratic societies make the distinction between members and nonmembers of political communities, globalism does not require governments to treat foreigners in exactly the same way as citizens or to deny the reality of citizenship and nationhood. Where nationalists and their fellow travelers go wrong is in assuming that modern nation-states are the only communities featuring such shared habits—and in claiming, furthermore, that political nations are somehow time-invariant, primitive entities extending far back in history.

FANTASIES AND DEMONS OF THE PAST

Nationalist thinkers often embrace a romantic, ahistoric view of the nation's formation. In his recent book, *The Virtue of Nationalism*, the Israeli author Yoram Hazony conceptualizes the nation-state as a natural reflection of the reality of national communities built on the basis of family, clan, and tribal bonds. "[H]eads of tribes," writes Hazony, "can come together to form a nation whose members number in the millions. . . . Like ties of loyalty to the clan, the bond of loyalty to one's tribe or nation grows out of loyalty to one's parents."[10]

Modern European nations, much less the American one, did not arise through a coming together of different tribes or clans but through explicit projects of political unification. France, for example, succeeded in shedding its multiple regional identities, cultures, and linguistic traditions only as recently as the nineteenth century and *only thanks* to top-down centralism and deliberate efforts to uproot regional and minority languages through policies of forced assimilation.[11]

A similar story could be told about most other European countries. Massimo d'Azeglio, one of the pioneers of Italian unification, is famously (although mistakenly) cited as the author of the following quip: "We have made Italy. Now we must make Italians."[12] To the present day, Italy retains a number of distinctive regional identities and cultures that are also associated with diverging social and economic outcomes along with a tradition of political separatism, especially in the north. Likewise, notwithstanding the long history of political centralization in Spain, extending throughout much of the modern period, regional identities remain strong and periodically efforts at secession resurface—most notably in Catalonia, the Basque country, and Galicia. Whether either Spain or Italy will exist as a unitary state twenty or thirty years from now is anybody's guess.

Conversely, multiethnic political projects in Europe were not limited to the Holy Roman Empire, which Hazony mistakenly characterizes as an exercise in imperial domination while ignoring its polycentric and federalist features. Other decentralized, multiethnic polities in Europe include the Habsburg Empire, Switzerland, and Belgium. As an aside, present-day India, a multiethnic democracy with twenty-two official languages, does not seem to fit Hazony's model of nationhood very well.

The feudal political order that divided Europe into small political units for much of the Middle Ages and the early modern period, including during the so-called Westphalian era, paid little attention to the ethnic or tribal character of European populations. Hazony's idea of "nations-as-unions-of-tribes" flies in the face of the so-called European marriage pattern,[13] which asserted itself particularly in those countries that Hazony cites as prime illustrations of his thesis: England and the Low Countries. As Mark Koyama, an economic historian at George Mason University, notes in his review of Hazony's book, "[a]n extensive literature documents how the Catholic Church eroded tribal and clan-based loyalties by prohibiting cousin marriage, encouraging widows to remain unmarried, and advocating for marriage as an institution for consenting adults."[14] As a result, extended families, or clans, which were supposedly the basis of modern nationhood, had been displaced with much more agile nuclear family units *before* it made sense to identify the English or the Dutch as distinct political nations.

The mistake that modern conservative advocates of nationalism, such as Hazony or Scruton, commit is akin to that made by proponents of identity politics on the far left who believe that one's politics is inextricably linked to observable attributes such as gender, ethnicity, or religion. Just as being female, African American, or Muslim does not *lock* one into any particular set of political beliefs or allegiances (though it can predict them with a degree of reliability), there is no inherent reason why individual political loyalties should be tied exclusively and inextricably to the color of one's passport. Of course, nations and other "imagined communities"[15] are not arbitrary constructs that could be disposed of or reshaped by policymakers at will. Yet one can simultaneously be a citizen of New York City, the State of New York, and the United States (or of Bratislava, Slovakia, and the European Union) and feel strongly about each of those respective identities without necessarily seeing them as being in conflict and while allowing each facet of those identities to assert themselves in different contexts.[16]

To be sure, such individual allegiances can also clash with each other. Unsurprisingly, some actors actively exploit such tensions existing in human identities. The integration of Muslim immigrants into mainstream European societies has not been always straightforward, especially given the continent's sclerotic labor markets. It should not come as a surprise that thousands of predominantly unemployed and underemployed young men in such communities across the continent were radicalized thanks to the presence of Salafi-Jihadi networks and subsequently turned against their host countries. Over fifty-five hundred EU nationals migrated to Syria to join the so-called Islamic State[17] and a number of others committed acts of domestic terrorism in European countries.

Large Russian minorities live in countries across the former Soviet Union, and around sixty million ethnic Chinese live outside mainland China, mostly in other Asian countries. Russia's war against Georgia, interference in Moldova, annexation of Crimea, and invasion of Eastern Ukraine have been justified precisely on the grounds of defending the interests of the Russian-speaking minority. In 2014, Vladimir Putin articulated a doctrine under which Russia has the right and obligation to defend the interests of ethnic Russians anywhere in the world.[18] The Chinese regime has also invested heavily into ties with ethnic Chinese populations outside the mainland, arguably with the purpose of leveraging those ties politically. Since the times of Mao Tse-tung, the Chinese Communist Party (CCP) has relied on the policy known as "using civil actors to promote political ends." Although cultural and educational activities—under the umbrella of "Confucius Institutes" founded at Western universities, for example—have received attention in the West, potentially more pernicious are the CCP's attempts to "guide" overseas Chinese in the pursuit of Beijing's geopolitical influence. Except for the religious group Falungong, pro-Taiwan, Uighur, and Tibetan groups, it is hard to find organizations of overseas Chinese that would operate independently of any "guidance" from Beijing. President Xi Jinping called such efforts the CCP's "magic weapons."[19] Not even Chinese-language media overseas can escape Beijing's interest. There are numerous examples of boycotts, withdrawals of advertisement, and other activities that encourage a degree of self-censorship even among journalists working for mainstream Western outlets.[20]

The constant renegotiation of political identities is being exploited by other actors as well. Paradoxically, some governments that get high marks among conservatives for defending national sovereignty also tend to be active in seeking to expand their influence by leveraging ethnic minorities in neighboring countries. The governments of Hungary and Austria, for example, have encouraged ethnic minorities in neighboring countries to take on Hungarian and Austrian citizenships and provided local organizations with funding in pursuit of this objective. The current Austrian government, which features the nationalist Freedom Party of Austria as one of its coalition members, has reached out particularly to inhabitants of the South Tyrol region of Italy, putting it at loggerheads with the current populist government in Rome.[21] South Tyrol was, of course, a part of Austria until 1918 and still features a large community of German speakers.

Around 150,000 ethnic Hungarians in Ukraine have been encouraged by Budapest to demand political autonomy. The Hungarian minority present in Romania is even larger (over 1.2 million), accounting for over 6 percent of the country's total population. There, the Orbán government's efforts have followed similar lines. It is telling that the high-profile, Fidesz-organized Summer University—at which Viktor Orbán delivered his famous speech on "illiberal democracy" in 2014—has been taking place regularly at the Transylvanian spa town of Băile Tuşnad, known also as Tusnádfürdő in Hungarian.

Interestingly, Orbán's government has also slammed the US-Hungarian billionaire-philanthropist George Soros for his support of various progressive causes in Central Europe as indicative of an effort to undermine democracy in the region. Yet the same Hungarian government has vastly outspent Soros in its engagement with Hungarian ethnic minorities in neighboring countries, including in Romania, Ukraine, and Slovakia, under the umbrella of the country's "National Policy."[22] Needless to say, these efforts take place in the shadow of the trauma of the 1920 Trianon Agreement, which dramatically reduced Hungary's size and geopolitical clout and scattered ethnic Hungarians across the territories of multiple countries. But Europe already lived through one iteration of the same nationalist policies seeking to reverse the post–World War I settlement on the continent. Eighty years ago, those policies led to the Munich Agreement and the most destructive conflict in human history.

THE FRAYING FABRIC OF CIVIL SOCIETY

"Imagined communities" sustaining democratic politics are being reshaped by globalization. Western societies have grown more ethnically and culturally diverse. The worlds of academic inquiry, research, and civil society are more integrated globally than ever before. News and ideas travel faster than ever, thanks to cheap travel and the internet. Due to free capital flows, conversations in corporate boardrooms around the planet are less and less shaped by local sensitivities and more by sanitized corporate cultures that have taken root around the globe. If the lifestyles and values of the educated upper classes worldwide—the "anywheres," in Goodhart's terminology—have seen a degree of convergence, they have also detached themselves from the outlooks of their more parochial countrymen.

The resulting "coming apart"[23] of Western societies into mobile and cosmopolitan cognitive elites, with weak ties to particular locations and those "left behind," has not just created a new dividing political line. It has likely fueled resentment, partisan polarization, and authoritarian populism. That is especially true as the bulk of the benefits of a more interconnected world is seen as being reaped precisely by the mobile "elites," whereas economic outcomes for other parts of Western populations, typically less mobile ones with less education, have seen less improvement. The combination of economic hardship, and the perception that elites are cutting themselves loose from the rest of their countries, has thus created conditions for populist politics driven by resentment and bigotry,[24] while making it harder to maintain a healthy culture of civic engagement.

However, the reality of an increasingly interconnected world is not going away, regardless of whether one thinks that it is on balance desirable. Instead, democracies will have to adapt, including by responding effectively to the unwanted interference from authoritarian regimes and other unfriendly actors who seek to leverage ethnic, linguistic, or religious ties to their advantage. But most importantly, they need to restore the civic fabric that binds individuals together.

Should that restoration fail, the risk is not merely that the current backlash against "globalism" will continue, but that Western democratic societies will continue on their current path toward tribalism and its political cousin, authoritarianism. A long stream of conservative and classical liberal literature, from Friedrich von Hayek's *Law, Legislation, and Liberty*[25] to Jonah Goldberg's *Suicide of the West*,[26] reminds us that Western civilization's foundational principles of rule of law and impersonal market relations rely on tempering our tribal instincts and loyalties and instead embracing a highly "unnatural" moral outlook that relies on following abstract and generalizable rules of conduct. Such rules of conduct are embedded in political institutions that exist in people's minds as much as they exist in the form of written laws, formal court systems, and so forth. Ultimately, their survival is contingent on the ability of people to transcend their moral intuitions and deep-seated tribalistic instincts, which give preference to people of one's own family, clan, or tribe over outsiders.

Tribalism has now been on the rise on the political right, where divisive ethnonationalism has propelled authoritarian populists to electoral successes in the United States and Europe. A Republican member of the House of Representatives from Iowa, Steve King, advocated for "an America that's just so homogeneous that we look a lot the same"[27]—a distinctly repugnant vision deliberately leaving out large portions of America's population on ethnic grounds. A common conservative response seeks to distinguish between healthy patriotic sentiments and their pathological varieties, of which Representative King's views are a particularly abominable illustration. As Scruton argues, "[t]he nation state should not be understood in terms of the French nation at the Revolution or the German nation in its twentieth-century frenzy. For those were nations gone mad, in which the springs of civil peace had been poisoned and the social organism colonized by anger, resentment and fear."[28]

That is a valid point, but it does not relieve conservatives and advocates of nationalism of their duty to consider the second-order effects of their political actions and advocacy. Are those who now sing paeans to the virtues of nationalism or seek to come up with elaborate accounts for why the current populist moment is in fact a healthy correction to decades of globalist overreach steering the conversation in a benign direction, or are they "normalizing" (as the common turn of the phrase goes) attitudes and policies that for good reasons have been long seen as inadmissible in a civilized society?

This question is particularly salient because, in political life, pursuing seemingly legitimate nationalist and sovereigntist causes, such as Brexit, has often involved forming political coalitions with bigots, racists, and worse. In August 2014, the cerebral, free-market, euroskeptic member of the UK Parliament for the Conservative Party, Douglas Carswell, famously defected to Nigel Farage's United Kingdom Independence Party (UKIP). Back then,

UKIP's reputation was tainted by bigotry, and by Carswell's own admission, his move was motivated by an effort to detoxify its brand in order to build a broader political coalition to facilitate the United Kingdom's exit from the European Union.[29] Of course, this "detoxification" was only partly successful. While the 2016 referendum was a triumph for Carswell and his free-market euroskeptic allies, it came at the price of a highly illiberal framing of Brexit, in which UKIP's anti-immigration agenda took center stage. And it was that agenda, alas, that also informed the United Kingdom's approach to negotiations, most prominently its red line on free movement of people, which precluded a form of Brexit that would include a future membership in the European common market, favored by a number of prominent free-market figures such Daniel Hannan.[30]

The same criticism can be addressed at Republicans in the United States who have either decided to look the other way or been very mild in their criticisms of Donald Trump's racist and would-be authoritarian antics, hoping that the president is, for all his flaws, still the best vehicle for their agenda of reducing taxes, deregulation, appointing conservative judges, and restoring America's sovereignty. Compromises are an inherent part of political life. Yet in both cases, the result has been less a material advancement of legitimate conservative causes and more a poisoning of political life by a tribalistic mindset that seeks to make excuses or ignore the worst political impulses seen in the Western world in a long time.

Needless to say, the political left is not immune to the same problem. In the United Kingdom, the Labour Party has become a cult built around the personality of its leader, Jeremy Corbyn. Corbyn prides himself at being an unreconstructed member of the 1970s-style hard left. He hosted a television program on Iran's state TV and has well-documented ties to Islamists, Holocaust deniers, and anti-Semites.[31] During his tenure, what was once a broad-based center-left party has become a place that is unwelcoming of its Jewish members. In fact, according to a poll organized by the United Kingdom's *Jewish Chronicle* in 2017, only 13 percent of British Jews would consider voting Labour.[32]

In the United States, the fight over the character of the Democratic Party is underway too, with ever-stronger voices emerging on the populist, hard left. Not only has there been a revival of statist approaches to economic policy under the umbrella of "democratic socialism," the left has also become increasingly interested in categorizing people based on their gender, ethnic, and religious backgrounds in order to place them in a hierarchy of oppression that is inevitably coming from white males.[33] A greater sensitivity to the cultural norms, expectations, and prejudices that hold back women and people of color is welcome. But approaching *all* politics through the lenses of a structural source of oppression has its perils. First, it extends the political to realms that had once been private and intimate—sex, family life, and consumer habits—entrenching already existing political divides. Second, symmetrical to the problem existing on the political right, the elevation of real or imagined oppression above all other political causes makes otherwise decent people oblivious to extremism and bigotry in their midst, especially if it comes from individuals or groups that are identified as oppressed. Linda Sarsour, a female Muslim-American activist, was a key figure of the mass Women's March that followed President Trump's inauguration, notwithstanding her long history of virulent anti-Semitism and hate.[34] There was also an eerie silence on the political left when Rashida Tlaib, the first Palestinian-American member of US Congress, accused senators opposed to boycotts of Israel of "double identity"—one of the most common anti-Semitic smears. "They forgot what country they represent," she wrote on Twitter.[35]

The problem is not just that tribal politics facilitates the resurfacing of the ugliest streaks of political imagination both on the left and right. The divisiveness inherent in tribalism also places politicians and the voting public into increasingly rigid political camps wherein members of differing camps end up seeing each other not as fellow citizens but as mortal enemies—that is true also of the emerging camps of "somewheres" and "anywheres." Similar forms of tribalism have taken many countries to unhappy destinations—including Rwanda, Lebanon, and the former Yugoslavia. Lest Western democracies suffer a similar fate, it is necessary to renew the bonds that tie our societies together and enable people to self-organize, politically and otherwise. That should not be read as an abstract wish but rather as a concrete plea to people on all ends of the political spectrum: Talk to your neighbors, engage with those who disagree with you, do not lose friends over politics. Without a critical mass of individuals who are willing to push against the growing balkanization of the West's public sphere, it will be hard to change the current direction.

The present moment is not only one of threat but also of opportunity. The emergence of new transnational actors,[36] for example, provides opportunities to address the shortcomings of existing international institutions by exercising coordinated pressure on those institutions and national governments. To the extent to which institutional sclerosis is a real problem of international (and national) bureaucracies, it is a result of the abdication of democratic leaders to act as effective "principals" of such organizations. Political incentives to do so have often been weak, as electorates rarely express genuine interest in questions of international cooperation, which are often arcane, technical, and seemingly detached from everyday life. With the sudden salience of such questions in the era of populism, the functioning of international institutions has now become a subject of intense public scrutiny. That also means that the defenders of international cooperation have no choice but to make an explicit, political case for them—and to articulate reforms that would address the voters' legitimate grievances.

Because of its cultural and economic heterogeneity, the world lacks a coherent "demos" to sustain a global democracy. Yet much the same observation could be made about the newly emerged nation-states of the nineteenth century. It was the shared institutions, the shared perception of outside threats and common policy challenges, and often the heavy-handed government fiat that led to the emergence of coherent bodies of public opinion in European countries. Likewise, it takes a process of interaction between policy challenges, institutions, and democratic contestation—much like the churn already underway—to create political communities extending beyond national borders. In contrast to the theoretical literature that considers the possibility of democracy beyond the nation-state as an either-or question,[37] the polycentric, covenantal approach toward "patterns of associated relationships [transcending] national boundaries,"[38] as Vincent Ostrom called them, is much more modest. Specifically, it recognizes that there are many partly overlapping *demoi* of which the same individuals can be members—some local, some national, and some international or transnational.[39] The endgame is not to build a single world polity with a homogenous body of public opinion—a positively utopian and unrealistic project—but rather to encourage a plurality of competing governance mechanisms dealing with different and sometimes overlapping subject matters, all open to contestation.

Pushing back against tribalism and building a political culture, in which such a fluidity of political identities can flourish, instead of being a source of conflict, are two sides of the same coin. An effective pushback on the political, cultural, and intellectual fronts seems to be the mother of all collective action problems—but that does not mean that it is impossible. Self-governing societies have displayed a remarkable aptitude for renewal in times of hardship, precisely because of their social capital and the possibility for political entrepreneurship granted by the open nature of their political systems. The question is whether the public and budding political entrepreneurs equipped with sound policy ideas can mobilize themselves toward such a renewal, equipped with sound policy ideas, or whether the West needs to slide further on its current dangerous path for such political renewal to take place.

Chapter Eight

A Globalism for the People

The West has reached an impasse. The preservation of the bland, sanitized status quo touted by the Davos class is not politically viable, yet the alternatives proposed by its populist disruptors are almost invariably terrible. The solution proposed in this book is to embed globalism in a covenantal, polycentric view of governance. The same fundamental institutions that allow societies to govern themselves and solve collective-action problems locally ought to be extended more systematically to the transnational and international space. How that general guidance translates into specific reforms cannot be derived from abstract principles. Rather, institutional design requires a process of open-ended trial and error, competition, and contestation, which can lead to very different institutional and policy choices in different contexts.

Those who see the nation-state as the final and complete form of social organization are not going to be pleased by the call to open up states to covenantal arrangements that transcend national borders. At the same time, this book's message is meant to be disconcerting for those who assume that addressing international challenges necessarily involves the creation of formalized international organizations with a single center of decision-making.

In a complex and uncertain world populated by fallible human beings, even the most conspicuously *global* problems, such as climate change, are not amenable to easy, top-down, global solutions. The failure of the Copenhagen Summit of 2009 illustrates just how unrealistic the hope that carbon emissions could be reduced by a single binding global agreement was.[1] That lesson was internalized in the Paris Agreement, where a much looser framework of "pledge and review" was adopted instead of centralized bargaining. National governments are thus free to set their emissions targets every five years on the basis of their domestic economic and political realities.[2] A number of other developments, with little connection to the high-profile summits of global leaders, are also helping to avoid catastrophic climate change. Technological advances are already making renewable energy economically competitive. Between 2010 and 2018, for example, the cost of wind energy fell by around 23 percent, while the cost of solar photovoltaic electricity decreased by 73 percent.[3] New forms of cooperation between local levels of government authorities have emerged as well. Several US states, most prominently California,[4] have unveiled ambitious plans for decarbonization. Cities are experimenting and learning from each other's examples in encouraging mass transit, deploying hydrogen-powered buses, encouraging cycling, supporting community gardening, and other activities. While the jury is still out on how successful humankind will be in dealing with the threat of climate change, such examples illustrate that there is no one-to-one correspondence between *global* problems and *global* solutions.[5]

This book's contention is that in order to become more effective at solving international problems such as climate change and regain the trust of voters in Western democracies, advocates of globalism must become more comfortable with polycentrism, as opposed to technocratic, top-down decision-making. As a general rule, the more distant institutions ought to play only a *subsidiary* role to local arrangements. Application of the principle of subsidiarity requires one to embrace the diversity and fragmented nature of the institutional forms that international cooperation takes. More importantly, the design of international institutions needs to ensure a correspondence between the chosen set of tools and the problems to be addressed. Effective feedback mechanisms, space for experimentation, and accountability are also needed to overcome principal-agent problems in any organizational context, including in international settings.

The remainder of this chapter outlines several directions in which polycentric governance could limit the shortcomings of existing international institutions. The one increasingly plausible alternative to this reform agenda is that existing structures will decay, atrophy, and ultimately become irrelevant in an increasingly chaotic and dangerous world. The reassertion of nation-states interested in the pursuit of a narrowly defined national interest and no longer heeding any authority—only crude power—is a source of risks as it weakens the commitment of states to predictable international norms, making some of them more aggressive. Without shared expectations that norms provide, the danger of miscalculation and interstate conflict increases. Furthermore, humankind will be unable to address emerging challenges, driven by factors outside the control of national governments without effective international institutions. Here are six suggestions for how to keep such risks at bay.

1. LIMIT THE REACH OF
INTERNATIONAL INSTITUTIONS

International cooperation cannot be all-encompassing. Governance is always a means to an end, not a goal in itself. In its transnational and international incarnations, its primary purpose is to serve as a vehicle for resolving collective-action problems that transcend national borders, especially externalities and coordination problems, as well as providing a commitment device and a backstop against the failure of governments to uphold basic human rights. Because of subsidiarity considerations and the need to curb the principal-agent problems involved, such institutions ought to be built as close as possible to individuals affected by the issues they purport to address. To avoid the cycles of hubris and underdelivery, which have long characterized the functioning of international organizations, clear mandates and boundaries need to be imposed on such platforms for cooperation. Their mandates ought to be limited to questions that genuinely cross national borders, instead of including worthwhile yet broad aspirations or policy goals that properly belong to the purview of national governments. That is not to say that a razor sharp separation of power between different levels of government is the only possible way of organizing international cooperation. There may well be functional overlap between activities pursued by national governments, international organizations, and transnational networks, for example. The purpose of such overlap is to create redundancy, foster competition, and prevent any layer of governance from dominating or arbitrarily commandeering the others.

Many international institutions fail this test. The European Union's institutional infrastructure is famously a result of strategic efforts to shape incentives facing national governments in favor of ever more integration.[6] Yet contrary to the ambitions of its founders, the premise of a continual evolution toward "ever-closer union" has not led to the establishment of a European superstate. Instead, it has led to a pooling of sovereignty in areas where common decision-making yields only questionable benefits, ignoring the principle of subsidiarity. Simultaneously, the perception that the European Union's institutional setup is skewed in the direction of ever-tighter integration has played an important role in fueling resistance against the European project across member states—especially in those states such as the United Kingdom where large sways of the electorate did not view EU membership as a carte blanche for further political integration.

The European Union is an idiosyncratic organization, but its overreach is hardly unique. It has been hypothesized that bureaucrats face incentives to expand their budgets and purview, especially without effective supervision by their principals.[7] In the international realm, where such problems are pervasive, overreach can thus be expected to be the norm. If serving as a backstop to protect basic human rights, especially in cases of serious state failure or state-sponsored violence (*jus cogens*), is indeed one of the key tasks of international cooperation, such a task needs to be limited in scope and matched by appropriate policy instruments, up to and including coercive ones.[8] If the commitment to human rights is instead broad but toothless, it will inevitably erode both the efficacy and the legitimacy of action in areas where there is a strong rationale for action.

Numerous UN-sponsored declarations and conventions on human rights pursue laudable goals but carry very little practical meaning. The 1966 International Covenant on Economic, Social and Cultural Rights, for example, commits countries "to take steps" toward "full realization" of a variety of positive rights, including "[r]est, leisure and reasonable limitation of working hours and periodic holidays with pay, as well as remuneration for public holidays."[9] Given the dramatic differences in levels of economic development among signatory countries, it is hard to see what goal is served by making such broad and largely vacuous promises. An obvious one, of course, is that it provides an agenda for international civil servants to convene meetings and issue reports monitoring progress achieved in a fundamentally domestic area of policymaking.

Or consider a 2011 report by the UN High Commissioner for Human Rights that gives evidence of often horrific abuses directed against LGBT persons worldwide, especially in countries where homosexuality is criminalized or provides grounds for targeted violence. Those certainly provide the foundation for strongly worded condemnation and perhaps even for coercive measures. At the same time, it is not obvious why a global body sees it as a mandate to opine about domestic media policies, which "have a role to play by eliminating negative stereotyping of LGBT people, including in television programmes popular among young people"; sexual education, which "must pay special attention to diversity, since everyone has the right to deal with his or her own sexuality"; or school playgrounds where "boys deemed by others to be too effeminate or young girls seen as tomboys endure teasing and sometimes the first blows linked to their appearance and behaviour, perceived as failing to fit in with the heteronormative gender identity."[10]

This is not to deny the substantive validity of points made in the report or to downplay the value of progress already achieved globally in the treatment of LGBT persons. However, throughout the Western world, durable progress has come from a bottom-up change of norms of communities, slowly building up to create pressure for systemic change at the national level. An international organization with a global mandate to step into politically and emotionally charged domestic debates is unlikely to serve as a catalyst for progress. Instead, it risks providing ammunition to political forces that are trying to depict globalism as an inherently left-wing program that seeks to circumvent domestic policymaking. Furthermore, the combination of unbounded, high-minded ambitions and the utter lack of the tools needed to deliver any results is eroding the credibility of international institutions, reducing them in popular imagination to expensive talking shops or make-work employment schemes for overachieving graduates of public policy programs at the world's leading universities.

In short, globalism needs a dose of humility. International cooperation exists neither to solve all of humankind's problems, nor to make policymakers feel good about themselves. Its proper role is to effectively complement mechanisms of governance existing at a lower level. In that sense, subsidiarity represents both a principle of institutional design and enforcement, as well as a political guide for governments and other "principals" of international organizations.

While concrete prescriptions differ from case to case, as a general rule, governments and local actors ought to find it easier to limit mandates of existing organizations than to expand them. That can be done through asymmetric voting rules that would require supermajorities in favor of positive action. It can also be done with explicit, binding charters outlining which subjects are off limits to such organizations. In the EU context, the Early Warning System could be expanded along the lines proposed by the UK government in 2015—that is, by introducing the institution of a red card that would enable national parliaments to stop unwanted legislative action by European institutions. A new European treaty could also provide a list of policy areas in which European institutions are prevented from legislating. That would alleviate the common concerns, founded or not, that the bloc is acting as a vehicle for a progressive social and cultural agenda.

2. IMPROVE DECISION-MAKING AND ADAPTATION

Accountability, adaptability, and responsiveness of institutions of "global governance"—from military alliances through trade agreements to formal international organizations—is a reflection of their design. Every institution needs avenues for contestation and renegotiation. In international ones, the need is amplified by the presence of principal-agent problems.

Unfortunately, the manner in which international organizations change is often a result of bureaucratic discretion. The UN Children's Fund (UNICEF) is currently seeking to extend its support to the more nebulous category of "youth," as opposed to its original mission confined to children's rights, needs, and opportunities.[11] The International Monetary Fund, initially tasked with managing balance of payment problems within the Bretton-Woods system of fixed exchange rates, later reinvented itself as the chief supervisor of global financial stability. As of late, it has also become busy promoting the financial and economic empowerment of women, among other causes.[12] The first loans extended and guaranteed by the World Bank revolved almost exclusively around infrastructure investment. Over time, the organization expanded its ambitions to include a much wider array of questions of economic development, including health and education. Besides being simply a vehicle for financing, the bank has also become a major player, providing policy advice to countries and facilitating international agreements to reduce poverty.[13]

Substantively, those changes of focus and the adaptation to new realities might be perfectly defensible. What is questionable, however, is the extent to which such decisions reflect conscious choices of the organization's principals. To ensure greater responsiveness, one avenue worth exploring is experimentation with decision-making rules. For a long time, voting weights, or quotas, of individual countries in international organizations such as the International Monetary Fund have been criticized as no longer reflecting the relative importance of developed and emerging economies around the world. Simultaneously, one may be concerned that changes reflecting the new distribution of economic weight around the world could marginalize smaller Western democracies that have contributed disproportionately to the good functioning of such organizations. One possible way around such problems is a decision-making system that provides flexibility for actors, small and big ones, to assign different salience to their votes. Under quadratic voting rules, for example, countries would be each allocated a fixed amount of "voting credits" that they could use to participate in collective decisions. That would enable them to cast more votes in decisions that actually matter to them, empowering even small countries and their coalitions to stand up against large ones on matters of importance to them.[14]

In addition to the use of voice, the ability to exit is also important. Sunset provisions can provide for an automatic shutdown of organizations and treaties at a specified future time unless their further existence is agreed upon and possibly ratified again by member countries or other participants. Accordingly, the Kyoto Protocol had an explicit sunset provision, as do the International Air Transport Association and the 1962 International Coffee Agreement.[15] Another mechanism pointing in the same general direction consists of lowering the costs of exit by explicit escape clauses, which allow governments and other participants to vote with their feet. The European Union's institutional architecture famously features a provision for an orderly exit of a member state—Article 50 of the Treaty on the European Union— as does the Rome Statute which underpins the International Criminal Court.

The availability of mechanisms for renegotiation and for easy exit is important particularly in international settings that involve disagreements over the division of surplus—especially the category of interactions that could be described as "battles of the sexes," to use the vocabulary introduced in chapter 3. In such situations, long time horizons and inflexibility are likely to inhibit cooperation from those actors who believe that they should be getting a larger fraction of the surplus and are unwilling to make open-ended commitments that they might perceive as unfair. In contrast, shortening time horizons and preserving the ability to change the terms of agreements later enables participants to make less demanding commitments and cooperate with the expectation of receiving a larger portion of the surplus in the future.

Easier exit and the effective use of voice by governments and other principals of international and transnational organizations are thus connected. Yet even the cleverest institutional fixes are no substitute for leadership and ownership of international institutions by their principals. In the past, the United States underwrote the operation of numerous global organizations, steering them in ways that were generally benign for the wider world. With the turn inward taken by the current administration, more such agencies are on autopilot or vulnerable to capture by rising powers, such as China. And, of course, in the case of the European Union, the lack of political leadership has been a festering problem for decades. A revitalization of globalism will not succeed with national governments stepping up their level of international engagement, instead of seeking to retreat home.

3. INTERNATIONAL INSTITUTIONS HAVE TO BE A TWO-WAY STREET

Another weakness of international organizations driven by bureaucratic incentives is the stasis in their membership. As a result, even when some participants cease to contribute to effective common governance or go "rogue," only weak mechanisms are available to penalize or expel them. To some extent, this flaw reflects also the optimistic mindset, which prevailed after the fall of communism when the integration of new countries into international structures was seen as a part of an irreversible global march toward democracy, markets, and liberal values.

On balance, the enlargements of the North Atlantic Treaty Organization (NATO) and the European Union, driven by this underlying sense of optimism, have been successful. The "Westernized" Central and Eastern Europe of today is a far more prosperous and democratic place than those parts of the post-Soviet space that did not face a realistic prospect of joining such international structures. However, this success has also created significant challenges for both organizations. In the European Union, Poland and Hungary have defied basic principles of rule of law and democracy by stacking courts, cracking down on civil society organizations, and silencing opposition media. The bloc's response has been slow and largely ineffective, contributing to a real risk that the European Union will become home to genuinely auto-cratic regimes.

The same problem exists, perhaps even more acutely, within NATO. If the alliance was created primarily to defend Europe against a common ene-my, the Soviet Union, following the end of communism it became primarily a community based on shared values—and by extension on a shared percep-tion of external threats. Especially as Turkey embraces autocratic rule, it is hard to argue that those shared values (and shared strategic outlook) are still there. Are Turkey's Western allies ready to come to the country's defense if Recep Tayyip Erdoğan's regime becomes involved in a conflict through its own recklessness?

No form of polycentric governance can function without sanctions against members who break agreed-upon rules. In some cases, they may be present, at least on paper. Yet the mere existence of such formal provisions is no guarantee of their effective application. The European Commission, for ex-ample, has launched proceedings under Article 7 of the Treaty on European Union against Hungary, Poland, and Romania. Those could culminate with the suspension of voting rights of each country in the European Council. But the European Union's current predicament is that the authors of the legal procedure did not really consider the possibility of two or more countries going off the rails simultaneously and coming to each other's defense in the European Council to prevent the emergence of unanimity needed for the procedure to be effective. It is also telling that to the present day, Fidesz, Viktor Orbán's ruling party, is a member of the European People's Party, alongside its supposed political nemesis, Angela Merkel's Christian Demo-cratic Union. If not even the most powerful family of political parties in the European Union can exclude an unruly member, it is hard to see the political leadership needed to effectively sanction national governments of countries such as Poland and Hungary.

A different example has to do with China's joining the World Trade Organization (WTO) in 2001. At the time, the move was motivated by the hope that Chinese economic reforms would continue to progress and move the country closer to the market. However, since its accession, the opposite has happened. Especially in recent years, China's regime has become protec-tionist and mercantilist in its outlook, contributing to the populist wave in the United States. This is not to necessarily suggest that China should be ex-pelled from the WTO. However, the possibility of ejection of unruly or rogue members, alongside a system of escalating sanctions, has to become a part of the institutional design of international institutions, instead of a naive hope that dialogue and multilateralism are in and of themselves guarantees of good outcomes. But institutional design does not obviate the need for responsible political leadership—or for the courage needed to disrupt complacency by applying the existing rules.

4. LEVERAGE INSTITUTIONAL DIVERSITY, EXPERIMENTATION, AND MARKET INCENTIVES

Instead of looking for one-size-fits-all solutions to international problems, globalism needs to be about facilitating the emergence of solutions, adapted to local conditions, through a process of trial and error by those actors who are best positioned to address such problems. Sometimes, such actors might be national governments acting in concert; at other times, they could be international organizations staffed with technical experts, transnational networks of regulators, local governments, or groups of private businesses and individuals. If globalism is to work, it has to embrace a much greater diversity of flexible arrangements, instead of limiting itself to formal multilateral institutions. It must involve more "coalitions of the willing," composed of national governments and other actors, addressing problems that large international organizations have been unable or unwilling to tackle. Likewise, cross-border problems can often be best dealt with by transnational networks of local governments, regulators, universities, and others. When embedded in shared norms of behavior, the multiplicity of different initiatives and forms of cooperation is not a liability—in fact, redundancies increase the resilience of the overall system and furthermore stimulate competition and discovery of best practices.

International cooperation should also leverage competition and market incentives more explicitly. It seems beyond any doubt that technological change is rapidly outpacing innovation in the production and application of legal rules. Platforms such as Uber and Airbnb have left local governments dumbfounded. As a result, in many places they have often either operated outside the law or become victims of blanket bans by municipalities. National and local policymakers have displayed only a limited understanding of the regulatory dimension of driverless cars, drones, or advanced facial recognition technologies. Relatedly, software users routinely accept voluminous terms of conditions without ever learning their content, often giving away valuable personal data to companies for free. The notion that the only way to address these emerging challenges is through political deliberation in national parliaments is hardly compelling, particularly given the unpredictable nature of technological platforms and business models and the fact that the effects of such innovations are spilling across borders.

The legal scholar Gillian Hadfield of the University of Toronto argues that appropriate legal frameworks for a "flat" global economy cannot solely be the creations of national governments or of top-down decisions. Instead, market competition ought to be introduced to a number of critical areas. Within federal systems, such as the United States, there is a scope for rules-shopping and competition across states as state courts are obligated to give "[f]ull faith and credit" to the legal instruments of other states.[16] Even in situations where private parties have no connection to a state, they can often have recourse to its law. For example, a 1984 New York statute allows business deals worth over $250,000 to be governed by state law, regardless of where and by whom such contracts are concluded. As a result, courts in other states, such as California, can easily find themselves applying New York law.[17] With some caveats, that practice could be extended to private providers of rules governing contracts (where blockchain could play an important role too) and to corporate, employment, and consumer law. Without effective oversight, one may perhaps worry about capture. Yet it is the current practice that often makes consumers captive to terms and conditions they rarely read and understand. The existence of real competition between rules providers, naturally supervised by antitrust and other authorities, would create strong pressures to simplify rules and make them transparent, as well as to continuously develop legal instruments adapted to newly emerging technologies.

Even in the area of regulation, where capture is an even stronger concern, new markets in rules could add value.[18] As of now, many areas of regulation rely on technical standards for their granular details. Such standards are voluntary, created by bodies built by private businesses themselves, and the system helps lessen the burden on the government, which is absolved of the need to micromanage economic sectors it hardly understands and encourages cross-border trade as most relevant standards are international and often global. The downside is that standardization agencies often enjoy monopolies granted to them by national regulators or international bodies such as the European Union. Wherever the size of the market allows it, a competition between different producers of standards would be preferable. That way, national governments (and the European Union) would take on the role of "superregulators," focusing on whether privately provided regulatory frameworks lead to desired outcomes and making democratically informed decisions about what outcomes matter, while being shielded from facing the overwhelming complexity of the underlying technological and economic relationships.

The merit of such "markets for rules" in different areas of law is that they can help provide a stronger legal basis for businesses operating in countries that lack robust rule of law—in much the same way as ISO 9000 certification has facilitated the rise of exports from developing countries and facilitated the inflow of foreign direct investment.[19] A market-based approach would also provide a viable decentralized alternative to the currently stalled efforts at government-led regulatory cooperation involved in trade agreements, contributing to a spontaneous, bottom-up convergence in norms and behaviors of economic actors worldwide.

5. BE WARY OF AUTHORITARIANS

Globalism cannot be approached as a value-free enterprise. There is a fundamental difference between international structures created by free, self-governing societies and those set up by authoritarian regimes. Furthermore, while mixing the two categories together in shared international settings is sometimes necessary, it is also fraught with difficulties—not least by exacerbating the extent of principal-agent problems. More importantly, there is no substitute for the leading role that Western democracies play in setting international norms and standards and providing solutions to collective-action problems.

If Western democracies, driven by a misguided quest to recapture national sovereignty, resign their roles as movers and shakers of the international institutions, others will fill the void. Vladimir Putin's Russia, Xi Jinping's China, and other authoritarian powers are seeking to assert themselves on the world stage. It is not a coincidence that at a time when traditional, democratic underwriters of formal structures of international cooperation are retreating, authoritarian regimes are setting up international structures that mimic those created by the United States and other democracies in the aftermath of World War II.

China's Belt and Road initiative in particular seeks to foster investment connections and infrastructure that would tie a number of countries to Beijing economically and politically. Although the initiative provides funding for investment that is often of only marginal economic value—there is, after all, a reason why land connections between China and Europe were viable in the past—it is filling a real void left in Central Asia and Eastern Europe by Western powers. It is also contributing to a path dependency for poorer economies that may not be able to extricate themselves from Chinese influence in the future. For example, when economic conditions of such countries worsen, the Chinese regime can alleviate the newly incurred debt burdens of relatively poor countries within the program in exchange for further contracts or political concessions.

The "Digital Silk Road," a subset of the Belt and Road initiative, consists of purchases of Chinese telecommunication equipment, fiberoptic cables, and surveillance systems by governments and the private sector around the globe. In many countries, such purchases prompt fears about importing the intrusive, Orwellian characteristics of the Chinese political system, as well as about the risks of espionage. After all, both Huawei and ZTE have been under close scrutiny in a number of Western countries, including Australia and New Zealand.[20]

It is easy to spot the parallels between Chinese investment outreach and that of the United States' Marshall Plan after World War II and other efforts to bolster transatlantic relations. Yet the key difference is that the US-led entrenchment of a social contract based on democratic capitalism has led to a period of unprecedented peace, stability, and openness in Europe. The efforts of a communist regime to bring Asian and European countries into China's orbit are bound to produce very different outcomes, domestically and internationally.

Emulating the United States, China and Russia have also sought to create a multilateralist façade for what are essentially their projects of power projection. Similar to the World Bank's initial role, China has set up a multilateral investment bank, the Asian Infrastructure Investment Bank, to provide a new source of infrastructure financing. While the World Bank's track record in promoting actual economic development in poorer parts of the world is limited, the organization has accumulated useful technical expertise and is generally seen as a politically neutral, substance-driven organization. Beyond superficial similarities, the Asian Infrastructure Investment Bank cannot really offer either—nor can the same benefits be provided by the International Investment Bank, a relic of the Cold War era revived by Vladimir Putin's regime. Today, the International Investment Bank functions as a multilateral bank featuring a small number of EU members (Bulgaria, Czech Republic, Hungary, Romania, Slovakia), alongside Cuba, Vietnam, Mongolia, and Russia. For one, the "technical" expertise needed to sustain economic growth beyond just a process of investment-driven catching-up would necessarily rub against the institutional and political realities of both China and Russia. By their nature, unfree societies are not reliable sources of the innovation, new technologies, and new ideas that drive economic growth in the long run. Policy advice that could genuinely lead to long-run growth would necessarily involve an opening up of politics and an elimination of authoritarian patronage and rent-seeking that characterizes both regimes.

To be sure, in an economically integrated world, extricating ourselves from authoritarian regimes is easier said than done. A large part of democratic and free Europe runs on Russian energy. Chinese companies in private hands, yet with ties to the Communist Party, are an integral part of the Western business landscape, and leading Western companies have large operations in China. Severing those ties would be economically damaging and likely counterproductive.

However, scrutinizing investment coming from autocratic regimes on security grounds is simply prudent policy. But more importantly, the West has to demonstrate that it has the capacity to push back effectively against behavior that runs contrary to its interests, instead of systematically retreating because of the fear of escalation. NATO has to present its adversaries with overwhelming deterrent force on its Eastern flank and be able to respond adequately to provocations even beyond the alliance's borders. The fact that Ukraine is not a NATO member does not mean that the Western powers should not respond to Russian aggression in Luhansk and Donetsk, or the recent incident in the Kerch Straits. The same is true of various transgressions against international norms by China. [21]

The purpose is not to go "abroad in search of monsters to destroy" nor to sever all forms of cooperation with unfree societies. There are often compelling reasons for marriages of convenience, including the possibility that Western influence may eventually lead to political and economic opening up. At the same time, there are strong reasons not to treat authoritarian regimes, which lack accountability toward their citizens, as equals, especially in those international fora whose functioning relies on shared goals and values. Western democracies, furthermore, cannot just check out of the globalized world populated also by autocrats. If they seek to do so, they will allow their adversaries to write the rules of the game.

Neither can the West be oblivious to the changing security environment, in which revisionist powers including Russia and China are increasingly astute at leveraging their hard, economic, and soft power. So far, responses by Western governments have generally been lackluster, lacking discipline, strategy, and follow through. The first step toward addressing the problem lies in making the distinction between self-governing societies and those ruled by unaccountable autocrats the main compass of foreign and security policy across the Western world, as well as its engagement in platforms of international cooperation.

6. MUCH OF THE PROBLEM IS DOMESTIC

A large part of the current backlash against globalism has less to do with international institutions themselves and more to do with a broader crisis of politics and identity in the Western world. Most voters do not harbor strong opinions about the organizational dysfunction at the World Bank, the democratic deficit at the International Electrotechnical Commission, or the minutiae of Basel III rules. Although bashing opaque international agreements and organizations has long been an effective political strategy for antiestablishment figures, the current blowback is driven primarily by domestic forces— most importantly by the sense that the existing social contracts in Western liberal democracies are not delivering for large segments of their populations. Western electorates are increasingly polarized and segregated geographically, [22] culturally, and along the lines of educational achievement. [23] Without a compelling story about what binds citizens of democratic societies together, our politics risk becoming ever more dysfunctional and extreme.

As a result, the agenda of reconstructing and reforming the existing international order cannot be separated from the broader challenge of restoring trust in democratic politics in the West. The healing process is unlikely to be facilitated by leaders linked with the status quo; nor are they likely to be offered by authoritarian populists feeding on the popular discontent without offering much in terms of solutions. Instead, they will have to come from a new wave of political disruptors who can develop policy agendas that can effectively address the sources of voters' anger.

Needless to say, many of the "international" solutions proposed by populists to address domestic problems—economic protectionism, highly restrictive immigration policy, reclaiming sovereignty from international organizations—are likely to do a lot of damage without providing any corrective to what has gone wrong in the Western world. Dismantling NATO, Western countries withdrawing from multilateral cooperative structures such as the European Union or WTO, and tariffs are not going to do *anything* to improve the condition of working-class voters or restore their social status—quite the contrary. Instead of trying to retreat from the modern, globalized world, political entrepreneurs need to offer a reconciliation of its reality with the interests of those who feel left behind by impersonal market forces operating on an international scale.

Such bargains can take many different forms. One possibility is a wave of structural reforms that would both restore the West's dynamism and even the playing field in the economy. Priorities should involve removing obstacles to economic and social mobility, especially in the poor and the working classes—repealing unnecessary licensing laws, eliminating arbitrary zoning restrictions in economically prosperous areas, and clamping down on excessive intellectual property legislation[24]—while simultaneously providing Western citizenries with a guarantee of a robust social safety net, for example, in the form of a universal basic income.[25]

To both combat wealth inequality and stasis in the economy, a common ownership self-assessed tax could be imposed on some fixed assets such as land, radio frequencies, patents, and internet domain names, as proposed by the legal scholar Eric Posner and the economist Glen Weyl in their recent book.[26] The idea of common ownership self-assessed tax consists of asking the owners of such assets to declare their monetary value and then *enable anyone* to purchase the asset in question at the declared price. Because owners would be taxed at a percentage of the declared value, they would no longer have the incentive to inflate the self-declared value of their assets, as patent trolls or property owners in the Bay Area do. Such a policy move would simultaneously limit rent-seeking in the economy in the form of patent trolling and excessively restrictive zoning laws, increase the churn in the economy by effectively allocating resources to their most valued uses, and provide a significant mechanism for redistribution because the tax would be levied on assets *and* related liabilities (resulting thus in a subsidy for homeowners whose property has suddenly fallen in value). Posner and Weyl offer other ideas, including a more effective application of antitrust policy to limit the influence of institutional investors, which arguably reduces competitive pressures across large segments of the US economy.

To be sure, outlining a wholesale policy agenda to revitalize democratic politics in the West goes far beyond the scope of this book. Its main message is simpler. There is nothing inevitable or preordained about the extraordinary human progress witnessed since the end of the Second World War. Even setting aside the current nationalist alternatives, the status quo has long been an unstable and fragile one. As Vincent Ostrom put it, "[t]he world cannot remain half free and half in servitude. Each is a threat to the other."[27] In order to preserve and build on the achievements of an open, rules-based international order underwritten by the world's leading free societies and to prevail over short-sighted populist nationalism, international cooperation must shed its reputation as a sanitized, technocratic endeavor detached of politics and values. Instead, globalism has to become an extension of the broader exercise of self-governance by free and responsible individuals. International and transnational institutions must be traceable back to the consent of individuals affected by them and provide space for the resolution of collective-action problems through adaptation and experimentation by groups of actors transcending national borders. Instead of seeking to provide remedies for everything that is ailing the world, institutions extending across national borders need to be limited in their scope, primarily to address questions that cannot be adequately dealt with at more local levels of government.

If such a conception of globalism is much more humble in its prescriptions than most of its contemporary advocates and critics, it is also a far more demanding one because it insists on a sharp distinction between the friends and enemies of free, self-governing societies. That distinction was once a cornerstone of foreign policy thinking on the political right—it was typically the radical left that was frivolous and naive in its dealings with authoritarians, especially during the Cold War. The decision of many on the right to discard this distinction in the wake of the current populist revolt, alongside a blind veneration for the unitary nation-state, has now become one of the main threats to peace and prosperity in the world and a danger to the future of free societies. Here's to hoping that we can do better.

Notes

PREFACE

1. Bandow, "How Many Enemies Does America Want?"
2. Bandow, "How Many Enemies Does America Want?"
3. Sally, *Classical Liberalism and International Economic Order*, 177.
4. Hayek, *Individualism and Economic Order*, 270.
5. Rohac, "The Libertarian Case for the European Union."
6. Rohac, *Towards an Imperfect Union*.
7. Rohac, "Classical Liberals and Foreign Policy."
8. Rohac, "Time for a Rethink?"
9. Birnbaum, "European Leaders Shocked as Trump Slams NATO and E.U."
10. Galindo, "Trump: EU Was 'Set Up to Take Advantage' of US."
11. Berger, "Why Withdrawing from Syria and Afghanistan Won't Save Much Money."
12. Deutsche Welle, "US and South Korea to Scrap Major Military Exercises in Spring."
13. Shane, "Trump's Budget Calls for New Base Closing Round in 2021."
14. Kazianis, "Trump Is Right—NATO Is Obsolete."
15. Thiessen, "Trump Is Using Tariffs to Advance a Radical Free-Trade Agenda."
16. Rohac, "Indiana's Gift to the International Order."

1. EVERY COUNTRY FOR ITSELF?

1. Hartwich, "Neoliberalism," 21–25.
2. Hartwell, *A History of the Mont Pelerin Society*, 21.
3. Mises, *Omnipotent Government*, 265.
4. Mises, *Omnipotent Government*, 266.
5. Hayek, *Individualism and Economic Order*, 269.
6. Röpke, *International Economic Disintegration*, 266.
7. Ostrom, *The Meaning of Democracy and the Vulnerabilities of Democracies*, 12.
8. Gallup, "Confidence in Institutions."
9. For an overview of the moves toward authoritarianism in Hungary and Poland, see Rohac, "Authoritarianism in the Heart of Europe."
10. Associated Press, "Trump Says Other Countries 'Taking Advantage' of US—Video."

11. Cited in Matthews, "Zero Sum Trump."
12. Galindo, "Trump."
13. Rohr, "I Don't Want This European Soviet Union."
14. Orbán, "Orbán Viktor's Ceremonial Speech."
15. Buchanan, "Is the West Disintegrating?"
16. Scruton, "England and the Need for Nations."
17. O'Sullivan, "Global Governance v Democratic Sovereignty."
18. Hazony, *The Virtue of Nationalism.*
19. Rabkin, *Law without Nations?*
20. Ku and Yoo, *Taming Globalization.*
21. Bolton, "Should We Take Global Governance Seriously?"
22. Bolton, "Should We Take Global Governance Seriously?" 221.
23. O'Sullivan, "Global Governance v Democratic Sovereignty."
24. Helms, Letter to US Trade Representative Mickey Cantor.
25. Rabkin, *Law without Nations?* 96.
26. Clemens, "Economics and Emigration."
27. See Salam, "Melting Pot or Civil War?"
28. Franck, "Trump Doubles Down."
29. Furceri et al., "Macroeconomic Consequences of Tariffs."
30. Hufbauer and Lowry, "US Tire Tariffs."
31. Bown, Jung, and Zhang, "Trump's Steel Tariffs Have Hit Smaller and Poorer Countries the Hardest."
32. Hammond, "The Future of Capital Mobility."
33. Friedman, *The World Is Flat.*
34. Hadfield, *Rules for a Flat World,* 131.
35. Hadfield, *Rules for a Flat World,* 144.
36. Hadfield, *Rules for a Flat World,* 135.
37. Hadfield, *Rules for a Flat World,* 5.
38. McKinsey Global Institute, *Navigating a World of Disruption,* 2.
39. Bostrom, "The Vulnerable World Hypothesis," 1.
40. Bostrom, "The Vulnerable World Hypothesis," 14.
41. Morgenthau, *Politics among Nations.*
42. Waltz, *Theory of International Politics.*
43. See Pavel, *Divided Sovereignty,* 171–90.
44. See Kolev, "Ordoliberalism."
45. For a popularized yet research-based and essentially uncontroversial account of the importance of institutions, see Acemoglu and Robinson, *Why Nations Fail.*
46. Coase, "The Problem of Social Cost."

2. WHAT SLIPPERY SLOPE?

1. Tuccille, "This Is the Number of Innocent People Murdered by Governments."
2. See, for example, Besley and Persson, *Pillars of Prosperity.*
3. Wilkinson, "What If We Can't Make Government Smaller?"
4. Patrick, *The Sovereignty Wars,* 40.
5. Grice-Hutchison, *The School of Salamanca.*
6. See Niemelä, "A Cosmopolitan World Order?"
7. See Benoist, "The First Federalist."
8. Kant, *Perpetual Peace.*
9. Tennyson, "Locksley Hall."
10. Willkie, *One World,* 133.
11. Reves, *The Anatomy of Peace.*
12. See Patrick, *The Sovereignty Wars,* 75.
13. Einstein, "Towards a World Government," 146.

14. Thatcher, "Speech in Hendon."

15. Slaughter, "Everyday Global Governance," 84.

16. See Howard-Jones, "The Scientific Background of the International Sanitary Conferences."

17. Covenant of the League of Nations.

18. "The Members of the League undertake to respect and preserve as against external aggression the territorial integrity and existing political independence of all Members of the League. In case of any such aggression or in case of any threat or danger of such aggression the Council shall advise upon the means by which this obligation shall be fulfilled." Covenant of the League of Nations, Article 10. See also Hewes, "Henry Cabot Lodge and the League of Nations."

19. Cited in Patrick, *The Sovereignty Wars*, 66.

20. Patrick, *The Sovereignty Wars*, 66.

21. Campbell, "The Struggle for Upper Silesia."

22. Woolsey, "The Leticia Dispute between Colombia and Peru."

23. See Covenant of the League of Nations, Article 22.

24. Kellogg-Briand Pact, 1928.

25. Covenant of the League of Nations, Article 8.

26. See Pavel, *Divided Sovereignty*.

27. UN Dag Hammarskjöld Library, "Security Council."

28. UN Security Council, Draft Resolution S/8761.

29. UN Security Council, Draft Resolution S/2018/321.

30. Neuer, "Reform or Regression?"

31. Freedom House, "Freedom in the World 2018."

32. Goldberg, "When Beheading Won't Do the Job."

33. Convention on the Prevention and Punishment of the Crime of Genocide.

34. See https://en.unpacampaign.org/proposal/.

35. Freedom House, "Freedom in the World 2018."

36. North Atlantic Treaty.

37. De Long and Eichengreen, "The Marshall Plan."

38. De Long and Eichengreen, "The Marshall Plan," 2.

39. Kagan, *The World That America Made*.

40. Pinker, *Better Angels of Our Nature*.

41. See Our World in Data, "The Visual History of Decreasing War and Violence."

42. See Human Progress, "Battle-Related Deaths, High Estimate."

43. Eisner, "Long-Term Historical Trends in Violent Crime." See Our World in Data, "The Visual History of Decreasing War and Violence."

44. See Center for Systemic Peace, Polity IV Database.

45. See Oneal and Russett, "The Kantian Peace."

46. Penciakova, Chandy, and Ledlie, *The Final Countdown*.

47. Ortiz-Ospina and Roser, "International Trade."

48. World Bank, *World Development Report*, 134–35.

49. Bown and Irwin, "The GATT's Starting Point," 1.

50. Ausubel, *Nature Rebounds*. See also Follett, "Seven Ways in Which Human Ingenuity Helps the Planet."

51. DeSombre, "The Experience of the Montreal Protocol."

52. Cited in Dreher, "Dying for Montenegro."

53. Swann, "International Standards and Trade."

54. Bartsch, "The Global Fund to Fight AIDS, Tuberculosis and Malaria."

55. See Tallberg et al., *The Opening Up of International Organizations*.

56. Fischer-Lescano and Teubner, "Regime-Collisions," 1000.

57. Biermann, Pattberg, and van Asselt, "The Fragmentation of Global Governance Architectures," 31.

58. See Park, "Enforcing International Trade Agreements."

59. Besedeš, Johnson, and Tian, "Economic Determinants of Multilateral Environmental Agreements." A theoretical rationale for this regularity is discussed in Barrett, "Self-Enforcing International Environmental Agreements."

60. Young, "Effectiveness of International Environmental Regimes."

61. Mansfield, Milner, and Rosendorff, "Why Democracies Cooperate More."

3. THE ANATOMY OF GLOBALISM

1. Keohane and Victor, "The Regime Complex for Climate Change," 12.

2. Ostrom, "Beyond Market and States," 645.

3. Shivakoti et al., *Improving Irrigation in Asia*.

4. Boettke, Palagashvili, and Lemke, "Riding in Cars with Boys," 409.

5. Aligica and Boettke, *Challenging Institutional Analysis and Development*, 31.

6. See, for example, Ostrom, Parks, and Whitaker, "Do We Really Want to Consolidate Urban Police Forces?"

7. Ostrom and Ostrom, "Behavioral Approach to the Study of Intergovernmental Relations," 135–36.

8. Polanyi, *The Logic of Liberty*.

9. Ostrom, Tiebout, and Warren, "The Organization of Government in Metropolitan Areas," 831.

10. Ostrom, *The Meaning of American Federalism*, 243.

11. Barry, "The Tradition of Spontaneous Order."

12. Fennell, "Ostrom's Law," 9.

13. Boettke, Palagashvili, and Lemke, "Riding in Cars with Boys," 409.

14. Ostrom, *The Meaning of American Federalism*, 227.

15. Ostrom, *The Meaning of American Federalism*, 242–43.

16. Ostrom, *The Meaning of American Federalism*, 242.

17. Cited in Ostrom, *The Meaning of American Federalism*, 224.

18. Cited in Tarko, *Elinor Ostrom*, 16.

19. For an overview, see, for example, Kinsky, "Personalism and Federalism."

20. Burgess, *Federalism and European Union*, 152.

21. McGinnis and Ostrom, "Design Principles for Local and Global Commons," 2.

22. Ostrom, *The Meaning of American Federalism*, 225.

23. Hazony, *The Virtue of Nationalism*.

24. Ostrom, *The Meaning of American Federalism*, 257.

25. Berg, Nakueira, and Shearing, "Global Non-State Auspices of Security Governance."

26. Roe, "Multi-Level and Polycentric Governance."

27. Van Zeben and Bobić, *Polycentricity in the European Union*.

28. Jordan et al., *Governing Climate Change*.

29. Shackelford, "On Climate Change and Cyber Attacks."

30. Backer, "Private Actors and Public Governance Beyond the State."

31. Black, "Constructing and Contesting Legitimacy and Accountability."

32. Ostrom, *Understanding Institutional Diversity*, 282.

33. Ostrom, Tiebout, and Warren, "The Organization of Government in Metropolitan Areas," 836.

34. Hayek, *Individualism and Economic Order*, 267.

35. Pavel, *Divided Sovereignty*.

36. Elinor Ostrom cited in Tarko, *Elinor Ostrom*, 97.

37. See Fernández-Huertas Moraga and Rapoport, "Tradable Refugee-Admission Quotas and EU Asylum Policy." For the original formulation, see Schuck, "Refugee Burden-Sharing."

38. See Fearon, "Domestic Politics, Foreign Policy, and Theories of International Relations."

39. Alchian, "Uncertainty, Evolution, and Economic Theory."

40. See Morgenthau, *Politics among Nations*; and Waltz, *Theory of International Politics*.

41. Mearsheimer, "The False Promise of International Institutions," 48.

42. See Black, "On the Rationale of Group Decision-Making"; and Arrow, *Social Choice and Individual Values.*

43. In economics, Douglass C. North and Ronald Coase made seminal contributions to the study of institutions. In the field of international relations, perhaps the most influential school of thought emphasizing institutions has been that of rational functionalism, associated with Robert Keohane, especially with his book *After Hegemony* (1984).

44. Ostrom, *Governing the Commons.*

45. Compare with Aligica and Boettke, *Challenging Institutional Analysis and Development*, 22.

46. Koremenos, Lipson, and Snidal, "The Rational Design of International Institutions."

47. Ostrom, *The Meaning of American Federalism*, 2226.

48. McGinnis and Ostrom, "Design Principles for Local and Global Commons."

49. McGinnis and Ostrom, "Design Principles for Local and Global Commons," 9.

50. Buchanan and Tullock, *Calculus of Consent*, 63–91.

51. Aligica and Boettke, *Challenging Institutional Analysis and Development*, 47.

52. McGinnis and Ostrom, "Design Principles for Local and Global Commons," 9.

53. See Rabkin, *Why Sovereignty Matters*, 30–31.

54. McGinnis and Ostrom, "Design Principles for Local and Global Commons," 9.

55. One of Ostrom's most famous studies, that of lobster fisheries in Maine, highlights the dynamic that can be set in motion by from the bottom up. Following the transformation of informal local organizations overseeing the management of lobster stock into formalized, territorially defined council with democratic accountability, almost immediately an overarching "council of council" emerged to address problems of larger-than-local scale. See Tarko, *Elinor Ostrom*, 131.

56. Tarko, *Elinor Ostrom*, 113.

57. Ostrom et al., "Revisiting the Commons."

58. Ostrom et al., "Revisiting the Commons," 242.

59. See, for example, Kindleberger, "Dominance and Leadership in the International Economy."

4. THE WEST'S GLOBALIST HISTORY

1. Irwin, "Multilateral and Bilateral Trade Policies in the World Trading System."

2. See Mokyr, *A Culture of Growth.*

3. Friedrichs, "The Meaning of New Medievalism."

4. See Neff, "Short History of International Law," 5–7.

5. Orford, "Jurisdiction without Territory."

6. Hills, "Federalism as Westphalian Liberalism."

7. Cited in Schröder, "The Constitution of the Holy Roman Empire After 1648," 966.

8. Eulau, "Federalism under the Holy Roman Empire."

9. Ostrom, *The Meaning of American Federalism*, 240–41.

10. See Krasner, *Sovereignty*; and Osiander, "Sovereignty, International Relations, and the Westphalian Myth."

11. Avalon Project, "The Golden Bull of the Emperor Charles IV."

12. Straumann, "The Peace of Westphalia as a Secular Constitution."

13. Avalon Project, "The Golden Bull of the Emperor Charles IV."

14. Osiander, "Sovereignty, International Relations, and the Westphalian Myth," 276.

15. Epstein, "The Rise and Decline of Italian City States"; Raccagni, "The Teaching of Rhetoric and the Magna Carta of the Lombard Cities"; and Raccagni, "When the Emperor Submitted to His Rebellious Subjects."

16. Huffman, "Urban Diplomacy, Cologne, the Rhenish League."

17. A *commenda* ("trust" or "custody" in Low Latin) was a common type of contract in which one of the partners provided investment capital and the other acted as business agent, particularly in the context of long-distance trade.

18. Greif, "Contract Enforceability and Economic Institutions in Early Trade."

19. Ewert and Selzer, "Commercial Super Trust or Virtual Organisation?"; and Ewert and Sunder. "Trading Networks, Monopoly and Economic Development."

20. Fink, "Under What Conditions May Social Contracts Arise?"

21. Ewert and Selzer, "Commercial Super Trust or Virtual Organisation?" 15.

22. Sellers, "Transnational Urban Associations and the State."

23. Pedersen, "Trade and Politics in the Medieval Baltic"; and Postan, "The Economic and Political Relations of England and the Hanse."

24. Postan, "The Economic and Political Relations of England and the Hanse," 93.

25. Pedersen, "Trade and Politics in the Medieval Baltic," 164–65.

26. Postan, "The Economic and Political Relations of England and the Hanse," 101.

27. Fink, "The Hanseatic League."

28. Sellers, "Transnational Urban Associations and the State," 9.

29. Sarnowsky, "The 'Golden Age' of the Hanseatic League."

30. McNamara, "The Euro Is an Experiment."

31. For a precrisis overview, see Lane, "The Real Effects of European Monetary Union."

32. See his seminal piece: Mundell, "A Theory of Optimum Currency Areas."

33. See Cipolla, "Currency Depreciation in Medieval Europe."

34. See Selgin, "The Rise and Fall of the Gold Standard in the United States."

35. Salter and Tarko, "Polycentric Banking and Macroeconomic Stability."

36. In her seminal study, Romer finds that the output losses linked to recessions were the same before and after 1913. Romer, "Changes in Business Cycles." Selgin and colleagues arrive at even more flattering conclusions about the operation of the pre-1913 monetary system. Selgin, Lastrapes, and White, "Has the Fed Been a Failure?"

37. Keynes, *The Economic Consequences of Peace*, 11.

38. See Eichengreen, *Golden Fetters*.

39. See, for example, Wicksell, *Interest and Prices*; and Mises, *The Theory of Money and Credit*.

5. FREE TRADE AND ITS DISCONTENTS

1. Krugman, "Is Free Trade Passé?" 131.

2. Chicago Booth Initiative on Global Markets, Free Trade Survey.

3. Smeltz and Kafura, "Record Number of Americans Endorse Benefits of Trade."

4. European Commission, Special Eurobarometer 461.

5. Palmer, "Clinton Raved about Trans-Pacific Partnership."

6. Navarro and Autry, *Death by China*. See also, for example, Williamson, "Peter Navarro."

7. Corporate Europe Observatory, "Public Services Under Attack through TTIP and CETA." At the time of writing, the talks have been relaunched on a smaller scale, focused on a limited number of sectors.

8. Rodrik, *Straight Talk on Trade*.

9. Chang, *Bad Samaritans*.

10. Irwin, "Tariffs and Growth in Late Nineteenth Century America."

11. See, for example, Deardorff, "Testing Trade Theories and Predicting Trade Flows."

12. See, for example, Bhagwati and Srinivasan, "Trade and Poverty in the Poor Countries."

13. For an overview, see Helpman, "The Structure of Foreign Trade."

14. Bastiat, *What Is Seen and What Is Not Seen*.

15. Krugman, "Oh, What a Trumpy Trade War!"

16. See, for example, Lemieux, *What's Wrong with Protectionism*; and Sally, *Classical Liberalism and International Economic Order*, 198–200.

17. Smith, *An Inquiry into the Nature and Causes of the Wealth of Nations*, 471.

18. See, for example, O'Rourke and Williamson, *Globalization and History*; and Bairoch, "European Trade Policy."

19. Lampe, Fernandes, and Tena-Junguito, "How Much Trade Liberalization Was There?"

20. Kindleberger, "The Rise of Free Trade in Western Europe."

21. The most prominent example was the 1858 Treaty of Amity and Commerce concluded between Japan and the United States.

22. Starting with the 1842 Treaty of Nanking, Qing-dynasty China concluded a series of "unequal treaties" with Western powers, which later became a source of great resentment in the country.

23. See, for example, Bolsinger, "The Foundation of Mercantile Realism."

24. Bolsinger, "The Foundation of Mercantile Realism."

25. See Madsen, "Trade Barriers and the Collapse of World Trade," 850.

26. Hynes, Jacks, and O'Rourke, "Commodity Market Disintegration in the Interwar Period." Röpke notes that global trade flows in 1934 were smaller than in 1913. Röpke, *International Economic Disintegration*, 24.

27. Eichengreen and Irwin, "The Slide to Protectionism in the Great Depression."

28. World Trade Organization, *World Trade Report 2007*, 39–43.

29. Bown and Irwin, "The GATT's Starting Point."

30. General Agreement on Tariffs and Trade, Article 24.

31. Bacchus, "Was Buenos Aires the Beginning of the End" (emphasis added).

32. Busch, "Overlapping Institutions, Forum Shopping, and Dispute Settlement."

33. David, "Overlapping Institutions in Trade Policy."

34. Rose, "Do We Really Know That the WTO Increases Trade?"

35. Goldstein, Rivers, and Tomz, "Institutions in International Relations"; Tomz, Goldstein, and Rivers, "Do We Really Know That the WTO Increases Trade?"

36. Goldstein, Rivers, and Tomz, "Institutions in International Relations," 39.

37. For the landmark contribution, see Lipsey and Lancaster, "The General Theory of Second Best."

38. Freund and Ornelas, "Regional Trade Agreements." See also Pauwelyn, "Not As Preferential As You May Think."

39. Wellhausen, "Recent Trends in Investor-State Dispute Settlement."

40. Wellhausen, "Recent Trends in Investor-State Dispute Settlement." See also Franck, "Empirically Evaluating Claims about Investment Treaty Arbitration."

41. European Commission, "Report of the 15th Round of Negotiations."

42. Quinn, "TTIP Deal Poses 'Real and Serious Risk.'"

43. Eaton and Kortum, "Technology, Geography, and Trade."

44. Anderson and von Wincoop, "Trade Costs."

45. Harford, "The Simple Steel Box."

46. Melitz, "Language and Foreign Trade"; and Melitz and Toubal, "Native Language, Spoken Language, Translation and Trade."

47. Rauch, "Business and Social Networks in International Trade."

48. Estrin, Baghdasaryan, and Meyer, "The Impact of Institutional and Human Resource Distance."

49. Baldwin, *The Great Convergence*.

50. Orefice, Piermartini, and Rocha, "Harmonization and Mutual Recognition."

51. Organisation for Economic Co-operation and Development. *International Regulatory Co-operation and Trade*, 9.

52. Akhtar and Jones, "Proposed Transatlantic Trade and Investment Partnership," 8.

53. Maskus, Otsuki, and Wilson, "The Cost of Compliance," 22.

54. Agreement on Technical Barriers to Trade.

55. Agreement on the Application of Sanitary and Phytosanitary Measures.

56. The recently agreed United States–Canada–Mexico Agreement is an exception by addressing this question explicitly. See Manak, "Regulatory Issues in the New NAFTA."

57. Basedow and Kauffman, "International Trade and Good Regulatory Practices," 8.

58. Basedow and Kauffman, "International Trade and Good Regulatory Practices," 8.

59. Clougherty and Grajek, "The Impact of ISO 9000 Diffusion on Trade and FDI."

60. Fliess et al., "The Use of International Standards in Technical Regulation."

61. Orefice, Piermartini, and Rocha, "Harmonization and Mutual Recognition."

62. Pelkmans, "The New Approach to Technical Harmonization and Standardization."

63. Pelkmans, "Mutual Recognition in Goods and Services," 3.

64. Correia De Brito, Kauffmann, and Pelkmans, "The Contribution of Mutual Recognition," 73–83.

65. Correia De Brito, Kauffmann, and Pelkmans, "The Contribution of Mutual Recognition," 71.

66. Davies, "Is Mutual Recognition an Alternative to Harmonization?"

67. Bronk and Jacoby, "Uncertainty and the Dangers of Monocultures in Regulation." See also Elliott and Litan, "Identifying and Regulating Systemically Important Financial Institutions."

68. Rodrik, *Straight Talk on Trade*, 121.

69. Rodrik, *Straight Talk on Trade*, 121.

70. Furman, *Wal-Mart*.

71. Amiti et al., "How Did China's WTO Entry Benefit U.S. Consumers?" 3.

72. Autor, Dorn, and Hanson, "The China Syndrome"; and Acemoglu et al., "Import Competition."

73. Feenstra and Sasahara, "The 'China Shock,' Exports and U.S. Employment."

74. Autor et al., "Importing Political Polarization?"

75. Bisbee, "What Is Out Your Back Door."

76. Cerrato, Ferrara, and Ruggieri, "Why Does Import Competition Favor Republicans?"

77. For a debunking of the notion that the pre-1913 global economy was particularly tightly integrated, see Bairoch and Kozul-Wright, "Globalization Myths."

6. THE MIRAGE OF SOVEREIGNTY

1. Parker, "Brexit 'Museum of Sovereignty' to Tell Story of Leaving the EU."

2. The website (https://www.museumofbrexit.uk/) administrators did not respond to the author's query for more details about the museum's prospective opening.

3. Anton, "The Flight 93 Election."

4. Smith, "The 'Extremists' on Both Sides of the Brexit Debate."

5. Stone, "Families Losing £150 a Month Is a Price Worth Paying for Brexit."

6. *Economist*, "Dreaming of Sovereignty."

7. *Merriam-Webster*, "sovereignty."

8. Krasner, *Sovereignty*, 3–43.

9. For an excellent exploration of this idea and its implications, see Pavel, *Divided Sovereignty*.

10. Helms, "American Sovereignty and the UN."

11. See, for example, Deyermond, "The Uses of Sovereignty in Twenty-First Century Russian Foreign Policy."

12. Cited in Schwartz, "Khrushchev/Brezhnev Doctrine at Helsinki." See also Jones, *The Soviet Concept of "Limited Sovereignty" from Lenin to Gorbachev.*

13. Charter of the United Nations.

14. See Lynch, "Woodrow Wilson and the Principle of 'National Self-Determination.'"

15. Rabkin, *Law without Nations?* 68.

16. Hulliung, "Rousseau, Voltaire and the Revenge of Pascal."

17. Slack, "The Enemies of the People."

18. Sparrow, "May Should Close Parliament If Necessary to Stop Bill Blocking No Deal Brexit, Says Rees-Mogg."

19. Donald Trump (@realDonaldTrump), Twitter, October 29, 2018, 5:03 a.m., https://twitter.com/realDonaldTrump/status/1056879122348195841.

20. BBC News, "Europe Referendum" (emphasis added).

21. Ashcroft, "How the United Kingdom Voted on Thursday . . . and Why."

22. Gaston and Hilhorst, *At Home in One's Past*, 20.

23. Pollard and Mendelsohn, "RAND Kicks Off 2016 Presidential Election Panel Survey."

24. Alloy and Abramson, "Judgments of Contingency in Depressed and Nondepressed Students." See also Moore, "What Is the Sense of Agency and Why Does It Matter?"

25. Geer, Davison, and Gatchel, "Reduction of Stress in Humans."

26. Ferguson, *An Essay on the History of Civil Society*.

27. Hayek, "The Use of Knowledge in Society."

28. See William Easterly's work for a Hayek-inspired critique of top-down development policy promoted by large donors and international organizations. Easterly, *Tyranny of Experts*.

29. See also Levy, "The Sovereign Myth."

30. Ostrom, *The Meaning of American Federalism*, 226.

31. US Constitution, Article 6.

32. Cited in Ku and Yoon, *Taming Globalization*, 92–93.

33. See Flaherty, "History Right?"

34. *Rutgers v. Waddington*.

35. Vázquez, "The Four Doctrines of Self-Executing Treaties."

36. Yoon, "Globalism and the Constitution"; Flaherty, "History Right?"; and Vázquez, "Judicial Enforcement of Treaties."

37. Ku and Yoon, *Taming Globalization*, 96–97.

38. See, for example, Connelly, Pitney Jr., and Schmitt, *Is Congress Broken?*

39. Rabkin, *Law without Nations?* 68.

40. Ku and Yoon, *Taming Globalization*, 49.

41. See, for example, *United States v. Curtiss-Wright Export Corp.*

42. Guzman and Landsidle, "The Myth of International Delegation."

43. See Weingast, "The Economic Role of Political Institutions."

44. *New York v. United States*.

45. The full quote reads: "[T]he proposed government cannot be deemed a NATIONAL one; since its jurisdiction extends to certain enumerated objects only, and leaves to the several States a residuary and inviolable sovereignty over all other objects." Madison, "The Conformity of the Plan to Republican Principles."

46. Halper, "A California-Led Alliance." Similar initiatives were seen around the time when the United States refused to ratify the Kyoto Protocol, as various US states and Canadian provinces set joint targets to reduce greenhouse emissions, which were even more ambitious than those stipulated by Kyoto. See Ku and Yoon, *Taming Globalization*, 169.

47. Ku and Yoon, *Taming Globalization*, 173.

48. For the intellectual origins of this position, see Jessup, "The Doctrine of Erie Railroad v. Tompkins."

49. For an overview of the debate and an outline of a middle position between the two extremes, see Bellia and Clark, "The Law of Nations as Constitutional Law."

50. *Roper v. Simmons*.

51. See Douglass, "British Influence on the Abolition Movement in America."

52. Scholte, "Globalization and Governance."

53. *Roper v. Simmons*.

54. *Atkins v. Virginia*.

55. *Lawrence v. Texas*. All three examples singled out by Ku and Yoon, *Taming Globalization*, 227, alongside *Graham v. Florida*, which overturned a life sentence without the possibility of parole for juvenile when he committed a nonhomicide offense.

56. Hausalter, "L'euro?"

57. European Commission, Standard Eurobarometer 89.

58. Eisenhard, "Agency Theory."

59. Pavel, *Divided Sovereignty*, 46.

60. Tallberg et al., "Explaining the Transnational Design of International Organizations."

61. Oxford Living Dictionaries, "subsidiarity."

62. See Leo XIII, "Rerum Novarum"; and Pius XI, "Quadragesimo Anno."

63. Treaty on European Union and the Treaty on the Functioning of the European Union, Article 5(3).

64. *Consolidated Version of the Treaty on European Union.*

65. *Consolidated Version of the Treaty on European Union.*

66. Alesina, Angeloni, and Schuknecht, "What Does the European Union Do?"

7. CITIZENS OF NOWHERE, UNITE!

1. Goodhart, *The Road to Somewhere.*

2. Ward, "Read Trump's Speech to the UN General Assembly."

3. May, "Full Text."

4. Scruton, *England and the Need for Nations*, 22–23.

5. Ostrom, *The Meaning of American Federalism*, 226.

6. Goodin, "What Is So Special about Our Fellow Countrymen?" 682.

7. Levy and Peart, "The Secret History of the Dismal Science."

8. Mises, *Liberalism*, 105–06.

9. Bateman, "Patriotism Needn't Be a Dirty Word."

10. Hazony, *The Virtue of Nationalism*, 68.

11. Cole, "France."

12. In fact, the original quote was: "We have made Italy but unfortunately we haven't made Italians." The quote attributed to d'Azeglio was made in 1896 by Ferdinando Martini, after Italy's defeat at Adua. See Confino, "Review of *Making Italians*," 194.

13. Hajnal, "European Marriage Pattern in Historical Perspective."

14. Koyama, "A Nationalism Untethered to History."

15. A term coined in Anderson, *Imagined Communities.*

16. Tallberg and Uhlin, "Civil Society and Global Democracy."

17. Scherrer and Isaksson, *The Return of Foreign Fighters to EU Soil.*

18. Coalson, "Putin Pledges to Protect All Ethnic Russians Anywhere." For specifics of the Kremlin's use of the Russian diaspora, see Suslov, "'Russian World.'"

19. Brady, "Magic Weapons."

20. Freedom House, "New Report Shows Growing International Reach of Chinese Media Censorship."

21. Larin and Engl, "Granting Austrian Citizenship to German-Speaking Italians."

22. Sobják, "The Implications of Hungary's National Policy for Relations with Neighbouring States."

23. Murray, *Coming Apart.*

24. See Berman, "Why Identity Politics Benefits the Right More Than the Left."

25. Hayek, *Law, Legislation, and Liberty.*

26. Goldberg, *Suicide of the West.*

27. Rafferty, "Rep. Steve King Defends 'Somebody Else's Babies' Remarks."

28. Scruton, *England and the Need for Nations*, 3.

29. Shipman, "All Out War."

30. Hannan, "What Brexit Would Look Like for Britain."

31. Rohac, "Jeremy Corbyn and His Sinister Friends."

32. Dysch, "Labour Support Just 13 per Cent Among UK Jews."

33. Berman, "Why Identity Politics Benefits the Right More Than the Left."

34. Kirchick, "On Linda Sarsour's Politics of Hate."

35. Rashida Tlaib (@RashidaTlaib), Twitter, January 6, 2019, 9:03 p.m., https://twitter.com/RashidaTlaib/status/1082095303325609984.

36. Scholte, "Civil Society and Democracy in Global Governance."

37. See, for example, Koenig-Archibugi, "Is Global Democracy Possible?"; and List and Koenig-Archibugi, "Can There Be a Global Demos?"

38. Ostrom, *The Meaning of American Federalism*, 257.

39. Macdonald, *Global Stakeholder Democracy*; and Bäckstrand, "Democratising Global Environmental Governance."

8. A GLOBALISM FOR THE PEOPLE

1. Haug and Berkhout, "Learning the Hard Way?"
2. Victor, "Why Paris Worked."
3. International Renewable Energy Agency, *Renewable Power Generation Costs in 2017*.
4. Roberts, "California Gov. Jerry Brown Casually Unveils History's Most Ambitious Climate Target."
5. See Turnheim, Kivimaa, and Berkhout, *Innovating Climate Governance*.
6. See Featherston, "Jean Monnet and the 'Democratic Deficit' in the European Union."
7. Niskanen, "Bureaucrats and Politicians."
8. For a powerful argument in favor of *jus cogens*, see Pavel, *Divided Sovereignty*.
9. International Covenant on Economic, Social and Cultural Rights, Article 7(d).
10. UN Human Rights Council, "Discriminatory Laws and Practices and Acts of Violence," 19.
11. For a discussion of the UNICEF-support UPSHIFT program, aimed at expanding opportunities to young Sudanese, typically ages fourteen to twenty-four years, see Fricker and Zahir, "Youth Spark Innovation in Sudan."
12. International Monetary Fund, "Pursuing Women's Economic Empowerment."
13. Clemens and Kremer, "The New Role for the World Bank."
14. Quadratic voting also involves foregoing the square of the number of votes cast because of the quadratic nature of external effects involved in collective decision-making. For details, see Posner and Weyl, *Radical Markets*, 80–126.
15. Kuyper, "Designing Institutions for Global Democracy," 200.
16. US Constitution, Article 4, § 1.
17. Hadfield, *Rules for a Flat World*, 250.
18. Hadfield, *Rules for a Flat World*, 264ff.
19. Clougherty and Grajek, "The Impact of ISO 9000 Diffusion on Trade and FDI."
20. Prasso, "China's Digital Silk Road Is Looking More like an Iron Curtain."
21. Blumenthal and Scissors, "China Is a Dangerous Rival."
22. Kaplan, Spenkuch, and Sullivan, "Measuring Geographic Polarization."
23. Murray, *Coming Apart*.
24. Lindsey and Teles, *The Captured Economy*.
25. See Hammond, "The Pro-Work Case for Universal Basic Income."
26. See Posner and Weyl, *Radical Markets*.
27. Ostrom, *The Meaning of American Federalism*, 242.

Bibliography

Acemoglu, Daron, and James Robinson. *Why Nations Fail*. New York: Crown Publishing, 2012.

Acemoglu, Daron, David H. Autor, David Dorn, Gordon H. Hanson, and Brendan Price. "Import Competition and the Great US Employment Sag of the 2000s." *Journal of Labor Economics* 34, no. S1 (2016): 141–98.

Agreement on the Application of Sanitary and Phytosanitary Measures. https://www.wto.org/english/tratop_e/sps_e/spsagr_e.htm.

Agreement on Technical Barriers to Trade. https://www.wto.org/english/docs_e/legal_e/17-tbt_e.htm.

Akhtar, Shayerah Ilias, and Vivian C. Jones. "Proposed Transatlantic Trade and Investment Partnership (T-TIP): In Brief." Congressional Research Service, June 11, 2014. https://fas.org/sgp/crs/row/R43158.pdf.

Alchian, Armen A. "Uncertainty, Evolution, and Economic Theory." *Journal of Political Economy* 58, no. 3 (1950): 211–21.

Alesina, Alberto, Ignazio Angeloni, and Ludger Schuknecht. "What Does the European Union Do?" National Bureau of Economic Research, December 2001. http://www.nber.org/papers/w8647.

Aligica, Paul Dragos, and Peter J. Boettke. *Challenging Institutional Analysis and Development: The Bloomington School*. Abingdon, UK: Routledge, 2009.

Alloy, Lauren B., and Lyn Y. Abramson. "Judgments of Contingency in Depressed and Nondepressed Students: Sadder but Wiser?" *Journal of Experimental Psychology: General* 108, no. 4 (1979): 441–85.

Amiti, Mary, Mi Dai, Robert C. Feenstra, and John Romalis. "How Did China's WTO Entry Benefit U.S. Consumers?" National Bureau of Economic Research, December 2018. http://www.nber.org/papers/w23487.

Anderson, Benedict. *Imagined Communities: Reflections on the Origin and Spread of Nationalism*. London: Verso, 2016.

Anderson, James E., and Eric van Wincoop. "Trade Costs." *Journal of Economic Literature* 42, no. 3 (2004): 691–751.

Anton, Michael [Publius Decius Mus, pseud.]. "The Flight 93 Election." *Claremont Review of Books*, September 5, 2016. https://www.claremont.org/crb/basicpage/the-flight-93-election/.

Arrow, Kenneth J. *Social Choice and Individual Values*. Yale University Press, 1951.

Ashcroft, Michael. "How the United Kingdom Voted on Thursday . . . and Why." Lord Ashcroft Polls, June 24, 2016. http://lordashcroftpolls.com/2016/06/how-the-united-kingdom-voted-and-why/.

Associated Press. "Trump Says Other Countries 'Taking Advantage' of US—Video." *Guardian*, July 20, 2018. https://www.theguardian.com/us-news/video/2018/jul/20/trump-says-other-countries-advantage-of-us-china-surplus-video.

Atkins v. Virginia, 536 U.S. 304 (2002). https://www.law.cornell.edu/supremecourt/text/536/304.

Ausubel, Jesse. *Nature Rebounds*. New York: Rockefeller University, 2015. https://phe.rockefeller.edu/docs/Nature_Rebounds.pdf.

Autor, David H., David Dorn, and Gordon H. Hanson. "The China Syndrome: Local Labor Market Effects of Import Competition in the United States." *American Economic Review* 103, no. 6 (2013): 2121–68.

———, and Kaveh Majlesi. "Importing Political Polarization? The Electoral Consequences of Rising Trade Exposure." National Bureau of Economic Research, December 2017. http://www.nber.org/papers/w22637.

Avalon Project. "The Golden Bull of the Emperor Charles IV 1356 A.D." Yale Law School, Lillian Goldman Law Library. http://avalon.law.yale.edu/medieval/golden.asp.

Bacchus, James. "Was Buenos Aires the Beginning of the End or the End of the Beginning? The Future of the World Trade Organization." Cato Institute, May 8, 2018. https://www.cato.org/publications/policy-analysis/was-buenos-aires-beginning-end-or-end-beginning-future-world-trade.

Backer, Larry C. "Private Actors and Public Governance beyond the State: The Multinational Corporation, the Financial Stability Board, and the Global Governance Order." *Indiana Journal of Global Legal Studies* 18, no. 2 (2011): 751–802.

Bäckstrand, Karin. "Democratising Global Environmental Governance: Stakeholder Democracy after the World Summit on Sustainable Development." *European Journal of International Relations* 12, no. 3 (2006): 467–98.

Bairoch, Paul. "European Trade Policy, 1815–1914." In *The Cambridge Economic History of Europe VIII, The Industrial Economies: The Development of Economic and Social Policies*, edited by Peter Mathias and Sidney Pollard, 1–160. Cambridge, UK: Cambridge University Press, 1989.

———, and Richard Kozul-Wright. "Globalization Myths: Some Historical Reflections on Integration, Industrialization and Growth in the World Economy." UN Conference on Trade and Development, March 1996. https://unctad.org/en/docs/dp_113.en.pdf.

Baldwin, Richard. *The Great Convergence: Information Technology and the New Globalization*. Cambridge, MA: Harvard University Press, 2016.

Bandow, Doug. "How Many Enemies Does America Want? Congress Sacrifices U.S. Security with New Sanctions Against Russia." *Forbes*, December 15, 2014. https://www.forbes.com/sites/dougbandow/2014/12/15/how-many-enemies-does-america-want-congress-sacrifices-u-s-security-with-new-sanctions-against-russia/.

Barrett, Scott. "Self-Enforcing International Environmental Agreements." *Oxford Economic Papers* 46 (1994): 878–94.

Barry, Norman. "The Tradition of Spontaneous Order." *Literature of Liberty: A Review of Contemporary Liberal Thought* 5, no. 2 (1982): 7–58.

Bartsch, Sonja. "The Global Fund to Fight AIDS, Tuberculosis and Malaria." In *Global Health Governance and the Fight Against HIV/AIDS*, edited by Wolfgang Hein, Sonja Bartsch, and Lars Kohlmorgen, 146–71. London: Palgrave Macmillan, 2007.

Basedow, Robert, and Céline Kauffmann. "International Trade and Good Regulatory Practices: Assessing the Trade Impacts of Regulation." Organisation for Economic Cooperation and Development, July 20, 2016. http://dx.doi.org/10.1787/5jlv59hdgtf5-en.

Bastiat, Frédéric. *What Is Seen and What Is Not Seen, or Political Economy in One Lesson*. 1850; Online Library of Liberty, 2015. https://oll.libertyfund.org/pages/wswns.

Bateman, Victoria. "Patriotism Needn't Be a Dirty Word." CapX, December 29, 2016,https://capx.co/patriotism-neednt-be-a-dirty-word-2016/.

BBC News. "EU Agrees to Reform Services Plan." *BBC News*, March 23, 2005. http://news.bbc.co.uk/2/hi/europe/4374007.stm.

———. "Europe Referendum: Brexit 'Means More Money for Services.'" *BBC News*, April 16, 2016. https://www.bbc.com/news/uk-wales-politics-36057331.

Bellia, Anthony J., and Bradford R. Clark. "The Law of Nations as Constitutional Law." *Virginia Law Review* 98, no. 4 (2012): 729–838.

Benoist, Alain de. "The First Federalist: Johannes Althusius." *Telos* 118 (2000): 25–58.

Berg, Julie, Sophie Nakueira, and Clifford Shearing. "Global Non-State Auspices of Security Governance." In *The Routledge Handbook of International Crime and Justice Studies*, edited by Bruce A. Arrigo and Heather Y. Bersot, 77–97. New York: Routledge, 2013.

Berger, Rick. "Why Withdrawing from Syria and Afghanistan Won't Save Much Money." Defense One, February 26, 2019. https://www.defenseone.com/ideas/2019/02/why-withdrawing-syria-and-afghanistan-wont-save-much-money/155134/.

Berman, Sheri. "Why Identity Politics Benefits the Right More Than the Left." *Guardian*, July 14, 2018. https://www.theguardian.com/commentisfree/2018/jul/14/identity-politics-right-left-trump-racism.

Besedeš, Tibor, Erik P. Johnson, and Xinping Tian. "Economic Determinants of Multilateral Environmental Agreements." Working paper, Georgia Institute of Technology, School of Economics, January 2016. https://econ.gatech.edu/sites/default/files/attachments/Tian%20-%20JM%20Paper.pdf.

Besley, Tim, and Torsten Persson. *Pillars of Prosperity: The Political Economics of Development Clusters*. Princeton: Princeton University Press, 2013.

Bhagwati, Jagdish, and T. N. Srinivasan. "Trade and Poverty in the Poor Countries." *American Economic Review* 92, no. 2 (2002): 180–83.

Biermann, Frank, Philipp Pattberg, and Harro van Asselt. "The Fragmentation of Global Governance Architectures: A Framework for Analysis." *Global Environmental Politics* 9, no. 4 (2009): 14–40.

Birnbaum, Michael. "European Leaders Shocked as Trump Slams NATO and E.U., Raising Fears of Transatlantic Split." *Washington Post*, January 16, 2017. https://www.washingtonpost.com/world/europe-leaders-shocked-s-trump-slams-nato-eu-raising-fears-of-transatlantic-split/2017/01/16/82047072-dbe6-11e6-b2cf-b67fe3285cbc_story.html.

Bisbee, James. "What Is Out Your Back Door: How Policy Preferences Respond to Local Trade Shocks." 2018. https://www.dropbox.com/s/vacprfieznxzc9b/bisbee_jmp.pdf?dl=0.

Black, Duncan. "On the Rationale of Group Decision-Making." *Journal of Political Economy* 56 (1948): 23–34.

Black, Julia. "Constructing and Contesting Legitimacy and Accountability in Polycentric Regulatory Regimes." *Regulation and Governance* 2 (2009): 137–64.

Blumenthal, Dan, and Derek Scissors. "China Is a Dangerous Rival, and America Should Treat It Like One." *New York Times*, January 15, 2019. https://www.nytimes.com/2019/01/14/opinion/us-china-trade.html.

Boettke, Peter J., Liya Palagashvili, and Jayme Lemke. "Riding in Cars with Boys: Elinor Ostrom's Adventure with the Police." *Journal of Institutional Economics* 9, no. 1 (2013): 407–25.

Bolsinger, Eckard. "The Foundation of Mercantile Realism: Friedrich List and International Political Economy," 2004. https://web.archive.org/web/20080626025135/http://www.psa.ac.uk/journals/pdf/5/2004/Bolsinger.pdf.

Bolton, John R. "Should We Take Global Governance Seriously?" *Chicago Journal of International Law* 1, no. 2 (2000): 205–21.

Bostrom, Nick. "The Vulnerable World Hypothesis." University of Oxford, Future of Humanity Institute, 2018. https://nickbostrom.com/papers/vulnerable.pdf.

Bown, Chad P., and Douglas A. Irwin. "The GATT's Starting Point: Tariff Levels Circa 1947." Working paper, National Bureau of Economic Research, December 2015. http://www.nber.org/papers/w21782.

Bown, Chad P., Euijin Jung, and Eva (Yiwen) Zhang. "Trump's Steel Tariffs Have Hit Smaller and Poorer Countries the Hardest." Peterson Institute for International Economics, November 15, 2018. https://piie.com/blogs/trade-investment-policy-watch/trumps-steel-tariffs-have-hit-smaller-and-poorer-countries.

Brady, Marie-Anne. "Magic Weapons: China's Political Influence Activities Under Xi Jinping." Paper presented at the conference on "The Corrosion of Democracy Under China's

Global Influence," Arlington, VA, September 16–17, 2017. https://www.wilsoncenter.org/sites/default/files/magicweaponsanne-mariebradyseptember162017.pdf.

Bronk, Richard, and Wade Jacoby. "Uncertainty and the Dangers of Monocultures in Regulation, Analysis, and Practice." Max-Planck-Institut für Gesellschaftsforschung, 2016. http://pubman.mpdl.mpg.de/pubman/item/escidoc:2287051/component/escidoc:2287049/mpifg_dp16_6.pdf.

Buchanan, James M., and Gordon Tullock. *The Calculus of Consent: Logical Foundations of Constitutional Democracy*. Ann Arbor: University of Michigan Press, 1962.

Buchanan, Pat. "Is the West Disintegrating?" *UNZ Review*, December 29, 2015. https://www.unz.com/pbuchanan/topic/immigration/2015/12/.

———. "Will America Follow Europe into Dissolution?" *American Conservative*, December 29, 2015. http://www.theamericanconservative.com/buchanan/will-america-follow-europe-into-dissolution/.

Burgess, Michael. *Federalism and European Union: The Building of Europe, 1950–2000*. London: Routledge, 2000.

Busch, Marc L. "Overlapping Institutions, Forum Shopping, and Dispute Settlement in International Trade." *International Organization* 61, no. 4 (2007): 735–61.

Campbell, F. Gregory. "The Struggle for Upper Silesia, 1919–1922." *Journal of Modern History* 42, no. 3 (September 1970): 361–85.

Center for Systemic Peace. Polity IV Database. http://systemicpeace.org/inscrdata.html.

Cerrato, Andrea, Federico Maria Ferrara, and Francesco Ruggieri. "Why Does Import Competition Favor Republicans?" SSRN, September 30, 2018. https://ssrn.com/abstract=3147169.

Chang, Ha-Joon. *Bad Samaritans: The Myth of Free Trade and the Secret History of Capitalism*. London: Bloomsbury Press, 2008.

Charter of the United Nations. http://www.un.org/en/charter-united-nations/index.html.

Chicago Booth Initiative on Global Markets. Free Trade Survey, 2012. http://www.igmchicago.org/surveys/free-trade.

Cipolla, Carlo M. "Currency Depreciation in Medieval Europe." *Economic History Review* 15, no. 3 (1963): 413–22.

Clemens, Michael A. "Economics and Emigration: Trillion-Dollar Bills on the Sidewalk?" *Journal of Economic Perspectives* 25, no. 3 (2011): 83–106.

———, and Michael Kremer. "The New Role for the World Bank." *Journal of Economic Perspectives* 30, no. 1 (2016): 53–76.

Clougherty, Joseph A., and Michał Grajek. "The Impact of ISO 9000 Diffusion on Trade and FDI: A New Institutional Analysis." *Journal of International Business Studies* 39, no. 4 (2008): 613–33.

Coalson, Robert. "Putin Pledges to Protect All Ethnic Russians Anywhere. So, Where Are They?" Radio Free Europe/Radio Liberty, April 10, 2014. https://www.rferl.org/a/russia-ethnic-russification-baltics-kazakhstan-soviet/25328281.html.

Coase, Ronald. "The Problem of Social Cost," *Journal of Law and Economics* 3, no. 1 (1960): 1–44.

Cole, Alistair. "France: Between Centralization and Fragmentation." In *The Oxford Handbook of Local and Regional Democracy in Europe*, edited by Frank Hendriks, Anders Lidström, and John Loughlin, 307–30. Oxford, UK: Oxford University Press, 2010.

Confino, Alon. Review of *Making Italians: School and Culture in Modern Italy*, edited by Simonetta Soldani and Gabriele Turi. *Social History* 22, no. 2 (1997): 194–201.

Connelly, William F. Jr, John J. Pitney Jr., and Gary J. Schmitt, eds. *Is Congress Broken? The Virtues and Defects of Partisanship and Gridlock*. Washington, DC: Brookings Institution Press, 2018.

Consolidated Version of the Treaty on European Union, OJ C 326, 26.10.2012. https://eur-lex.europa.eu/legal-content/EN/TXT/?uri=celex%3A12012M%2FTXT.

Convention on the Prevention and Punishment of the Crime of Genocide. December 9, 1948. https://treaties.un.org/doc/publication/unts/volume%2078/volume-78-i-1021-english.pdf.

Corporate Europe Observatory. "Public Services Under Attack through TTIP and CETA." Corporate Europe Observatory, October 12, 2015. https://corporateeurope.org/international-trade/2015/10/public-services-under-attack-through-ttip-and-ceta.

Correia de Brito, Anabela, Céline Kauffmann, and Jacques Pelkmans. "The Contribution of Mutual Recognition to International Regulatory Co-operation." Working paper, Organisation for Economic Cooperation and Development, January 26, 2016. http://dx.doi.org/10.1787/5jm56fqsfxmx-en.

Covenant of the League of Nations. http://avalon.law.yale.edu/20th_century/leagcov.asp.

David, Christina L. "Overlapping Institutions in Trade Policy." *Perspectives on Politics* 7, no. 1 (2009): 25.

Davies, Gareth. "Is Mutual Recognition an Alternative to Harmonization? Lessons on Trade and Tolerance of Diversity from the EU." In *Regional Trade Agreements and the WTO Legal System*, edited by Lorand Bartels and Federico Ortino, 265–80. Oxford, UK: Oxford University Press, 2006.

De Long, J. Bradford, and Barry Eichengreen. "The Marshall Plan: History's Most Successful Structural Adjustment Program." Working paper, National Bureau of Economic Research, November 1991. http://www.nber.org/papers/w3899.

Deardorff, Alan V. "Testing Trade Theories and Predicting Trade Flows." In *International Trade*. Volume 1 of *Handbook of International Economics*, edited by Ronald Jones and Peter Kenen, 467–517. Amsterdam: North-Holland, 1984.

DeSombre, Elizabeth R. "The Experience of the Montreal Protocol: Particularly Remarkable, and Remarkably Particular." *UCLA Journal of Environmental Law and Policy* 19, no. 1 (2000): 49–81.

Deutsche Welle. "US and South Korea to Scrap Major Military Exercises in Spring." March 3, 2019. https://www.dw.com/en/us-and-south-korea-to-scrap-major-military-exercises-in-spring/a-47748887.

Deyermond, Ruth. "The Uses of Sovereignty in Twenty-first Century Russian Foreign Policy." *Europe-Asia Studies* 68, no. 6, 957–84.

Douglass, Frederick. "British Influence on the Abolition Movement in America: An Address Delivered in Paisley, Scotland, on April 17, 1846." In *The Frederick Douglass Papers: Series One—Speeches, Debates, and Interviews*, edited by John Blassingame et al. 1846; New Haven: Yale University Press, 1979. https://glc.yale.edu/british-influence-abolition-movement-america.

Dreher, Rod. "Dying for Montenegro." *The American Conservative*, July 17, 2018,https://www.theamericanconservative.com/dreher/trump-dying-for-montenegro/.

Dysch, Marcus. "Labour Support Just 13 per Cent Among UK Jews." *Jewish Chronicle*, May 30, 2017. https://www.thejc.com/news/uk-news/labour-support-just-13-per-cent-among-uk-jews-1.439325.

Easterly, William. *Tyranny of Experts: Economists, Dictators, and the Forgotten Rights of the Poor*. New York: Basic Books, 2014.

Eaton, Jonathan, and Samuel Kortum. "Technology, Geography, and Trade." *Econometrica* 70, no. 5 (2002): 1741–79.

Economist. "Dreaming of Sovereignty." March 19, 2016. https://www.economist.com/britain/2016/03/19/dreaming-of-sovereignty.

Eichengreen, Barry. *Golden Fetters: The Gold Standard and the Great Depression, 1919–1939*. Oxford, UK: Oxford University Press, 1992.

———, and Douglas A. Irwin. "The Slide to Protectionism in the Great Depression: Who Succumbed and Why?" National Bureau of Economic Research, July 2009. http://www.nber.org/papers/w15142.

Einstein, Albert. "Towards a World Government." In *Out of My Later Years: The Scientist, Philosopher and Man Portrayed through His Own Words*, A. Einstein, 146–48. New York: Wings Books, 1956.

Eisenhardt, Kathleen M. "Agency Theory: An Assessment and Review." *Academy of Management Review*, 14, no. (1989): 57–74.

Eisner, Manuel. "Long-Term Historical Trends in Violent Crime." *Crime and Justice* 30 (2003): 83–142. See also Our World in Data: https://ourworldindata.org/slides/war-and-violence/#/3.

Elliott, Douglas J., and Robert E. Litan. "Identifying and Regulating Systemically Important Financial Institutions: The Risks of Under and Over Identification and Regulation." Brookings Institution, January 16, 2011, https://www.brookings.edu/research/identifying-and-regulating-systemically-important-financial-institutions-the-risks-of-under-and-over-identification-and-regulation/.

Epstein, Stephan R. "The Rise and Decline of Italian City States." Working paper, London School of Economics, Department of Economic History, July 1999. http://eprints.lse.ac.uk/22389/.

Estrin, Saul, Delia Baghdasaryan, and Klaus E. Meyer. "The Impact of Institutional and Human Resource Distance on International Entry Strategies." *Journal of Management Studies* 46, no. 7 (2009): 1172–96.

Eulau, Heinz H. F. "Federalism under the Holy Roman Empire." *American Political Science Review* 35, no. 4 (1941): 643–64.

European Commission. "Report of the 15th Round of Negotiations for the Transatlantic Trade and Investment Partnership." October 2016. http://trade.ec.europa.eu/doclib/docs/2016/october/tradoc_155027.pdf.

———. Special Eurobarometer 461: Designing Europe's Future. April 2017. http://ec.europa.eu/commfrontoffice/publicopinion/index.cfm/Survey/getSurveyDetail/instruments/SPECIAL/surveyKy/2173.

———. Standard Eurobarometer 89. 2018. http://ec.europa.eu/commfrontoffice/publicopinion/index.cfm/Survey/getSurveyDetail/instruments/STANDARD/surveyKy/2180.

Ewert, Ulf Christian, and Marco Sunder. "Trading Networks, Monopoly and Economic Development in Medieval Northern Europe: An Agent-Based Simulation of Early Hanseatic Trade." Paper prepared for the 9th European Historical Economics Society Conference, Dublin, Ireland, September 2–3, 2011.

Ewert, Ulf Christian, and Stephan Selzer. "Commercial Super Trust or Virtual Organisation? An Institutional Economics Interpretation of the Late Medieval Hanse." Working paper prepared for the Eighth European Historical Economics Society Conference, Graduate Institute Geneva, September 4–5, 2009.

Fearon, James D. "Domestic Politics, Foreign Policy, and Theories of International Relations." *Annual Review of Political Science* 1 (1998): 289–313.

Featherstone, Kevin. "Jean Monnet and the 'Democratic Deficit' in the European Union." *Journal of Common Market Studies* 32, no. 2 (1994): 149–70.

Feenstra, Robert C., and Akira Sasahara. "The 'China Shock,' Exports and U.S. Employment: A Global Input-Output Analysis." National Bureau of Economic Research, November 2017. https://www.nber.org/papers/w24022.

Fennell, Lee Anne. "Ostrom's Law: Property Rights in the Commons." *International Journal of the Commons* 5, no. 1 (2011): 9–27.

Ferguson, Adam. *An Essay on the History of Civil Society.* London: T. Cadell, 1782. http://oll.libertyfund.org/titles/ferguson-an-essay-on-the-history-of-civil-society.

Fernández-Huertas Moraga, Jesús, and Hillel Rapoport. "Tradable Refugee-Admission Quotas and EU Asylum Policy." Discussion paper, Institute for the Study of Labor (Bonn): November 2014. http://ftp.iza.org/dp8683.pdf.

Fink, Alexander. "The Hanseatic League and the Concept of Functional Overlapping Competing Jurisdictions." *Kyklos* 65, no. 2 (2012): 194–217.

———. "Under What Conditions May Social Contracts Arise? Evidence from the Hanseatic League." *Constitutional Political Economy* 22 (2011): 173–90.

Fischer-Lescano, Andreas, and Gunther Teubner. "Regime-Collisions: The Vain Search for Legal Unity in the Fragmentation of Global Law." *Michigan Journal of International Law* 25, no. 4 (2004): 999–1046.

Flaherty, Martin. "History Right? Historical Scholarship, Original Understanding and Treaties as 'Supreme Law of the Land.'" *Columbia Law Review* 99, no. 8 (1999): 2095–153.

Fliess, Barbara, Frederic Gonzales, Jeonghoi Kim, and Raymond Schonfeld. "The Use of International Standards in Technical Regulation." Organisation for Economic Co-operation and Development, 2010. http://dx.doi.org/10.1787/5kmbjgkz1tzp-en.

Follett, Chelsea. "Seven Ways in Which Human Ingenuity Helps the Planet." *Human Progress*, September 14, 2016. https://humanprogress.org/article.php?p=420.

Fonte, John. *Sovereignty or Submission: Will Americans Rule Themselves or Be Ruled by Others?* New York: Encounter Books, 2011.

Franck, Susan D. "Empirically Evaluating Claims about Investment Treaty Arbitration." *North Carolina Law Review* 86 (2007): 1–88.

Franck, Thomas. "Trump Doubles Down: 'Trade Wars Are Good, and Easy to Win.'" CNBC, March 2, 2018. https://www.cnbc.com/2018/03/02/trump-trade-wars-are-good-and-easy-to-win.html.

Freedom House. "Freedom in the World 2018: Democracy in Crisis, 2018." https://freedomhouse.org/report/freedom-world/freedom-world-2018.

———. "New Report Shows Growing International Reach of Chinese Media Censorship." October 22, 2013, https://freedomhouse.org/article/new-report-shows-growing-international-reach-chinese-media-censorship.

Freund, Caroline L., and Emanuel Ornelas. "Regional Trade Agreements." *Annual Review of Economics* 2 (2010): 139–66.

Fricker, Toby, and Hadeel Zahir. "Youth Spark Innovation in Sudan." UNICEF, September 28, 2018. https://www.unicef.org/stories/youth-spark-innovation-sudan.

Friedman, Thomas L. *The World Is Flat: A Brief History of the Twenty-First Century.* New York: Farrar, Strauss and Giroux, 2005.

Friedrichs, Jörg. "The Meaning of New Medievalism." *European Journal of International Relations* 7, no. 4 (2001): 475–502.

Furceri, Davide, Swarnali A. Hannan, Jonathan D. Ostry, and Andrew K. Rose. "Macroeconomic Consequences of Tariffs." National Bureau of Economic Research, December 2018. https://www.nber.org/papers/w25402.

Furman, Jason. *Wal-Mart: A Progressive Success Story.* Mimeo, 2005, https://www.mackinac.org/archives/2006/walmart.pdf.

Galindo, Gabriela. "Trump: EU Was 'Set Up to Take Advantage' of US." *Politico*, June 28, 2018. https://www.politico.eu/article/donald-trump-eu-was-set-up-to-take-advantage-of-us-trade-tariffs-protectionism/.

Gallup. "Confidence in Institutions." 2018. https://news.gallup.com/poll/1597/confidence-institutions.aspx.

Gaston, Sophie, and Sacha Hilhorst. *At Home in One's Past: Nostalgia as a Cultural and Political Force in Britain, France and Germany.* London: Demos, 2018, 20. https://www.demos.co.uk/wp-content/uploads/2018/05/At-Home-in-Ones-Past-Report.pdf.

Geer, James H., Gerald C. Davison, and Robert I. Gatchel. "Reduction of Stress in Humans Through Nonveridical Perceived Control of Aversive Stimulation." *Journal of Personality and Social Psychology* 16, no. 4 (1970): 731–38.

General Agreement on Tariffs and Trade. 1986. https://www.wto.org/english/docs_e/legal_e/gatt47.pdf.

Goldberg, Jeffrey. "When Beheading Won't Do the Job, the Saudis Resort to Crucifixion." *Atlantic*, September 24, 2015. https://www.theatlantic.com/international/archive/2015/09/saudi-arabia-beheading-crucifixion-nimr/407221/.

Goldberg, Jonah. *Suicide of the West: How the Rebirth of Tribalism, Populism, Nationalism, and Identity Politics Is Destroying American Democracy.* New York: Crown Forum, 2018.

Goldstein, Judith L., Douglas Rivers, and Michael Tomz. "Institutions in International Relations: Understanding the Effects of the GATT and the WTO on World Trade." *International Organization* 61, no. 1 (2007): 37–67.

Goodhart, David. *The Road to Somewhere: The Populist Revolt and the Future of Politics.* London: Hurst, 2017.

Goodin, Robert E. "What Is So Special about Our Fellow Countrymen?" *Ethics* 98, no. 4 (1988): 663–86.

Graham v. Florida. 560 U.S. 48 (2010). https://www.law.cornell.edu/supct/html/08-7412.ZS.html.

Greif, Avner. "Contract Enforceability and Economic Institutions in Early Trade: The Maghribi Traders' Coalition." *American Economic Review* 83, no. 3 (1993): 525–48.

Grice-Hutchison, Marjorie. *The School of Salamanca.* Auburn, AL: Ludwig von Mises Institute, 2009.

Guzman, Andrew T, and Jennifer Landsidle. "The Myth of International Delegation." *California Law Review* 96, no. 6 (2008): 1692–723.

Hadfield, Gillian K. *Rules for a Flat World: Why Humans Invented Law and How to Reinvent It for a Complex Global Economy.* New York: Oxford University Press, 2017.

Hajnal, John. "European Marriage Pattern in Historical Perspective." In *Population in History*, edited by D. V. Glass and D. E. C. Eversley, 101–43. London: Arnold.

Halper, Evan. "A California-Led Alliance of Cities and States Vows to Keep the Paris Climate Accord Intact." *Los Angeles Times*, June 2, 2017. http://www.latimes.com/politics/la-na-pol-paris-states-20170602-story.html.

Hammond, Samuel. "The Future of Capital Mobility." *Plain Text*, March 30, 2016. https://readplaintext.com/the-future-of-capital-mobility-5c4675d987ac.

———. "The Pro-Work Case for Universal Basic Income." Niskanen Center, January 4, 2017. https://niskanencenter.org/blog/ubi-pro-work/.

Hannan, Daniel. "What Brexit Would Look Like for Britain." *Spectator*, January 23, 2016. https://www.spectator.co.uk/2016/01/what-brexit-would-look-like-for-britain/.

Harford, Tim. "The Simple Steel Box That Transformed Global Trade." BBC News, January 9, 2017. https://www.bbc.com/news/business-38305512.

Hartwell, Ronald M. *A History of the Mont Pelerin Society.* Indianapolis IN: Liberty Fund, 1995.

Hartwich, Oliver Marc. "Neoliberalism: The Genesis of a Political Swearword," *CIS Occasional Paper* 114. https://www.cis.org.au/app/uploads/2015/07/op114.pdf.

Haug, Constanze, and Frans Berkhout. "Learning the Hard Way? European Climate Policy After Copenhagen." *Environment: Science and Policy for Sustainable Development* 52, no. 3 (2010): 20–27.

Hausalter, Louis. "L'euro? Marine Le Pen ne veut plus en entendre parler (pour l'instant)." *Marianne*, May 22, 2017. https://www.marianne.net/politique/l-euro-marine-le-pen-ne-veut-plus-en-entendre-parler-pour-l-instant.

Hayek, Friedrich A. von. *Individualism and Economic Order.* Chicago: University of Chicago Press, 1948.

———. *Law, Legislation, and Liberty*, volumes 1–3. Chicago: University of Chicago Press, 1973.

———. "The Use of Knowledge in Society." *American Economic Review* 35, no. 4 (1945): 519–30.

Hazony, Yoram, *The Virtue of Nationalism.* New York: Basic Books, 2018.

Helms, Jesse. "American Sovereignty and the UN." *National Interest*, December 1, 2000. https://nationalinterest.org/article/american-sovereignty-and-the-un-283.

———. Letter to US Trade Representative Mickey Cantor. June 17, 1993. https://jessehelmscenter.org/new-page-2/.

Helpman, Elhanan. "The Structure of Foreign Trade." *Journal of Economic Perspectives* 13, no. 2 (1999): 121–44.

Hewes, James E. "Henry Cabot Lodge and the League of Nations." *Proceedings of the American Philosophical Society* 114, no. 4 (1970): 245–55.

Hills, Roderick M., Jr. "Federalism as Westphalian Liberalism." *Fordham Law Review* 75, no. 2 (2006): 769–98.

Howard-Jones, Norman. "The Scientific Background of the International Sanitary Conferences, 1851–1938." *WHO Chronicle* 28 (1974): 159–71.

Hufbauer, Gary Clyde, and Sean Lowry. "US Tire Tariffs: Saving Few Jobs at High Cost." Peterson Institute for International Economics, April 2012. https://piie.com/publications/pb/pb12-9.pdf.

Huffman, Joseph P. "Urban Diplomacy, Cologne, the Rhenish League (1254–1257) and the Rhenish Urban League (1381–1389)." *Anales de la Universidad de Alicante. Historia Medieval* 19 (2015): 193–219.

Hulliung, Mark. "Rousseau, Voltaire and the Revenge of Pascal." In *Cambridge Companion to Rousseau*, edited by Patrick Riley. Cambridge, UK: Cambridge University Press, 2000, 57–77.

Human Progress. "Battle-Related Deaths, High Estimate." https://humanprogress.org/dwworld?p=75&yf=1989&yl=2015.

Hynes, William, David S. Jacks, Kevin H. O'Rourke. "Commodity Market Disintegration in the Interwar Period." National Bureau of Economic Research, March 2009. http://www.nber.org/papers/w14767.

International Covenant on Economic, Social and Cultural Rights, 1966. https://www.ohchr.org/en/professionalinterest/pages/cescr.aspx.

International Monetary Fund. "Pursuing Women's Economic Empowerment." May 30, 2018. https://www.imf.org/en/Publications/Policy-Papers/Issues/2018/05/31/pp053118pursuing-womens-economic-empowerment.

International Renewable Energy Agency. *Renewable Power Generation Costs in 2017.* International Renewable Energy Agency, 2018. https://www.irena.org/-/media/Files/IRENA/Agency/Publication/2018/Jan/IRENA_2017_Power_Costs_2018.pdf.

Irwin, Doug A. "Multilateral and Bilateral Trade Policies in the World Trading System: An Historical Perspective." In *New Dimensions in Regional Integration*, by Jaime De Melo and Arvind Panagariya, 90–119. Cambridge, UK: Cambridge University Press, 1993.

———. "Tariffs and Growth in Late Nineteenth Century America." *The World Economy* 24, no. 1 (2001): 15–30.

Jessup, Philip C. "The Doctrine of Erie Railroad v. Tompkins Applied to International Law." *American Journal of International Law* 33, no. 740 (1939): 740–43.

Jones, Robert A. *The Soviet Concept of "Limited Sovereignty" from Lenin to Gorbachev: The Brezhnev Doctrine.* London: Palgrave Macmillan, 1990.

Jordan, Andrew, Dave Huitema, Harro van Asselt, and Johanna Forster, eds. *Governing Climate Change: Polycentricity in Action?* Cambridge, UK: Cambridge University Press, 2018.

Kagan, Robert. *The World That America Made.* New York: Alfred P. Knopf, 2012.

Kant, Immanuel. *Perpetual Peace: A Philosophical Sketch.* 1795. https://www.mtholyoke.edu/acad/intrel/kant/kant1.htm.

Kaplan, Ethan, Jörg L. Spenkuch, and Rebecca Sullivan. "Measuring Geographic Polarization: Theory and Long-Run Evidence." January 2019. http://econweb.umd.edu/~kaplan/big_sort_APSA.pdf.

Kazianis, Harry J. "Trump Is Right—NATO Is Obsolete, and He's Delivering That Message Loud and Clear." Fox News, July 10, 2018. https://www.foxnews.com/opinion/trump-is-right-nato-is-obsolete-and-hes-delivering-that-message-loud-and-clear.

Kellogg-Briand Pact, 1928. August 27, 1928. http://avalon.law.yale.edu/20th_century/kbpact.asp.

Keohane, Robert O. *After Hegemony: Cooperation and Discord in the World Political Economy.* Princeton, NJ: Princeton University Press, 1984.

Keohane, Robert O., and David G. Victor. "The Regime Complex for Climate Change." *Perspectives on Politics* 9, no. 1 (2011): 7–23.

Keohane, Robert O., and Lisa L. Martin. "The Promise of Institutionalist Theory." *International Security* 20, no. 1 (1995): 39–51.

Keynes, John Maynard. *The Economic Consequences of Peace.* New York: Harcourt, Brace, and Howe, 1920.

Kindleberger, Charles P. "Dominance and Leadership in the International Economy: Exploitation, Public Goods, and Free Rides." *International Studies Quarterly* 25, no. 2 (1981): 242–54.

———. "The Rise of Free Trade in Western Europe, 1820–1875." *Journal of Economic History* 35 (1975): 20–55.

Kinsky, Ferdinand. "Personalism and Federalism." *Publius* 9, no. 4 (1979): 131–56.

Kirchick, James. "On Linda Sarsour's Politics of Hate and the Pathos of Her Jewish Enablers." *Tablet Magazine*, June 14, 2017. https://www.tabletmag.com/jewish-news-and-politics/237149/linda-sarsour-jewish-enablers.

Koenig-Archibugi, Mathias. "Is Global Democracy Possible?" *European Journal of International Relations* 17, no. 3 (September 2011): 519–42.

Kolev, Stefan. "Ordoliberalism." In *Encyclopedia of Law and Economics*, edited by Alain Marciano and Giovanni Battista Ramello. New York: Springer, 2017. https://doi.org/10. 1007/978-1-4614-7883-6_618-3.

Koremenos, Barbara, Charles Lipson, and Duncan Snidal. "The Rational Design of International Institutions." *International Organization* 55, no. 4 (2001): 761–99.

Koyama, Mark. "A Nationalism Untethered to History." Liberal Currents, October 2018. https://www.liberalcurrents.com/a-nationalism-untethered-to-history/.

Krasner, Steven D. *Sovereignty: Organized Hypocrisy*. Princeton, NJ: Princeton University Press, 1999.

Krugman, Paul R. "Is Free Trade Passé?" *Journal of Economic Perspectives* 1, no. 2 (1987): 131–44.

———. "Oh, What a Trumpy Trade War!" *New York Times*, March 8, 2018. https://www.nytimes.com/2018/03/08/opinion/trump-trade-tariffs-steel.html.

Ku, Julian, and John C. Yoon. *Taming Globalization: International Law, the US Constitution, and the New World Order*. Oxford, UK: Oxford University Press, 2012.

Kuyper, Jonathan W. "Designing Institutions for Global Democracy: Flexibility through Escape Clauses and Sunset Provisions." *Ethics & Global Politics* 6, no. 4 (2013): 195–215. https://www.tandfonline.com/doi/full/10.3402/egp.v6i4.19163.

Lampe, Markus, Felipe Tâmega Fernandes, and Antonio Tena-Junguito. "How Much Trade Liberalization Was There in the World before and after Cobden-Chevalier?" Working paper, Universidad Carlos III de Madrid, February 2012. https://e-archivo.uc3m.es/bitstream/handle/10016/13345/wp_12-02.pdf.

Lane, Philip R. "The Real Effects of European Monetary Union." *Journal of Economic Perspectives* 20, no. 4 (2006): 47–66.

Larin, Stephen J., and Alice Engl. "Granting Austrian Citizenship to German-Speaking Italians Would Not Be a Victory for South Tyrol's Separatists." LSE EuroPP Blog, January 10, 2018,http://blogs.lse.ac.uk/europpblog/2018/01/10/granting-austrian-citizenship-to-german-speaking-italians-would-not-be-a-victory-for-south-tyrols-separatists/.

Lawrence v. Texas. 539 U.S. 558 (2003). https://www.law.cornell.edu/supct/html/02-102.ZO.html.

Lemieux, Pierre. *What's Wrong with Protectionism: Answering Common Objections to Free Trade*. Lanham, MD: Rowman & Littlefield, 2018.

Leo XIII. "Rerum Novarum." Libreria Editrice Vaticana, May 15, 1891. http://w2.vatican.va/content/leo-xiii/en/encyclicals/documents/hf_l-xiii_enc_15051891_rerum-novarum.html.

Levy, David M., and Sandra J. Peart. "The Secret History of the Dismal Science Part I. Economics, Religion and Race in the 19th Century." Library of Economics and Liberty, January 22, 2001. https://www.econlib.org/library/Columns/LevyPeartdismal.html.

Levy, Jacob T. "The Sovereign Myth." Niskanen Center, June 15, 2017. https://niskanencenter.org/blog/sovereign-myth/.

Lindsey, Brink, and Steven M. Teles. *The Captured Economy: How the Powerful Enrich Themselves, Slow Down Growth, and Increase Inequality*. Oxford, UK: Oxford University Press, 2017.

Lipsey, R. G., and Kelvin Lancaster. "The General Theory of Second Best." *Review of Economic Studies* 24, no. 1 (1956): 11–32.

List, Christian, and Koenig-Archibugi, Mathias. "Can There Be a Global Demos? an Agency-Based Approach." *Philosophy and Public Affairs* 38, no. 1 (2010): 76–110.

Lynch, Allen. "Woodrow Wilson and the Principle of 'National Self-Determination': A Reconsideration." *Review of International Studies* 28, no. 2 (2002): 419–36.

Macdonald, Terry. *Global Stakeholder Democracy: Power and Representation beyond Liberal States*. Oxford, UK: Oxford University Press, 2008.

Madison, James. "The Conformity of the Plan to Republican Principles." *Federalist*, no. 39. In *The Federalist Papers* (1788).

Madsen, Jacob B. "Trade Barriers and the Collapse of World Trade During the Great Depression." *Southern Economic Journal* 67, no. 4 (2001): 848–68.

Manak, Inu. "Regulatory Issues in the New NAFTA." International Economic Law and Policy Blog, October 10, 2018. http://worldtradelaw.typepad.com/ielpblog/2018/10/regulatory-cooperation-in-the-new-nafta.html.

Mansfield, Edward D., Helen V. Milner, and B. Peter Rosendorff. "Why Democracies Cooperate More: Electoral Control and International Trade Agreements." *International Organization* 56, no. 3 (2002): 477–513.

Maskus, Keith E., Tsunehiro Otsuki, and John S. Wilson. "The Cost of Compliance with Product Standards for Firms in Developing Countries: An Econometric Study." World Bank, May 2005. https://openknowledge.worldbank.org/handle/10986/8961.

Matthews, Dylan. "Zero Sum Trump. What You Learn from Reading 12 of Donald Trump's Books." Vox, January 19, 2017. https://www.vox.com/a/donald-trump-books.

Mauldin, William. "Trump's Big Gamble: Luring Countries into One-on-One Trade Deals." *Wall Street Journal*, February 27, 2017. https://www.wsj.com/articles/trumps-big-gamble-luring-countries-into-one-on-one-trade-deals-1485483628.

May, Theresa. "Full Text: Theresa May's Conference Speech." *Spectator*, October 5, 2016. https://blogs.spectator.co.uk/2016/10/full-text-theresa-mays-conference-speech/.

McGinnis, Michael, and Elinor Ostrom. "Design Principles for Local and Global Commons." Paper prepared for "Linking Local and Global Commons" conference, Cambridge MA, April 23–25, 1992.

McKinsey Global Institute. *Navigating a World of Disruption*. Briefing Note Prepared for the World Economic Forum in Davos, Switzerland, January 2019,https://www.mckinsey.com/featured-insights/innovation-and-growth/navigating-a-world-of-disruption.

McNamara, Kathleen. "The Euro Is an Experiment in Making a Currency without a Government. That's Why It's in Trouble." *Washington Post*, June 28, 2015. https://www.washingtonpost.com/news/monkey-cage/wp/2015/06/28/the-euro-is-an-experiment-in-making-a-currency-without-a-government-thats-why-its-in-trouble/.

Mearsheimer, John. "The False Promise of International Institutions." *International Security* 19, no. 3 (1995): 5–49.

Melitz, Jacques. "Language and Foreign Trade." Institut National de la Statistique et des Études Économiques, January 2003. http://crest.science/RePEc/wpstorage/2003-26.pdf.

———, and Farid Toubal. "Native Language, Spoken Language, Translation and Trade." Scottish Institute for Research in Economics, September 2012. http://repo.sire.ac.uk/bitstream/handle/10943/381/SIRE-DP-2012_82.pdf.

Merriam-Webster, online edition. https://www.merriam-webster.com/dictionary/sovereignty.

Mises, Ludwig von. *Liberalism. In the Classical Tradition*. San Francisco: Cobden Press and Irvington on Hudson: Foundation for Economic Education, 2002.

———. *Omnipotent Government: The Rise of the Total State and Total War*. New Haven, CT: Yale University Press, 1944.

———. *The Theory of Money and Credit*, 1912,https://mises.org/library/theory-money-and-credit.

Mokyr, Joel. *A Culture of Growth: Origins of the Modern Economy*. Princeton, NJ: Princeton University Press, 2016.

Moore, James W. "What Is the Sense of Agency and Why Does It Matter?" *Frontiers in Psychology* 7 (2016): 1272.

Morgenthau, Hans J. *Politics among Nations: The Struggle for Power and Peace*. New York: Alfred A. Knopf, 1944.

Mundell, Robert A. "A Theory of Optimum Currency Areas." *American Economic Review* 51, no. 4 (1961): 657–65.

Murray, Charles. *Coming Apart: The State of White America, 1960–2010*. New York: Crown Publishing, 2012.

Navarro, Peter, and Greg Autry. *Death by China: Confronting the Dragon—A Global Call to Action*. New York: Prentice Hall, 2011.

Neff, Stephen C. "Short History of International Law." In *International Law*, fourth edition, edited by Malcolm D. Evans, 3–32. Oxford, UK: Oxford University Press, 2014.

Neuer, Hillel C. "Reform or Regression? Ten Years of the UN Human Rights Council." Testimony to the Committee on Foreign Affairs, US House of Representatives, May 17, 2016. https://www.unwatch.org/10837-2/.

New York v. United States. 505 U.S. 144 (1992). https://www.law.cornell.edu/supremecourt/text/505/144.

Niemelä, Pekka. "A Cosmopolitan World Order? Perspectives on Francisco de Vitoria and the United Nations." *Max Planck Yearbook of United Nations Law* 12 (2008): 301–44. http://www.mpil.de/files/pdf3/mpunyb_08_niemelae_12.pdf.

Niskanen, William A. "Bureaucrats and Politicians." *Journal of Law and Economics* 18, no. 3 (1975): 617–43.

North Atlantic Treaty. 1949. https://www.nato.int/cps/ic/natohq/official_texts_17120.htm.

O'Rourke, Kevin H., and Jeffrey G. Williamson. *Globalization and History. The Evolution of a Nineteenth Century Atlantic Economy.* Cambridge, MA: MIT Press, 1999.

O'Sullivan, John. "Global Governance v Democratic Sovereignty." *Quadrant Online*, March 1, 2012. https://quadrant.org.au/magazine/2012/03/global-governance-v-democratic-sovereignty/.

Oneal, John R., and Bruce M. Russett. "The Kantian Peace: The Pacific Benefits of Democracy, Interdependence, and International Organizations, 1885–1992." *World Politics* 52, no.1 (1999): 1–37.

Orbán, Viktor. "Orbán Viktor's Ceremonial Speech on the 170th Anniversary of the Hungarian Revolution of 1848." Government of Hungary, March 16, 2018. http://www.kormany.hu/en/the-prime-minister/the-prime-minister-s-speeches/orban-viktor-s-ceremonial-speech-on-the-170th-anniversary-of-the-hungarian-revolution-of-1848.

Orefice, Gianluca, Roberta Piermartini, and Nadia Rocha. "Harmonization and Mutual Recognition: What Are the Effects on Trade?" Mimeo, April 30, 2012. https://www.gtap.agecon.purdue.edu/resources/download/5808.pdf.

Orford, Anne. "Jurisdiction without Territory: From the Holy Roman Empire to the Responsibility to Protect." *Michigan Journal of International Law* 30, no. 3 (2009): 981–1015.

Organisation for Economic Co-operation and Development. *International Regulatory Co-operation and Trade: Understanding the Trade Costs of Regulatory Divergence and the Remedies.* Paris: OECD Publishing, 2017. http://www.oecd.org/gov/international-regulatory-co-operation-and-trade-9789264275942-en.htm.

Ortiz-Ospina, Esteban, and Max Roser. "International Trade." OurWorldInData.org, 2018. https://ourworldindata.org/international-trade.

Osiander, Andreas. "Sovereignty, International Relations, and the Westphalian Myth." *International Organization* 55, no. 2 (2001): 251–87.

Ostrom, Elinor. "Beyond Market and States: Polycentric Governance of Complex Economic Systems." *American Economic Review* 100, no. 3 (2010): 641–72.

———. *Governing the Commons. The Evolution of Institutions for Collective Action.* Cambridge, UK: Cambridge University Press, 1990.

———. *Understanding Institutional Diversity.* Princeton, NJ: Princeton University Press, 2005.

———, Joanna Burger, Christopher B. Field, Richard B. Norgaard, and David Policansky. "Revisiting the Commons: Local Lessons, Global Challenges." *Science* 284, no. 5412 (1999): 278–82.

Ostrom, Elinor, Roger B. Parks, and Gordon P. Whitaker. "Do We Really Want to Consolidate Urban Police Forces? A Reappraisal of Some Old Assertions." *Public Administration Review* 33, no. 5 (1973): 423–32.

Ostrom, Vincent. *The Meaning of American Federalism: Constituting a Self-Governing Society.* San Francisco: Center for Contemporary Studies, 1991.

———, and Elinor Ostrom. "A Behavioral Approach to the Study of Intergovernmental Relations." *The Annals of the American Academy of Political and Social Science* 359 (1965): 135–46.

Ostrom, Vincent, Charles M. Tiebout, and Robert Warren. "The Organization of Government in Metropolitan Areas: A Theoretical Inquiry." *American Political Science Review* 55, no. 4 (1961): 831–42.

———. *The Meaning of Democracy and the Vulnerabilities of Democracies: A Response to Tocqueville's Challenge*. Ann Arbor, MI: University of Michigan Press, 1997.

Our World in Data. "The Visual History of Decreasing War and Violence." https://ourworldindata.org/slides/war-and-violence.

Oxford Living Dictionaries. https://en.oxforddictionaries.com/.

Palmer, Doug. "Clinton Raved about Trans-Pacific Partnership Before She Rejected It," Politico, October 8, 2016. https://www.politico.com/story/2016/10/hillary-clinton-trade-deal-229381.

Park, Jee-Hyeong. "Enforcing International Trade Agreements with Imperfect Private Monitoring." *Review of Economic Studies* 78, no. 3 (2011): 1102–34.

Parker, George. "Brexit 'Museum of Sovereignty' to Tell Story of Leaving the EU." *Financial Times*, April 9, 2018. https://www.ft.com/content/d4a3a5c8-3be9-11e8-b7e0-52972418fec4.

Patrick, Stewart. *The Sovereignty Wars: Reconciling America with the World*. Washington, DC: Brookings Institution, 2018.

Pauwelyn, Joost. "Not as Preferential as You May Think: How Mega-Regionals Can Benefit Third Countries." In *Mega-Regional Trade Agreements*, edited by Thilo Rensmann, 61–74. Cham, Switzerland: Springer, 2017.

Pavel, Carmen E. *Divided Sovereignty: International Institutions and the Limits of State Authority*. Oxford: Oxford University Press, 2015.

Pedersen, Fredrik. "Trade and Politics in the Medieval Baltic: English Merchants and England's Relations to the Hanseatic League 1370–1437." In *Public Power in Europe: Studies in Historical Transformations*, edited by J. Amelang and S. Beer, 161–81. Pisa, Italy: Edizione Plus, 2006.

Pelkmans, Jacques. "Mutual Recognition in Goods and Services: An Economic Perspective." European Network of Economic Policy Research Institutes, December 2002. https://pdfs.semanticscholar.org/8c51/8689930693ba999a1764a131c703a7b42400.pdf.

———. "The New Approach to Technical Harmonization and Standardization." *Journal of Common Market Studies* 25, no. 3 (1987): 249–69.

Penciakova, Veronika, Laurence Chandy, and Natasha Ledlie. *The Final Countdown: Prospects for Ending Extreme Poverty by 2030*. Washington DC: Brookings Institution, 2013,https://www.brookings.edu/research/the-final-countdown-prospects-for-ending-extreme-poverty-by-2030-report/.

Pinker, Steven. *Better Angels of Our Nature: Why Violence Has Declined*. New York: Viking Books, 2011.

Pius XI. "Quadragesimo Anno." Libreria Editrice Vaticana, May 15, 1931. http://w2.vatican.va/content/pius-xi/en/encyclicals/documents/hf_p-xi_enc_19310515_quadragesimo-anno.html.

Polanyi, Michael. *The Logic of Liberty*. Chicago: University of Chicago Press, 1951.

Pollard, Michael, and Joshua Mendelsohn. "RAND Kicks Off 2016 Presidential Election Panel Survey." RAND Blog, January 27, 2016. https://www.rand.org/blog/2016/01/rand-kicks-off-2016-presidential-election-panel-survey.html.

Posner, Eric A., and E. Glen Weyl. *Radical Markets: Uprooting Capitalism and Democracy for a Just Society*. Princeton, NJ: Princeton University Press, 2018.

Postan, Michael M. "The Economic and Political Relations of England and the Hanse (1400 to 1475)." In *Studies in English Trade in the Fifteenth Century*, by E. Power and M. M. Postan, 91–153. New York: Barnes & Noble, 1966.

Prasso, Sheridan. "China's Digital Silk Road Is Looking More like an Iron Curtain." *Bloomberg Businessweek*, January 10, 2019. https://www.bloomberg.com/news/features/2019-01-10/china-s-digital-silk-road-is-looking-more-like-an-iron-curtain.

Quinn, Ben. "TTIP Deal Poses 'Real and Serious Risk' to NHS, Says Leading QC." *The Guardian*, February 22, 2016. https://www.theguardian.com/business/2016/feb/22/ttip-deal-real-serious-risk-nhs-leading-qc.

Rabkin, Jeremy A. *Law without Nations? Why Constitutional Government Requires Sovereign States*. Princeton, NJ: Princeton University Press, 2005.

———. *Why Sovereignty Matters*. Washington, DC: AEI Press, 1998.

Raccagni, Gianluca. "The Teaching of Rhetoric and the Magna Carta of the Lombard Cities: The Peace of Constance, the Empire and the Papacy in the Works of Guido Faba and His Leading Contemporary Colleagues." *Journal of Medieval History* 39, no. 1 (2013): 61–79.

———."When the Emperor Submitted to His Rebellious Subjects: A Neglected and Innovative Legal Account of the Peace of Constance, 1183." *English Historical Review* 131, no. 550 (2016): 519–39.

Rafferty, Andrew. "Rep. Steve King Defends 'Somebody Else's Babies' Remarks." NBC News, March 13, 2017. https://www.nbcnews.com/politics/politics-news/steve-king-defends-somebody-else-s-babies-remarks-n732741.

Rauch, James E. "Business and Social Networks in International Trade." *Journal of Economic Literature* 39, no. 4 (2001): 1177–203.

Reves, Emery. *The Anatomy of Peace*. New York: Harper & Brothers Publishers, 1945.

Roberts, David. "California Gov. Jerry Brown Casually Unveils History's Most Ambitious Climate Target." Vox, September 12, 2018. https://www.vox.com/energy-and-environment/2018/9/11/17844896/california-jerry-brown-carbon-neutral-2045-climate-change.

Rodrik, Dani. *Straight Talk on Trade: Ideas for a Sane World Economy*. Princeton, NJ: Princeton University Press, 2018.

Roe, Michael. "Multi-Level and Polycentric Governance: Effective Policymaking for Shipping." *Maritime Policy and Management* 36, no. 1 (2009): 39–56.

Rohac, Dalibor. "Authoritarianism in the Heart of Europe." American Enterprise Institute, 2018. https://www.aei.org/publication/authoritarianism-in-the-heart-of-europe/.

———. "Classical Liberals and Foreign Policy: Time for a Rethink?" *Journal des Economistes Et des Etudes Humaines* 23, no. 1 (2017).

———. "Indiana's Gift to the International Order." *American Interest*, May 10, 2018. https://www.the-american-interest.com/2018/05/10/indianas-gift-to-the-international-order/.

———. "Jeremy Corbyn and His Sinister Friends." *Weekly Standard*, August 20, 2015. https://www.weeklystandard.com/dalibor-rohac/jeremy-corbyn-and-his-sinister-friends.

———. "The Libertarian Case for the European Union." *Reason*, September 9, 2014. https://reason.com/archives/2014/09/09/the-libertarian-case-for-the-european-un.

———. "Time for a Rethink? Libertarians and Foreign Policy." *World Affairs*, Summer 2015. http://www.worldaffairsjournal.org/article/time-rethink-libertarians-and-foreign-policy.

———. *Towards an Imperfect Union: A Conservative Case for the EU*. Lanham, MD: Rowman & Littlefield, 2016.

Rohr, Mathieu von. "'I Don't Want This European Soviet Union.'" *Der Spiegel*, June 3, 2014. http://www.spiegel.de/international/europe/interview-with-french-front-national-leader-marine-le-pen-a-972925.html.

Romer, Christina D. "Changes in Business Cycles: Evidence and Explanations." *Journal of Economic Perspectives* 13, no. 2 (1999): 23–44.

Roper v. Simmons. 543 U.S. 551 (2005). https://www.law.cornell.edu/supct/html/03-633.ZS.html.

Röpke, Wilhelm. *International Economic Disintegration*. London: William Hodge, 1942.

Rose, Andrew K. "Do We Really Know That the WTO Increases Trade?" *American Economic Review* 94, no. 1 (2004): 98–114.

Rutgers v. Waddington. Mayor's Court, City of New York, August 7, 1786. https://archive.org/details/caseofelizabethr00rutg.

Salam, Reihan. *Melting Pot or Civil War? A Son of Immigrants Makes the Case against Open Borders*. New York: Sentinel, 2018.

Sally, Razeen. *Classical Liberalism and International Economic Order: Studies in Theory and Intellectual History*. London: Routledge, 1998.

Salter, Alexander William, and Vlad Tarko. "Polycentric Banking and Macroeconomic Stability." *Business and Politics* 19, no. 2 (2017): 365–95.

Sarnowsky, Jürgen. "The 'Golden Age' of the Hanseatic League." In *A Companion to the Hanseatic League*, by Donald J. Harreld, 64–100. *Brill's Companions to European History*, volume 8. Leiden, Netherlands: Brill, 2015.

Scherrer, Amandine, and Cecilia Isaksson. *The Return of Foreign Fighters to EU Soil.* European Parliamentary Research Service, May 2018. http://www.europarl.europa.eu/RegData/etudes/STUD/2018/621811/EPRS_STU(2018)621811_EN.pdf.

Scholte, Jan Aart. "Civil Society and Democracy in Global Governance." Centre for the Study of Globalisation and Regionalisation, January 2001. http://wrap.warwick.ac.uk/2060/1/WRAP_Scholte_wp6501.pdf.

———. "Globalization and Governance: From Statism to Polycentrism." University of Warwick, Centre for the Study of Globalisation and Regionalisation, February 2004. http://wrap.warwick.ac.uk/1984/.

Schröder, Peter. "The Constitution of the Holy Roman Empire After 1648: Samuel Pufendorf's Assessment in His Monzambano." *Historical Journal* 42, no. 4 (1999): 961–83.

Schuck, Peter H. "Refugee Burden-Sharing: A Modest Proposal." *Yale Journal of International Law* 22 (1997): 243–97.

Schwartz, Harry. "The Khrushchev/Brezhnev Doctrine at Helsinki." *New York Times*, August 5, 1975. https://www.nytimes.com/1975/08/05/archives/the-khrushchevbrezhnev-doctrine-at-helsinki.html.

Scruton, Roger. *England and the Need for Nations*, second edition. London: Institute for the Study of Civil Society, 2006.

Selgin, George. "The Rise and Fall of the Gold Standard in the United States." *Cato Policy Analysis* 729 (2013),https://www.cato.org/publications/policy-analysis/rise-fall-gold-standard-united-states.

———, William D. Lastrapes, and Lawrence H. White. "Has the Fed Been a Failure?" *Journal of Macroeconomics* 34, no. 3 (2012): 569–96.

Sellers, J. M. "Transnational Urban Associations and the State: Contemporary Europe Compared with the Hanseatic League." *Yearbook of European Administrative History* 15 (2003): 289–308.

Shackelford, Scott J. "On Climate Change and Cyber Attacks: Leveraging Polycentric Governance to Mitigate Global Collective Action Problems." *Vanderbilt Journal of Entertainment and Technology Law* 18, no. 4 (2016): 653–711.

Shane III, Leo. "Trump's Budget Calls for New Base Closing Round in 2021." *Military Times*, May 23, 2017. https://www.militarytimes.com/news/pentagon-congress/2017/05/23/trumps-budget-calls-for-new-base-closing-round-in-2021/.

Shipman, Tim. *All Out War: The Full Story of How Brexit Sank Britain's Political Class.* London: William Collins, 2016.

Shivakoti, Ganesh P., Prachanda Pradhan, Wai Fung Lam, and Elinor Ostrom. *Improving Irrigation in Asia: Sustainable Performance of an Innovative Intervention in Nepal.* Cheltenham, UK: Edward Elgar, 2013.

Slack, James. "The Enemies of the People." *Daily Mail*, November 4, 2016. https://www.dailymail.co.uk/news/article-3903436/Enemies-people-Fury-touch-judges-defied-17-4m-Brexit-voters-trigger-constitutional-crisis.html.

Slaughter, Anne-Marie. "Everyday Global Governance." *Daedalus* 132, no. 1 (2003): 83–90.

Smeltz, Dina, and Craig Kafura. "Record Number of Americans Endorse Benefits of Trade." Chicago Council on Global Affairs, August 27, 2018. https://www.thechicagocouncil.org/publication/record-number-americans-endorse-benefits-trade.

Smith, Adam. *An Inquiry into the Nature and Causes of the Wealth of Nations*, volume 1. 1776; Oxford: Clarendon Press, 1979.

Smith, Matthew. "The 'Extremists' on Both Sides of the Brexit Debate." YouGov, August 1, 2017. https://yougov.co.uk/news/2017/08/01/britain-nation-brexit-extremists/.

Sobják, Anita. "The Implications of Hungary's National Policy for Relations with Neighbouring States." Polish Institute of International Affairs, June 2012. http://www.pism.pl/files/?id_plik=10996.

Sparrow, Andrew. "May Should Close Parliament If Necessary to Stop Bill Blocking No Deal Brexit, Says Rees-Mogg—as It Happened." *Guardian*, January 23, 2019. https://www.theguardian.com/politics/live/2019/jan/23/brexit-latest-news-developments-pmqs-may-corbyn-wont-be-able-to-use-vote-next-week-to-stop-no-deal-liam-fox-claims-politics-live.

Stone, Jon. "Families Losing £150 a Month Is a Price Worth Paying for Brexit, Leave.EU Campaign Chief Says." *Independent*, April 27, 2016. https://www.independent.co.uk/news/uk/politics/families-losing-150-a-month-is-a-price-worth-paying-for-brexit-leaveeu-campaign-chief-says-a7003616.html.

Straumann, Benjamin. "The Peace of Westphalia as a Secular Constitution." *Constellations* 15, no. 2 (2008): 173–88.

Suslov, Mikhail. "'Russian World': Russia's Policy Towards Its Diaspora." Centre for the Study of Globalisation and Regionalisation, July 2017. https://www.ifri.org/sites/default/files/atoms/files/suslov_russian_world_2017.pdf.

Swann, G. M. Peter. "International Standards and Trade: A Review of the Empirical Literature." Trade policy working paper, Organisation for Economic Cooperation and Development, 2010. https://search.oecd.org/trade/benefitlib/45500791.pdf.

Tallberg, Jonas, and Anders Uhlin. "Civil Society and Global Democracy: An Assessment." In *Global Democracy: Normative and Empirical Perspectives*, edited by Daniele Archibugi, Mathias Koenig-Archibugi, and Raffaele Marchetti, 210–32. Cambridge, UK: Cambridge University Press.

Tallberg, Jonas, Thomas Sommerer, Theresa Squatrito, and Christer Jönsson. "Explaining the Transnational Design of International Organization." *International Organization* 68, no. 4 (2014): 741–74.

———. *The Opening Up of International Organizations: Transnational Access in Global Governance*. Cambridge: Cambridge University Press, 2013.

Tarko, Vlad. *Elinor Ostrom: An Intellectual Biography*. Lanham MD: Rowman & Littlefield, 2017.

Tennyson, Alfred. "Locksley Hall." 1842. https://www.poetryfoundation.org/poems/45362/locksley-hall.

Thatcher, Margaret. "Speech in Hendon." May 19, 1975. https://www.margaretthatcher.org/document/102692.

Thiessen, Marc A. "Trump Is Using Tariffs to Advance a Radical Free-Trade Agenda." *Washington Post*, July 26, 2018. https://www.washingtonpost.com/opinions/trump-may-end-up-being-one-of-the-greatest-free-trade-presidents-in-history/2018/07/26/6eb6e65e-90fc-11e8-8322-b5482bf5e0f5_story.html.

Tlaib, Rashida (@RashidaTlaib). Twitter, January 6, 2019, 9:03 p.m. https://twitter.com/RashidaTlaib/status/1082095303325609984.

Tomz, Michael, Judith L. Goldstein, and Douglas Rivers. "Do We Really Know That the WTO Increases Trade? Comment." *American Economic Review* 97, no. 5 (2007): 2005–18.

Treaty on European Union and the Treaty on the Functioning of the European Union. 2012/C 326/01. http://eur-lex.europa.eu/legal-content/EN/TXT/?uri=celex%3A12012M%2FTXT.

Tuccille, J. D. "This Is the Number of Innocent People Murdered by Governments. Are You Anti-State Yet?" *Reason*, May 15, 2014,https://reason.com/archives/2014/05/15/be-antigovernment-and-proud.

Turnheim, Bruno, Paula Kivimaa, and Frans Berkhout, eds. *Innovating Climate Governance: Moving beyond Experiments*. Cambridge, UK: Cambridge University Press, 2018.

UN Dag Hammarskjöld Library. "Security Council: Vetos." http://research.un.org/en/docs/sc/quick.

UN Human Rights Council. "Discriminatory Laws and Practices and Acts of Violence Against Individuals Based on Their Sexual Orientation and Gender Identity." November 11, 2011. https://www.ohchr.org/documents/issues/discrimination/a.hrc.19.41_english.pdf.

UN Security Council. Draft Resolution S/2018/321. http://www.un.org/en/ga/search/view_doc.asp?symbol=S/2018/321.

———. Draft Resolution S/8761. http://www.un.org/en/ga/search/view_doc.asp?symbol=S/8761.

United States v. Curtiss-Wright Export Corp. 299 U.S. 304 (1936). https://www.law.cornell.edu/supremecourt/text/299/304.

US Constitution. https://www.law.cornell.edu/constitution.

Van Zeben, Josephine, and Ana Bobić (eds.). *Polycentricity in the European Union*. Cambridge: Cambridge University Press, 2019.

Vázquez, Carlos Manuel. "The Four Doctrines of Self-Executing Treaties." *American Journal of International Law* (1995): 695–723.

———. "Judicial Enforcement of Treaties: Self-Execution and Related Doctrines." *American Society of International Law Proceedings* 100 (2006): 439–48.

Victor, David G. "Why Paris Worked: A Different Approach to Climate Diplomacy." *Yale Environment 360*, December 15, 2015. https://e360.yale.edu/features/why_paris_worked_a_different_approach_to_climate_diplomacy.

Waltz, Kenneth. *Theory of International Politics*. Reading, MA: Addison-Wesley, 1979.

Ward, Alex. "Read Trump's Speech to the UN General Assembly." Vox, September 25, 2018. https://www.vox.com/2018/9/25/17901082/trump-un-2018-speech-full-text.

Weingast, Barry R. "The Economic Role of Political Institutions: Market-Preserving Federalism and Economic Development." *Journal of Law, Economics, and Organization* 11, no. 1 (1995): 1–31.

Wellhausen, Rachel L. "Recent Trends in Investor-State Dispute Settlement." *Journal of International Dispute Settlement* 7, no. 1 (2016): 117–35.

Wicksell, Knut. *Interest and Prices*. New York: Sentry Press, 1898; 1936. https://mises.org/library/interest-and-prices.

Wilkinson, Will. "What If We Can't Make Government Smaller?" Niskanen Center, October 19, 2016. https://niskanencenter.org/blog/cant-make-government-smaller/.

Williamson, Kevin D. "Peter Navarro: Trump's Nutty Economics Professor." *National Review*, April 14, 2017. https://www.nationalreview.com/2017/04/peter-navarro-trump-china-adviser-bad-economics/.

Willkie, Wendell L. *One World*. London: Cassell and Company, 1943.

Woolsey, L. H. "The Leticia Dispute between Colombia and Peru." *American Journal of International Law* 29, no. 1 (1935): 94–99.

World Bank. *World Development Report*. New York: Oxford University Press, 1987.

World Trade Organization. *World Trade Report 2007: Six Decades of Multilateral Trade Cooperation. What Have We Learnt?* Geneva: World Trade Organization, https://www.wto.org/english/res_e/booksp_e/anrep_e/world_trade_report07_e.pdf.

Yoon, John C. "Globalism and the Constitution: Treaties, Non-Self-Execution, and the Original Understanding." *Columbia Law Review* 99, no. 8 (1999): 1955–2094.

Young, Oran R. "Effectiveness of International Environmental Regimes: Existing Knowledge, Cutting-Edge Themes, and Research Strategies." *PNAS* 108, no. 50 (December 13, 2011): 19853–60.

Index

About the Author

Dalibor Rohac is a resident scholar at the American Enterprise Institute, where he studies the political economy of the European Union and transatlantic relations. He is concurrently a research associate at the Wilfried Martens Centre for European Studies in Brussels. His previous book, *Towards an Imperfect Union: A Conservative Case for the EU*, was included on *Foreign Affairs* magazine's list of best books of 2016. Rohac has written about European affairs for the *Washington Post*, the *New York Times*, *Financial Times*, the *Wall Street Journal*, *Foreign Affairs*, and other outlets, and has appeared on news outlets including BBC, Bloomberg Television, Fox News, and Fox Business. He holds a PhD in political economy from King's College London.

Made in the USA
Coppell, TX
04 February 2021

49484846R00099